HOUGHTON MIFFLIN

English

Authors
Robert Rueda
Tina Saldivar
Lynne Shapiro
Shane Templeton
C. Ann Terry
Catherine Valentino
Shelby A. Wolf

Consultants
Jeanneine P. Jones
Monette Coleman McIver
Rojulene Norris

 HOUGHTON MIFFLIN   BOSTON

Credits

Illustrations

Aaron Boyd: 248–249   **Lizi Boyd:** 27, 28, 79, 89, 99 (b), 103, 125 (t), 151, 178, 181, 207 **Wm. R. Brinkley & Associates (music)**: 229, 230, 231, 232   **Liz Callen**: 29, 52, 53 (t), 54, 76, 86, 99 (t), 100, 101 (t&b), 117, 129, 179 **Mircea Catusanu**: 232, 233   **Luisa D'Augusta**: 234   **Dagmar Fehlau**: 230, 231, 235   **Jennifer Harris**: 203, 205   **Dennis Hockerman**: 241 **Lily Toy Hong**: 246   **John Hovell**: 53 (b), 75, 101 (m), 125 (b), 126, 177, 178, 180, 195 **Darcia Labrosse**: 239   **Sharron O'Neil**: 229 **Darcy Schwartz**: 10, 13, 21, 22, 24, 26, 35, 38, 46, 48, 62, 64, 70, 72, 74, 94, 96, 106, 115, 120, 122, 130, 139, 146, 148, 156, 158, 167, 172, 176, 182, 187, 193, 198, 200, 208, 221   **Gerardo Suzán**: 243   **Brad Teare**: 252   **Linda Townshend**: 236, 237   **George Ulrich** 253

Photographs

Fine Art: 143 Anonymous/The Bridgeman Art Library   **223** Private Collection/Superstock

11, 12, 14, 17, 20, 21, 25, 26, 28, 41, 49, 51, 56, 65, 73, 77 (b), 89, 97, 105, 114, 123, 131, 140, 149, 150, 157, 166, 173, 183, 193, 201, 209, 221 Joel Benjamin   **19** (l) Barbara Peacock/FPG   **19** (m & r) Telegraph Colour Library/FPG   **203** Photodisc   **204** Photodisc   **223** (m) Adam Wolfitt/Corbis   **223** (b) Kennan Ward/Corbis   **254** (t) Brandon D. Cole/Corbis   **254** (b) Photodisc   **255** (t) W. Perry Conway/Corbis   **255** (b) The Purcell Team/Corbis

Printed in the U.S.A.

ISBN: 0-618-31006-1

1 2 3 4 5 6 7 8 9 10-B-11 10 09 08 07 06 05 04 03 02

TABLE OF CONTENTS

Unit 2 — Words We Know 46

Unit 3 — Sentences for Us 70

Unit 4 Personal Narrative 94

Unit 5 Description 120

Unit 6 Story 146

Unit 7 Instructions 172

Unit 8　Report　198

Introducing the Program

This level of *Houghton Mifflin English* provides a language arts program specifically designed for kindergarten children. The concepts, skills, and writing activities introduced at kindergarten set the foundation for formal composition instruction at the upper grades.

Units 1–3

In Units 1 through 3, the program presents activities to help children learn letters, words, numbers, colors, and kinds of sentences. Children build upon the hierarchy of letters as parts of words and words as parts of sentences.

Units begin with a read-aloud published model and a Modeled Writing lesson that support the concepts presented in each unit. Focus Skill lessons provide brief introductory instruction for skills in the following categories: oral language, viewing, grammar, vocabulary, writing, and study skills. Each unit ends with a Class Writing Project.

Units 4–8

Units 4 through 8 also begin with a read-aloud published model that reflects the following writing modes: **personal narrative, description, story, instructions,** and **report.** A Modeled Writing lesson helps to demonstrate the stages of the writing process appropriate to this level — prewriting, drafting, revising, publishing, and reflecting — for each unit's mode. Focus Skill lessons provide instruction in the areas of oral language, viewing, grammar, vocabulary, writing, and study skills. Grammar skills from Units 1 through 3 are repeated and further developed in these units. A Shared Writing lesson gives children the opportunity to collaborate with you to create a composition that reflects each writing mode.

Program Components

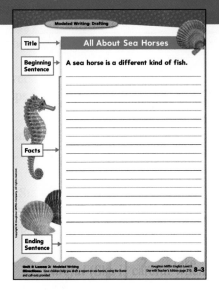

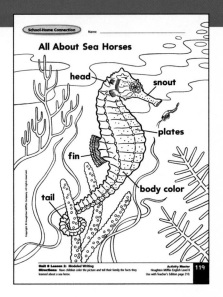

The **Poster Book** provides colorful, interactive pages that support instruction for each unit.

➡ **NOTE** Special paper in the Poster Book requires the use of a Sanford Expo 11, fine point, low order dry erase marker.

The **Overhead Transparencies** include background scenes to motivate oral language activities and writing graphic organizers and frames to support Modeled and Shared Writing. Every Poster Book page has been provided in transparency format.

The **Activity Masters** provide practice for Focus Skill lessons as well as activities to support School-Home Connections.

Instructional Sequence

All units follow a similar format.

 Daily Routines suggest oral language activities for an Interactive Bulletin Board and a Daily Discussion time.

 **Center Activities** are related to the unit concept or writing mode. Centers include Reading and Listening, Creative Arts, Writing, Science, Social Studies, and Math. The Reading and Listening Center and the Writing Center appear in every unit.

 **A Published Model** read-aloud serves as a model of the unit concept or writing mode.

 A **Modeled Writing** lesson introduces children to oral and written composition, using the concepts or the writing mode that is the focus for each unit.

 Focus Skill lessons provide instruction for oral language, viewing, grammar, vocabulary, writing, and study skills.

 A **Class Writing Project** in Units 1–3 provides a Big Book writing experience based on the unit concept.

 A **Shared Writing** lesson in Units 4–8 gives the structure for children to collaborate as they write a personal narrative, a description, a story, a set of instructions, and a report.

 **Independent Writing** in Units 4–8 provides the opportunity for children to tell, dictate, or write their own ideas, using the writing modes. It includes Writing Prompts.

 Meeting Individual Needs suggestions offer ideas for Reteaching, Challenge, and Students Acquiring English activities to support the Focus Skills.

Daily Routines

Language Arts concepts and skills build over time, especially the development of oral language. The **Daily Routines** feature at the beginning of each unit provides a daily oral language experience. Many teachers have a common routine of updating a calendar with children. By simply extending this routine to include additional **Interactive Bulletin Board** activities and then a **Daily Discussion**, children have the opportunity to develop a strong oral language foundation.

Interactive Bulletin Board

On pages 12–13 you will find directions for creating an Interactive Bulletin Board like the one shown in the photograph on the next page.

- The Interactive Bulletin Board has a calendar; an attendance list; a weather chart; color, number, size wheels; a daily message; and a bear that can be placed around the room to teach positional words.

- At the beginning of each unit you will find suggestions for how to vary one or more of the Interactive Bulletin Board activities to help address the content of that particular unit.

Daily Discussion

After updating the Interactive Bulletin Board each day, you will move into a Daily Discussion.

- At the beginning of each unit you will find topic suggestions with discussion prompts and resources that will help address that particular unit's content.

- Teach Lessons 1 through 8 in this Getting Started unit before beginning the Daily Routines in Unit 1 with children. Lessons 7 and 8 formally introduce children to these routines.

Daily Routines

Interactive Bulletin Board

The following are some suggestions for simple ways to enhance your current calendar routine or to create a calendar routine to build specific language arts skills. If you are already doing some of these activities, this will simply help you identify the language arts objectives you are addressing daily.

Attendance List

Anna	Bob	Carlos
Ellen	Fran	James
Kenji	Maria	Rosa
Sam	Terry	Vinny

CALENDAR
September

SUNDAY	MONDAY	TUESDAY	WEDNESDAY	THURSDAY	FRIDAY	SATURDAY
		1	**2**	**3**	**4**	**5**
6	**7**					

| YESTERDAY | TODAY | TOMORROW | DAYS OF THE WEEK |

① Attendance List

Create and post an alphabetical list of children's names on your calendar bulletin board.

HOW TO USE Have children help you check who is present or absent each day. Place a picture of each child next to his or her name to assist children in reading all the names with you.

② The Calendar

HOW TO MAKE Prepare color, size, and shape paper cutouts with a different date written on each cutout. These will form a pattern when the numerals are placed on the calendar. For example, triangle, circle, square or yellow, blue, red. Add pockets near the calendar labeled *yesterday, today,* and *tomorrow.* Then write the days of the week on index cards.

HOW TO USE Ask a volunteer to update the calendar daily, using the pattern cutouts. Together recite the day of the week, the month, and date. As the pattern is revealed, ask volunteers to identify what will come next in the pattern. Then ask one child to identify the day of the week, what day it was yesterday, and what day it will be tomorrow by placing the correct day of the week index card in each pocket.

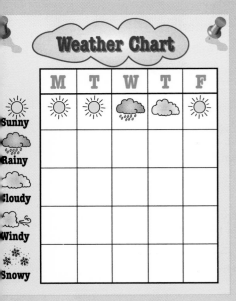

Weather Chart

M	T	W	T	F
☀	☀	🌧	☁	☀

☀ Sunny
⛅ Rainy
☁ Cloudy
🍃 Windy
❄ Snowy

3 Weather Chart

Create a weather chart similar to the one shown above but based on weather in your area.

HOW TO USE Each day ask a volunteer to mark an X next to the conditions. Then have a child identify what he or she picked and what type of clothing he or she feels would be appropriate to wear on such a day.

Daily Message

Today is Monday, September 7.

5 Daily Message

Children can help you compose a sentence each day related to the unit concept or mode.

4 Color, Number, Size Wheels

HOW TO MAKE Using paper plates, brads, and construction paper arrows, create three large spinners. On one plate, put colors labeled with color words; on the second plate, put numerals and number words; and on the third plate, put size words with helpful pictures.

HOW TO USE Each day have volunteers spin each spinner, identify the word, and use it in a complete sentence. You can have volunteers identify class objects that are the same color, line up a number of objects to show the number, and name the opposite of the size word.

6 Where Is the Bear?

HOW TO MAKE Use Activity Master 48. Glue it to tag board and then color and cut out Claire Bear.

HOW TO USE Before children arrive, place Claire Bear somewhere in your classroom. During Daily Routines have a volunteer follow your instructions to help locate the bear. Use positional terms, such as *in, on, out, above, below, in front of, behind, top, middle,* and *bottom*. Once the bear is found, have the volunteer post the bear on the bulletin board.

Where is the Bear?

Poster Book p. GS-A

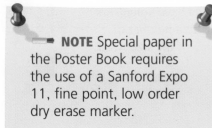

NOTE Special paper in the Poster Book requires the use of a Sanford Expo 11, fine point, low order dry erase marker.

① Communicating Together

Lesson Objective

Children will:
- discuss the different ways people communicate

Materials

Poster Book p. GS–A, magazine and newspaper pictures

Focus on Instruction

Tell children that every day people speak, listen, view, and write to learn about each other and the places and things around them.

Think and Discuss

Display Poster Book page GS–A and introduce children to Claire Bear. Explain that Claire Bear will remind them to use certain behaviors. Ask volunteers to identify whether Claire Bear is listening, speaking, viewing, or writing in each picture and why. Then use the following discussion prompts.

LISTENING
- When do you listen?
- What do you use to listen?
- To whom or to what do you listen?
- Why do you listen?

SPEAKING
- When do you speak?
- When do you speak loudly? softly?
- What do you use to speak?
- To whom do you speak?
- Why do you speak?

VIEWING
- When do you view?
- What do you use to view?
- What do you view?
- Why do you view?

WRITING
- When do you or others you know write?
- What do they use to write?
- To whom do they write? why?

Try It Together

Show various pictures from magazines or newspapers that depict people using one or more forms of communication. Ask volunteers to tell whether the people in the pictures are speaking, viewing, listening, and/or writing and explain their reasons.

Being a Good Listener

Lesson Objectives

Children will:
- recognize what it means to be a good listener
- apply listening tips

Materials

Poster Book p. GS–B, dry erase marker, Activity Master 49, cue card

Focus on Instruction

Tell children that they listen for many reasons—they listen to stories or music for fun and enjoyment, they listen to teachers and parents to learn new things and to stay safe, and they listen to their friends to show they care and to understand their feelings and/or problems. Explain to children that they can become better listeners by following some simple tips.

Think and Discuss

Display Poster Book page GS–B. Ask children to listen as you read the tips. Pause after reading each tip to have different children come up to the Poster Book page and circle the children in the photograph who appear to be following the tips.

> ## Listening Tips
> ✔ Listen carefully to the words.
> ✔ Think about what you hear.
> ✔ If you are listening to a person, look at the speaker's face and hands.
> ✔ Ask questions if you do not understand.

Try It Together

Now ask children to try to use the listening tips as you review your fire alarm procedure or other safety procedures with them. After finishing, discuss why it was important for them to be good listeners.

Tell children that throughout the school year they will have many opportunities to be good listeners. Display Activity Master 49, and explain that whenever you hold up Claire the Listening Bear it will be the signal for them to stop what they are doing and be good listeners. Reread the tips one more time as you hold up Claire the Listening Bear.

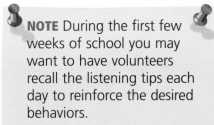

NOTE During the first few weeks of school you may want to have volunteers recall the listening tips each day to reinforce the desired behaviors.

Poster Book p. GS–C

③ Being a Good Speaker

Lesson Objectives

Children will:
- recognize what it means to be a good speaker
- apply speaking tips

Materials

Poster Book p. GS–C, Activity Masters 50–51

Focus on Instruction

Review with children some reasons why people speak—to share ideas, news, or problems and solutions and to give directions, for example. Then ask children to tell how speaking to adults can be different from speaking to other children. Tell children that people change how they speak and what they say to make the message clear to their listeners. Then discuss the speaking tips.

Think and Discuss

Read aloud the tips for being a good speaker. Pause after reading each tip to discuss with children why they think each tip is important.

> **Speaking Tips**
> ✔ Think about what you will say.
> ✔ Look at your listeners.
> ✔ Speak loudly and clearly.
> ✔ Use your face and hands to help your listeners understand.

Try It Together

Next Display Poster Book page GS–C. Explain to children that you will be the audience or the listener and you want volunteers to tell you about the picture. Give all children the opportunity to speak.

Display Activity Masters 50–51. Explain that whenever you hold up Claire the Speaking Bear with the megaphone in her hand it means you would like children to speak louder because you or others cannot hear them. If you hold up Claire the Speaking Bear giving the "Sh" gesture, it means you would like them to speak softly or stop talking, either because someone else is talking or because the room is too noisy.

> **NOTE** During the first weeks of school, review the Speaking Tips and practice using the different Claire Bear cue cards to reinforce the desired behaviors. As the school year progresses, note the development of children's speaking vocabulary. For example, do they use exact nouns, verbs, or adjectives?

④ Having a Conversation

Lesson Objectives

Children will:
- understand what it means to have a conversation
- apply conversation tips

Focus on Instruction

Tell children that a conversation is a talk between two or more people who take turns listening and speaking. Explain that when people have a conversation they can talk about many different things—they share ideas, ask questions, and tell their feelings. Explain to children that they can have better conversations by following some simple tips.

Think and Discuss

Read the tips for children. Pause after reading each tip to discuss why it is important.

Conversation Tips

✔ Listen carefully and speak clearly.

✔ Take turns.

✔ Ask questions if you do not understand.

✔ Look at the others in the group.

Try It Together

Role-play having a conversation with a volunteer in your classroom. Ask the volunteer what he or she wants to do after school that day and continue the conversation for a few minutes, modeling the tips.

Then ask pairs of children to have a conversation about what they want to do after school that day. As children converse, walk around the room helping them to stay on topic or to extend their conversations by asking questions. Throughout the year you can monitor children's progress in acquiring an expanded speaking vocabulary by having informal conversations.

Tell children that throughout the school year they will have many opportunities to have conversations with each other.

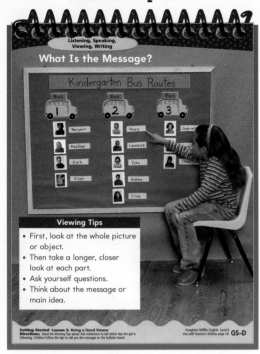

Poster Book p. GS–D

Listening, Speaking, Viewing, Writing

What Is the Message?

Kindergarten Bus Routes

Viewing Tips
- First, look at the whole picture or object.
- Then take a longer, closer look at each part.
- Ask yourself questions.
- Think about the message or main idea.

Getting Started Lesson 5: Being a Good Viewer
Directions: Read the Viewing Tips aloud. Ask volunteers to tell which tips the girl is following. Children follow the tips to tell you the message on the bulletin board.

Houghton Mifflin English Level K
Use with Teacher's Edition page 18. **GS–D**

⑤ Being a Good Viewer

Lesson Objectives

Children will:
- recognize what it means to be a good viewer
- apply viewing tips

Materials

Poster Book p. GS–D, Activity Master 52

Focus on Instruction

Remind children that they view many things every day and for many different reasons. For example, they may view pictures in a book to help them read, they may view signs on the street to help them stay safe, or they may watch videos, CD-ROMs, or television at home to learn new things or to enjoy themselves.

Explain that viewing is more than just looking at something or someone. It means thinking about what you are seeing so that you can get information. Explain to children that they can become better viewers by following some simple tips.

Think and Discuss

Read aloud the tips for being a good viewer. Display Poster Book page GS–D and discuss which tips the child seems to be following.

> Viewing Tips
> ✔ First, look at the whole picture or object.
> ✔ Then take a longer, closer look at each part.
> ✔ Ask yourself questions.
> ✔ Think about the message or main idea.

Activity Master 52

Daily Communication Links   Name _____

Being a Good Viewer

52 **Getting Started Daily Communication Links**
Directions: Color, cut out, and paste picture onto tag board to cue children that they should use their eyes to be good viewers.

Activity Master
Houghton Mifflin English Level K
Use with Teacher's Edition page 18.

Try It Together

Ask children to look at the bulletin board the child is looking at in the picture on Poster Book page GS–D. Then tell them to look at each part. Ask volunteers to tell what they think is the main idea or message. If necessary, model for children by asking yourself questions and making some conjectures aloud about the visual's message. (Sample answer: Who rides the bus to school?)

Then tell children that throughout the school year they will have numerous opportunities to be good viewers. Display Activity Master 52. Explain that whenever you hold up Claire the Viewing Bear holding the magnifying glass to her eye, it means you would like them to be good viewers.

⑥ Being a Good Writer

Lesson Objective

Children will:
• recognize where and why people write

Materials

Poster Book p. GS–E, Activity Master 53

Focus on Instruction

Remind children that people they know write every day and for many different reasons. People write lists to remember things to do. They write letters to family or friends. Some people write stories or reports. Tell them that during this school year they will begin to write with your help. Explain that they can begin to look for different types of writing they see at home and at school. They can start to think about why people write and for whom they write.

Think and Discuss

Use the following prompts with children. Say:

• *Do you see people writing at home, at school, or other places?*
• *To whom are they writing? Why are they writing?*

Try It Together

Display Poster Book page GS–E. Explain that each picture shows different types of writing. Ask volunteers to identify each type of writing and to talk about its purpose and audience. (Sample answers: 1. It is a letter written to share news with a friend. 2. It is a picture book written for children to enjoy. 3. These are labels written to help children in a classroom know where to put away different materials. 4. It is a name tag written to help children and a teacher remember where a person's desk is in the classroom. 5. It is a sign written to let people know where to leave the room or building. 6. It is a sign written to let people passing by know that lemonade is for sale.)

Then tell children that they will have many opportunities to be good writers. Display Activity Master 53. Explain that whenever you hold up Claire the Writing Bear, it means you will be working together to become good writers.

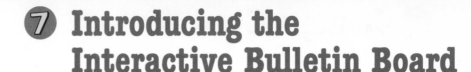

NOTE You may want to focus on a new element on the **Interactive Bulletin Board** each day until children understand the routine.

7 Introducing the Interactive Bulletin Board

Lesson Objective

Children will:
• learn routines, using the Interactive Bulletin Board

Materials

Interactive Bulletin Board, see pages 12–13, Activity Master 52

Focus on Instruction

Have children sit in a semicircle on the floor in front of the Interactive Bulletin Board.

Tell children that each day when they come to school they will put away their things and then come and sit as they are now in front of this bulletin board. Explain to children that they will help you to use this board to talk about different topics each day.

Think and Discuss

Hold up Claire the Viewing Bear. Tell children that you want them to be good viewers and think about what they might do with each element on the bulletin board. Then invite a few volunteers to tell what they think.

Try It Together

Model for children how to use each element on the Interactive Bulletin Board. Ask volunteers to help you as appropriate. See How-to-Use Instructions on pages 12–13.

⑧ Introducing Daily Discussion

Lesson Objectives

Children will:
- understand what it means to have a discussion
- apply discussion tips

Focus on Instruction

Have children sit in a semicircle on the floor in front of the Interactive Bulletin Board. Remind them that each day when they come to school they will put away their things and then come and sit as they are now in front of the board. Explain to children that after they work with the activities on the board they will then have a discussion together. Tell them that a discussion is a talk in which people share their ideas on one main idea or subject. Explain that you will have good discussions each day if together you follow some simple tips.

Think and Discuss

Read and discuss the importance of the following tips.

> Discussion Tips
> ✔ Share your ideas. They are important!
> ✔ Take turns listening and speaking.
> ✔ Speak clearly and loudly enough for everyone to hear.
> ✔ Keep to the topic or subject.
> ✔ Let others share ideas.
> ✔ If you are listening to a person, look at the speaker's face and hands.
> ✔ Think about what each person says.
> ✔ Raise your hand to ask questions if you do not understand.

Try It Together

Each morning before beginning your Daily Discussion, remind children of one or two of the Discussion Tips. Encourage them to focus on following these tips during your discussion. Soon children will grow accustomed to following all of the tips.

Unit 1
The Alphabet and Me

In this unit, children learn about letters and the alphabet. By listening to and discussing an alphabet book, they are introduced to the alphabet and its use in creating a language pattern. Children participate in the modeled writing of an alphabetical name book and then work together with you to create an alphabet Big Book. Unit skills develop language and relate to the published model and/or the unit focus.

What You Will Find in This Unit . . .

Unit 1 Planning Guide
The Alphabet and Me

	Poster Book	Transparency	Activity Masters Plus
DAILY COMMUNICATION LINKS			
Daily Routines *(26–27)*			
The oral language activities provide daily opportunities for children to develop their understanding of the alphabet and the relationship of letters to words.			
• **Interactive Bulletin Board:** Attendance List, Where Is the Bear?, Daily Message			
• **Daily Discussion Activity:** In the Spotlight Bulletin Board			
See also Additional Resources *(229)*			
Center Activities *(28–29)*			
• Reading and Listening Center • Writing Center			18–43
• Creative Arts Center • Social Studies Center			56–57
A Published Model ⏱ *1 day, 20 minutes*			
Lesson 1 Listening to an Alphabet Book *(30–31)* ABC and You: An Alphabet Book	1A		
Modeled Writing ⏱ *about 2 days, 20 minutes each day*			
Lesson 2 Making a Name Book *(32–33)*	1B–1C		59
Focus Skills ⏱ *about 6 days, 2 lessons a day, 20 minutes each day*			
Lesson 3 Oral Language: Making Introductions *(34)*			
Lesson 4 Oral Language: Following Directions *(34)*			60
Lesson 5 Viewing: Nonverbal Cues *(35)*			
Lesson 6 Viewing: Same and Different *(35)*			61
Lesson 7 Grammar: Nouns: People and Places *(36)*	1D		
Lesson 8 Grammar: Special Nouns and I *(36)*			62
Lesson 9 Vocabulary: Words for Feelings *(37)*			63
Lesson 10 Vocabulary: Positional Words: *Top, Middle, Bottom (37)*	1E		
Lesson 11 Writing: Writing the Alphabet *(38)*	1A		56–57
Lesson 12 Writing: Writing Names *(38)*			
Lesson 13 Study Skills: Parts of a Book *(39)*			
Lesson 14 Study Skills: Letters on a Keyboard *(39)*	1F		
Class Writing Project ⏱ *about 2–3 days, 20 minutes each day*			
Lesson 15 Our Big Book of Names *(40–41)*	1G		64–65

 MEETING INDIVIDUAL NEEDS *(42–45)*

Activities for Special Needs/Inclusion, for Students Acquiring English, for Reteaching, and for Enrichment/Challenge

Meeting Individual Needs

▶ **FOR SPECIAL NEEDS/INCLUSION:** *Houghton Mifflin English* Audiotape ▭ ; *See also* Reteaching.

▶ **FOR STUDENTS ACQUIRING ENGLISH:**
• Notes and activities are included in this Teacher's Edition throughout the unit to help you adapt or use lessons with students acquiring English.
• Students can listen to the published model *ABC and You: An Alphabet Book* on audiotape. ▭

▶ **RETEACHING**
• Activities for reteaching the focus skills are included on pages 42–45.

▶ **ENRICHMENT/CHALLENGE**
• Activities for challenge/enrichment that are correlated to focus skill lessons are included on pages 42–45.

 All audiotape recordings are also available on CD.

Additional Resources

Audiotapes

 Technology Tools
CD-ROM: Curious George® Paint & Print Studio
Paint, Write & Play! (published by The Learning Company)
*Type to Learn Jr.™

*©Sunburst Technology Corporation, a Houghton Mifflin Company. All rights reserved.

INTERNET: http://www.eduplace.com/rdg/hme/
Visit Education Place for these additional support materials and activities:
• author biographies
• patterns for shape booklets

 Informal Assessment
Activity Masters Plus, Assessment Checklists, pages 45–47

Keeping a Journal
In kindergarten, journals can be blank notebooks or folders filled with paper. As children draw and write about school activities, important events, and special thoughts, they can watch their writing growth as the year progresses.

 School-Home Connection
Suggestions for informing or involving family members in learning related to this unit are included in the Teacher's Edition throughout the unit.

Daily Routines

The oral language activities suggested here provide daily opportunities for children to develop their understanding of the alphabet and the relationship of letters to words. Refer to the **Interactive Bulletin Board** and **Daily Discussion** ideas on pages 10–13 and 20–21 for help in establishing Daily Routines for your classroom.

Interactive Bulletin Board

Attendance List

Anna   Bob   Carlos

Ⓔllen   Fran   Maria

Attendance List

Each day as children help you check the Attendance List, pick one Letter of the Day by pointing out new capital letters at the beginning of children's names. Ask children whose names also begin with that letter to stand up and say their names. Have other children give examples of words that begin with that letter.

Where is the Bear?

Daily Message

Print the day's capital letter. Name the letter, and describe the strokes you use to write it. Then retrace the letter on the board while children trace it in the air with their fingers.

Explain that names begin with a capital letter. Write a child's first name that begins with the day's letter. Ask a volunteer to say something positive about the child whose name was chosen. Record the statement, and read it aloud.

Where Is the Bear?

Place Claire Bear near an object whose name begins with the letter of the day. Have children guess the object by finding Claire Bear.

Daily Message

A
Amanda always shares her crayons.

Daily Discussion

Put a different child "in the spotlight" each day, following the order of the Attendance List. Ask each child to bring an item to school or to draw a picture of an activity that tells something about themselves. Children can use their item or picture as a prop as they share personal information, such as a special hobby, a fun trip, or a favorite family activity. Have other children ask questions to learn more about the speaker. Use the Think and Discuss questions below to prompt the discussion.

Make an **In the Spotlight Bulletin Board** to display the children's items from home and drawings. The day before a child will be in the spotlight, have that child draw a picture that shows his or her family, favorite place, or favorite thing to do. Help the child label the picture and write his or her name on it. Then have the child share the picture and add it to the bulletin board when he or she is in the spotlight.

NOTE To help children learn to follow the Rules for Discussion introduced in Getting Started, use the Claire Bear cue cards on Activity Masters 50–51.

Think and Discuss

- What is your full name?
- When is your birthday? How old are you?
- Do you have any brothers or sisters? What are their names?
- What is your favorite game? food? place? Why is it your favorite?
- What makes you feel happy?
- Who helps you? How do they help you?

NOUNS: PEOPLE Create an ongoing class picture list titled "People Who Help Us." Have children tell about people who help them and then draw pictures of them. (Examples: dad, sister, grandmother, teacher, firefighter, crossing guard, bus driver) Children can dictate nouns for you to write and label the pictures. Post the picture list on the Word Wall.

NOUNS: PLACES Create a second class picture list of "Our Favorite Places." Ask children to tell about and draw their favorite places. (Examples: park, library, beach, lake, restaurant, kitchen) Children can dictate nouns for you to label the pictures. Post this list on the Word Wall as well.

Daily Discussion Activity

In the Spotlight Bulletin Board

Center Activities

Center Activities provide additional daily opportunities for children to develop their understanding of the alphabet and the relationship of letters to words.

Reading and Listening Center

PUBLISHED MODEL Children can listen to the audiotape of *ABC and You* as they follow along in the book. **Listening**

LETTER MATCH Provide a double ordered set of six capital letter cards. Partners spread the 12 cards face down on a table. Each child alternates turning over two letter cards to try to make a match. If a match is made, the cards are taken out of play. If no match is made, the child replaces the cards in the same places on the table. Provide a different set of six ordered letter cards each day.

ALPHABET FAVORITES Provide various alphabet books for children to view when they come to this center. Place a strip of paper inside each book to serve as a bookmark and a ballot for children to show their preferences for particular books. Have children write the first letter of their name on the strip of their favorite book. At the end of the week you could have children help you tally the votes. Announce which alphabet book received the most votes.

Creative Arts Center

LETTER LISTS Provide several lists of names of objects that begin with consecutive letters of the alphabet. Make each first letter red and the rest of the letters black. For example, using the letters a, b, c, and d, the list could be; **a**pple, **b**at, **c**ap, and **d**og. Have children use tempera paints to paint the first letter for each word on the list.

NAME IN THE NEWS Have children write the first initial of their name at the top of a white sheet of construction paper. Then provide a sheet of newspaper. Have children write their first initial again and then cut around the letter to make a letter shape. Then they can paste the letter under their handwritten letter.

FINGER PAINTING Have children finger-paint using one letter of the alphabet. They can finger-paint the first letter of their names. When children are satisfied with their paintings, hang their papers up to dry.

CLAY-DOUGH LETTER PINS Have children use self-hardening clay or salt dough to form the capital and lowercase letters in their names. Help them attach jewelry pin backs (available at craft stores) to the clay letters. Allow the letters to harden, and then have children paint them. Tell children to use their fingers to trace the clay letters to practice how to write their names.

Writing Center

LETTER BOOKS Use Activity Masters 18–43 to provide Letter Books for all the letters of the alphabet. Each day, have children complete one or more Letter Books for the Letters of the Day. Then children can take home the Letter Books to share with family members.

HANDWRITING PRACTICE Have children practice writing the Letters of the Day by using your school's handwriting models. Review the correct formation of the day's letters by demonstrating on the board while children write the letters on ruled paper. Activity Masters 56–57 provide samples of traditional and modern handwriting models. **Viewing**

WRITING LETTER LISTS Have each child write the letter that begins his or her name at the top of a sheet of paper. Then they use pictures and/or words to list things whose names begin with that letter. Have them repeat the activity, using a letter of their choice. Provide sample lists, such as *fan, feather, fun,* and *fox* for *F.*

MATCHING LETTER LABELS Make labels for various objects in the Writing Center. Help children write the correct letters for the beginning letter of each labeled object on a self-stick note. They can place the letter label under the label you've created. For example, a child could use a self-stick note to match the label for *table* with a *t.* **Viewing**

 JOURNAL Have children make a journal using writing paper for the pages and construction paper for the cover. Encourage children to write the letters of the alphabet in their journals.

Social Studies Center

NAME TAGS Provide materials for making name tags. Help children write their names. Then have them sit in a circle and take turns introducing themselves to the person to their right, using the following model: "K, my name is Kate, and I like kangaroos." The person who sits next to Kate says, "Hello, Kate. B, my name is Bill, and I like baseball." **Viewing/Listening/Speaking**

A Published Model

About the Author

Eugenie Fernandes

Eugenie Fernandes has written several children's books. *Sleepy Little Mouse* was illustrated by her daughter, Kim Fernandes. This mother and daughter have worked together on other books, too.

Bibliography

You may also wish to read aloud these alphabet books.

- *Miss Bindergarten Gets Ready for Kindergarten* by Joseph Slate
- *Chicka Chicka Boom Boom* by Bill Martin Jr and John Archambault

Poster Book p. 1A

1 # Listening to an Alphabet Book

Lesson Objectives

Children will:
- listen to and discuss the characteristics of an alphabet book
- listen for and identify a language pattern
- evaluate the relationship of visuals and text
- respond personally and critically to the selection

Materials

ABC and You: An Alphabet Book, Poster Book p. 1A, Additional Resources p. 229

Optional Materials

tagboard, crayons or markers

Reading the Model

ABC and You: An Alphabet Book follows a pattern of letter, adjective, and child's name for every letter of the alphabet.

Building Background

Have children learn and sing "The Alphabet Song," using Poster Book page 1A and the music on Additional Resources page 229. Sing the song again, pointing to each letter on the Poster Book as you sing it.

Introducing Vocabulary

- As you display the appropriate page in *ABC and You*, discuss with children the meaning of each key vocabulary word: *brave* page 6, "strong and courageous"; *curious* page 7, "interested in everything"; *energetic* page 9, "full of energy"; *graceful* page 11, "moving with beauty"; and *organized* page 18, "putting everything in order."

- Ask volunteers to explain or show how they would act or what they would do if they were *brave, curious, energetic, graceful,* or *organized.*

Predicting and Purpose Setting

PICTURE WALK Display *ABC and You: An Alphabet Book* and read the title aloud. Identify the author and illustrator, Eugenie Fernandes. Preview the first four pages. Have children describe what they see for each letter, including a letter in a box, two words beginning with that letter, and a picture of a child. Then ask volunteers to predict what letter will come after C and why. Point out that the letters are in the order of the alphabet. Then continue the preview, having children identify the letters and discussing the pictures.

PURPOSE Explain that in *ABC and You* the author uses words the same way over and over to make a pattern. Tell children that the words are in pairs. Have children listen to find out what is the same about the second word in each pair as you read the book.

This selection is also available on audiotape.

Listening As a Writer

Think About Language

PROPER NOUNS Display pages 4–5 of *ABC and You*. Point to the two words. Tell children to listen as you read the words. Then ask: *What kind of word comes second in the pair?* (a person's name) Have children recall some of the names they heard. Then page through *ABC and You*, rereading the children's names.

LANGUAGE PATTERN: ADJECTIVES AND NOUNS Display pages 4–5 and reread the text. Ask: *What is the child's name?* (Amanda) *What word does the author use to describe her?* (amazing)

Repeat with pages 6 and 7 and then show a few pages for letters later in the book. Guide children to see that the author introduces each letter of the alphabet by using a pattern: a describing word and a name.

ALLITERATION Draw children's attention to the fact that the two words for each letter begin with the same letter and have the same sound. Explain that by doing this the author not only emphasizes that letter but also makes the words fun to hear and say.

Think About the Pictures

- Explain to children that looking at the pictures in *ABC and You* can help them understand the meanings of words. Turn to page 18 and read the name *Proud Peter*. Point out that Peter is smiling and waving, and his pony has a ribbon. Explain that a person feels proud when he or she won something or has done something well. Have children use the pictures in the book to help them define other words that may be unfamiliar, such as *royal* (page 20, "like a king or a queen") and *victorious* (page 24, "winning").

- Turn to page 6. Ask children if they can find anything else in the picture whose name begins with the same sound that they hear at the beginning of the name Ben. (baseball, bee, bird, bunny, butterfly) Continue with other examples.

NOTE If children are discussing and responding to the selection on a day following your initial reading of *ABC and You*, reread the book.

 FOR STUDENTS ACQUIRING ENGLISH

Make sure children acquiring English understand that the letters in the alphabet book represent the first letter of the words on that page in English. Use realia, actions, and additional examples to aid comprehension.

Responding

- **Personal Response** Tell each child to look at the page that begins with the same letter as his or her first name. Have children tell, dictate, or write what they liked or disliked about this page. Did they like the describing word? the illustration? Why or why not?

- **Critical Thinking** Tell children that you would like to replace a page in the book, such as page 10 about Freckled Freddie. Ask children to suggest what a replacement page for *F* might look like. What name could they use? What word could come before the name? What would the illustration show?

Modeled Writing

NOTE Unit 1 gives an overview of the alphabet for children beginning to learn letter-sound associations. Children are not expected to have mastery at the completion of this unit. Use Activity Masters 18–43, which provide booklets for each letter, throughout the year to support ongoing instruction with the alphabet.

Poster Book p. 1B

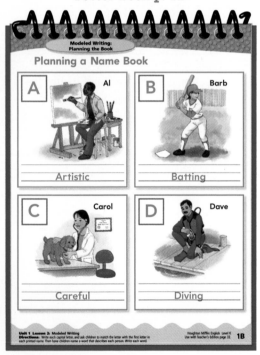

NOTE: Special paper in the Poster Book requires the use of a Sanford Expo 11, fine point, low odor dry erase marker.

② Making a Name Book

Lesson Objectives

Children will:
- help plan and draft a name book
- recognize and use proper nouns in alphabetical order

Materials

Poster Book pp. 1B, 1C, dry erase marker, crayons or colored markers, Activity Master 59

Optional Materials

scissors, glue, hole punch, yarn or string

Focus on Instruction

Recall with children that *ABC and You* includes children's names that begin with each letter of the alphabet. Explain that the letters of the alphabet follow an order, or pattern. The book shows the letters in order from A to Z. Explain that letters have their own names. Recite the names of the letters together. Tell children that you want to write a name book, using the first four letters of the alphabet: A, B, C, and D.

Planning the Book Poster Book p. 1B

- Tell children that first you must plan what you are going to write and decide who will want to read the name book.

Think Aloud I have four friends whose names begin with the first four letters of the alphabet: A, Al; B, Barb; C, Carol; and D, Dave. I could make a Name Book for them.

- Display Poster Book page 1B and read the title aloud. Explain to children that you will need their help to plan what you will write in this name book.

- Point to the small box at the top of each of the four large boxes. Explain that first you will write the first four letters of the alphabet that match the first letter of your friends' names. Write a capital *A* in the small box. Then guide children to name each of the next three letters: *B*, *C*, and *D*.

- Point to the name *Al* and read the name. Have children look at the picture and discuss what they see. Guide them to see that a good word to describe Al is *artistic* because he is an artist. Write the word *Artistic* on the line under the picture. Continue in the same way for each of the other names: B, *Batting*; C, *Careful* (She is careful when handling pets.); D, *Diving*.

Writing the Book Poster Book p. 1C

Explain to children that now you are ready to make your name book. Point out that the title tells what your book will be about.

Reread the first five pages of *ABC and You*, tracking each letter and the two words as you read them.

- Then review with children the planning you did on Poster Book page 1B. Explain that you will use the words from the planning page to write your name book so that it matches the pattern in *ABC and You*.

DRAFTING THE TEXT Display Poster Book page 1C and point out the letters at the top of each square. Help children identify each letter, and then ask volunteers to trace over the letter outlines. Point out that the letters are in the order of the alphabet.

- Explain that you want to write a describing word next to each of your friends' names to tell more about each one. You will use the words from the planning page that begin with the same first letter as the friend's name.

Think Aloud We said that Al is artistic. I will add the word *Artistic* before *Al* to tell about my friend the artist: *A Artistic Al*. We said that Barb is batting the ball. I will add the word *Batting* before *Barb*: *B Batting Barb*. We said that Carol was careful when she handles pets. I will write the word *Careful* before *Carol*: *C Careful Carol*. We said that Dave is diving. I will add the word *Diving* before *Dave*: *D Diving Dave*.

MODELING CONCEPTS OF PRINT Help children become familiar with concepts of print by modeling as you draft the page.

- Point out that you are moving from **left to right** as you write letters and words. As you read a word aloud, follow the text with your finger, using a sweeping motion from left to right.
- Reinforce the **concept of a word** by explaining that the group of letters you have written stands for a word. Name the word. Point out that you have left a space before and after it.
- Reinforce **capitalizing proper nouns**. As you are writing, pause to ask volunteers how you should begin a name.

Sharing the Book

- Read the Poster Book page 1C aloud, emphasizing the alliterative letter, the describing word, and the name. Tell children you will make a copy to give to your friends.
- Tell children that this book only uses four letters of the alphabet in order. Explain that in a few days they will work together to make a class name book that uses their own names in the ABC pattern.

 SCHOOL-HOME CONNECTION Activity Master 59

Have children make a name book page of their own to take home and share with family members. Have them draw a self-portrait and help them write their initial capital letter and first name, for example, *M Molly*.

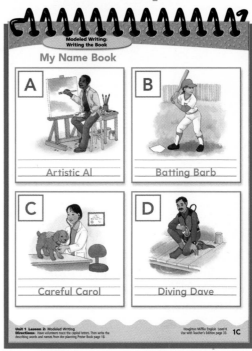

Poster Book p. 1C

My Name Book

A — Artistic Al
B — Batting Barb
C — Careful Carol
D — Diving Dave

Unit 1 Lesson 2: Modeled Writing
Directions: Have volunteers trace the capital letters. Then write the describing words and names from the planning Poster Book page 1B.

Houghton Mifflin English Level K
Use with Teacher's Edition page 33. 1C

 FOR STUDENTS ACQUIRING ENGLISH

To help children associate letters with sounds in English, have each child say his or her own name. Assist each child in identifying the first letter in English. Model using the children's names as in "T is for Tran," "P is for Petra," and have children repeat after you.

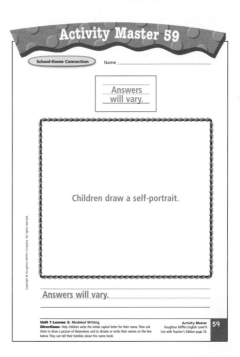

Activity Master 59

School-Home Connection   Name _____

Answers will vary.

Children draw a self-portrait.

Answers will vary.

Unit 1 Lesson 2: Modeled Writing
Directions: Help children write the initial capital letter for their name. Then ask them to draw a picture of themselves and to dictate or write their names on the line below. They can tell their families about the name book.

Activity Master
Houghton Mifflin English Level K
Use with Teacher's Edition page 33. 59

Focus Skill Oral Language

③ Making Introductions

Lesson Objectives

Children will:
- introduce themselves to peers
- introduce two children to each other

Ask volunteers to tell about meeting someone new. What did they say first? What did they tell about themselves?

- Model how to introduce yourself by saying your name and telling something about yourself. (Example: "Hello. My name is Mrs. Foster. I am a kindergarten teacher.") Ask children to take turns following your example.

- Use two volunteers to demonstrate how to introduce people. (Example: "Tim, this is Molly. She likes to play soccer. Molly, this is Tim. Tim plays soccer too.") Have the volunteers give appropriate responses. (Example: "Hi, Molly. It's nice to meet you." "Hello, Tim. It's nice to meet you too.") Point out that you tell each person's name and something about that person. Have groups of three take turns introducing and responding to each other.

④ Following Directions

Lesson Objective

Children will:
- follow one- and two-step oral directions

Materials

Activity Master 60, yellow and blue crayons

Ask children when they follow directions. (Sample answers: playing games, baking cookies) Tell them that listening carefully helps them follow directions.

- Play Simon Says with children, giving them one-step directions. (Examples: Simon says, "Stand up. Sit down.") Point out that by listening carefully and doing what Simon says, they were following directions.

- Play Simon Says again, giving two-step directions. (Examples: Put your hands over your head and tap. Simon says, "Raise your hand and wave.") Point out that children have followed directions to do two things.

- Distribute Activity Master 60. Explain that children should listen for two things to do as you read directions aloud. 1. Point to the circle under the pigs, and color it yellow. 2. Point to the circle under the farmer, and mark an X in it. 3. Point to the circle under the goats, and make a blue dot in it.

- Have children take turns giving and following one- and two-step directions.

 INFORMAL ASSESSMENT (See Activity Masters Plus p. 45)

 MEETING INDIVIDUAL NEEDS (See p. 42)

 FOR STUDENTS ACQUIRING ENGLISH

Allow children to watch several introductions between more proficient classmates and between yourself and others. Provide a simpler model as needed. Say: *Hello. My name is ____. What is your name?* Allow children acquiring English ample opportunity to practice. Then have them move about the room introducing themselves and asking classmates' names.

Activity Master 60

Focus Skill: Oral Language   Name _____

Listen and Do Too!

60 Unit 1 Lesson 4: Following Directions
Directions: Have children listen to follow two-step directions that you read aloud from the Teacher's Edition.

Activity Master
Houghton Mifflin English Level K
Use with Teacher's Edition page 34.

 **Viewing**

⑤ Nonverbal Cues

Lesson Objectives

Children will:
- use visual cues to identify feelings
- identify meanings of gestures and use gestures to communicate

 **FOR STUDENTS ACQUIRING ENGLISH**

Keep in mind that nonverbal cues and meanings of gestures vary considerably among cultures. As volunteers share expressions or gestures, say the corresponding words in English. Have children acquiring English repeat the words and make the faces or gestures with you. Do this several times for each word.

Ask volunteers to share happy experiences. Have them show how their faces look when they are happy. Ask children what they might do with their hands to show they loved a good catch in a baseball game. (clap)

- Point out that facial expressions can also show a person's feelings. Ask a volunteer to pantomime looking sad. Have children identify the feeling and point out the features that show the child is sad. Repeat with *excited*, *bored*, and other feelings.

- Tell children that another way people express themselves is by moving their hands. Demonstrate by raising your hand, and have children tell what you are "saying." Have pairs of children take turns using their hands to give these directions: *Be quiet!* (finger on lips) *Come here.* (hand motion toward yourself) *Stop!* (arm stretched out with hand facing forward)

⑥ Same and Different

Lesson Objective

Children will:
- use the terms *same* and *different* to compare letter forms

Materials

Activity Master 61, two alphabet cards for *A, C, E, Q, S, X*; six blocks; including two that are the same shape

Show six blocks, including one identical pair. Ask volunteers to find two blocks that are the same shape and two blocks that are different shapes. Discuss with children how the blocks are the same or different, focusing on shape.

- Point out that letters can also be the same shape or different shapes. Mix up and display the alphabet cards. Help children identify the letters and then compare the letter forms, finding pairs that are the same and different.

- Distribute Activity Master 61. In the top row, have children find the two shapes that are the same and circle them. Then have children identify the letter Claire Bear is holding and circle the same letter in each row.

 INFORMAL ASSESSMENT (*See* Activity Masters Plus p. 45)

 MEETING INDIVIDUAL NEEDS (*See* p. 42)

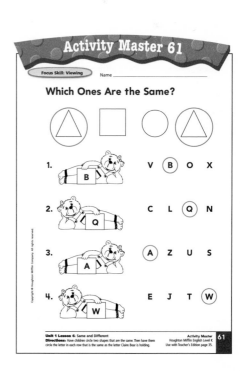

Activity Master 61

Focus Skill: Viewing   Name _____

Which Ones Are the Same?

1. B   V Ⓑ O X
2. Q   C L Ⓠ N
3. A   Ⓐ Z U S
4. W   E J T Ⓦ

Unit 1 Lesson 6: Same and Different
Directions: Have children circle two shapes that are the same. Then have them circle the letter in each row that is the same as the letter Claire Bear is holding.
Houghton Mifflin English Level K
Use with Teacher's Edition page 35.
Activity Master **61**

FOR STUDENTS ACQUIRING ENGLISH

Use the Picture Dictionary and the Poster Book to teach or review naming words for people and places that more proficient children give as examples. Plan to give extra practice in distinguishing between *he* and *she* and other gender-related pronouns.

Poster Book p. 1D

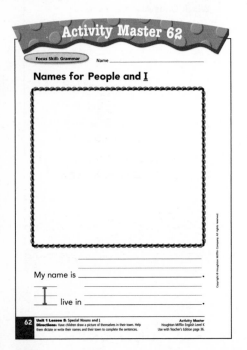

Activity Master 62

 Focus Skill **Grammar**

⑦ Nouns

Lesson Objectives

Children will:
• identify nouns for people and places
• match people with their workplaces

Materials

Poster Book p. 1D, dry erase marker

PEOPLE AND PLACES Ask children to name some kinds of people they know at school; for example, you are a *teacher*. (Sample answers: librarian, boy, girl) Then have them name some places they know well. (Sample answers: home, park) Tell children that words for people or places are naming words, or nouns.

● Display Poster Book page 1D. Point to the picture of the doctor. Ask children to identify the person and discuss what she does. Write a naming word to label the person. Repeat with the remaining pictures.

● Point to the picture of the hospital and discuss it with children. Write a naming word to label the place. Repeat with the remaining pictures.

● Talk with children about which person works in each place. Have volunteers draw lines to match the people with the appropriate places.

⑧ Special Nouns and I

Lesson Objectives

Children will:
• write or dictate proper nouns for people and places with a capital letter
• trace I with a capital letter

Materials

ABC and You, chart paper, markers, Activity Master 62

Tell children you are thinking of a girl in the class. Tell them that this girl has a name. Print the girl's name on the board and read it aloud, saying that the name tells exactly which girl. Say: *A person's name begins with a capital letter.*

● Display pages 8–9 *ABC and You*. Point to and read the names *Dan* and *Emily*. Ask children what kind of letter begins each name. (a capital letter)

● Explain that some nouns name special places. Have children name their town and school to complete these sentences: *I live in ___. I go to ___.* Record the sentences on chart paper and point out the capital letters.

● Circle the *I* in each sentence. Point out that *I* is a capital letter.

● Have children complete Activity Master 62. Tell children to draw a picture of themselves in a favorite place in their town or city. Then have them dictate or write the missing words to complete the sentences.

 INFORMAL ASSESSMENT (*See* Activity Masters Plus p. 46)

MEETING INDIVIDUAL NEEDS (*See* p. 43)

Focus Skill Vocabulary

⑨ Words for Feelings

Lesson Objective

Children will:
• learn words that describe feelings

Materials

ABC and You, Activity Master 63

Ask: *Have you ever felt excited? grumpy? What other feelings can you name?*

• Tell children that some words name feelings. Display page 6 in *ABC and You* featuring Brave Ben, and ask what it is like to feel brave. Have children give examples of when someone might feel brave. Repeat with other illustrations, such as Proud Peter and Excited Xavier.

• For Activity Master 63, give these directions in turn: Draw a circle around the <u>tired</u> child. Put an X under the <u>surprised</u> child. Draw a red line under the <u>proud</u> child. Then have children identify and discuss the other feelings pictured: <u>silly</u>, <u>upset</u>, and <u>cheerful</u>.

⑩ Positional Words

Lesson Objective

Children will:
• recognize the terms *top*, *middle*, and *bottom*

Materials

Poster Book p. 1E, dry erase marker

Ask: *Who can point to the <u>top</u> of the door? the <u>middle</u>? the <u>bottom</u>?* Tell children that understanding the words *top*, *middle*, and *bottom* will help them when they learn to write the letters of the alphabet.

• Display Poster Book page 1E. Use the words *top*, *middle*, and *bottom* to identify each shelf as you point to it. Have children use the words to locate toys in the picture. Ask: *What is on the top shelf? Where is the teddy bear?*

• Ask volunteers to draw simple toys, such as balls, on the top, middle, and bottom shelves.

• Point to the write-on line at the bottom of Poster Book page 1E. Explain that the write-on line is set up like the shelves above. Ask volunteers to point to the top, middle, and bottom rules of the write-on line.

• Explain that the rules can help them write letters correctly. Some letters begin at the top line, all letters touch the middle line, and some letters go below the bottom line. Write *l*, *a*, and *p* to demonstrate. Help children use the classroom alphabet banner to find other examples.

 INFORMAL ASSESSMENT (*See* Activity Masters Plus p. 47)

 MEETING INDIVIDUAL NEEDS (*See* p. 43)

Activity Master 63

How Do You Feel?

Poster Book p. 1E

FOR STUDENTS ACQUIRING ENGLISH

Say each letter and key word as you point to the drawing, and have the children repeat after you. To reinforce the letter-sound relationships, use the simpler "A is for apple." Call on children to come up and point to the object or letter. For example, say: *Point to the letter B.*

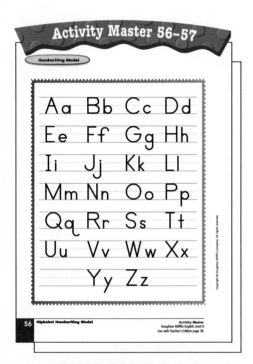

Activity Master 56–57

Handwriting Model

Aa Bb Cc Dd
Ee Ff Gg Hh
Ii Jj Kk Ll
Mm Nn Oo Pp
Qq Rr Ss Tt
Uu Vv Ww Xx
Yy Zz

56 Alphabet Handwriting Model   **Activity Master**
Houghton Mifflin English Level K
Use with Teacher's Edition page 38.

Focus Skill   **Writing**

11 Writing the Alphabet

Lesson Objective

Children will:
• recite and write the alphabet

Materials

Poster Book p. 1A

Optional Materials

Activity Masters 56–57

Sing "The Alphabet Song" on Poster Book page 1A. Tell children that now that they know the names of the letters in the alphabet, they will learn to write the letters.

• Display an alphabet strip of your school's handwriting style. Have children recite the alphabet.

• Have children write the alphabet by following your school's handwriting models. See Activity Masters 56–57 for traditional and modern handwriting models.

12 Writing Names

Lesson Objectives

Children will:
• dictate or write their names, beginning with capital letters
• dictate or write other proper nouns correctly

Materials

chart paper, markers, drawing paper, crayons

Ask a child to tell you his or her name. Tell children that everyone's name is special. Explain that today they'll write their own name and some special names of other people.

• Remind children that they have learned about special names for people and places. Write a child's name on chart paper, and read it aloud. Ask a volunteer to identify and underline the capital letter that begins this special name.

• Discuss common proper names children should know, such as the names of their teacher, principal, school, street, town or city. Write the names on chart paper. Ask volunteers to underline the capital letters.

• Tell children to draw a picture of themselves having fun with family members or friends. Have children dictate or write their own name to label themselves in the picture. Then ask children to dictate or write the special names of the other people in the picture.

 INFORMAL ASSESSMENT (*See* Activity Masters Plus p. 46)

 MEETING INDIVIDUAL NEEDS (*See* p. 44)

Focus Skill **Study Skills**

⑬ Parts of a Book

Lesson Objective

Children will:
• identify the parts of a book

Materials

ABC and You, picture books with a table of contents

Display the book *ABC and You*. Point to the cover and say: *Name one thing you like on the cover of this book. What does the cover tell us about the book?* Explain that knowing the parts of a book will help children find different kinds of information.

● Display the cover of *ABC and You,* reading the book's title and author/illustrator. Show children the title page, and read the information found there. Then display a picture book. Have children point out the cover, title, title page, and names of the author and illustrator.

● Next, show children a classroom textbook. Ask them to find the cover, title, and title page. Show them the table of contents, and explain its purpose.

⑭ Letters on a Keyboard

Lesson Objectives

Children will:
• learn the basic parts of a computer
• type and print the alphabet and their names

Materials

Poster Book p. 1F

Optional Materials

computer

Ask children if any of them have seen or used a computer. Have them talk about their experiences. Ask: *Who can tell us about a computer mouse? Is it a little furry animal?* Have a volunteer explain how a computer mouse is used.

● Display Poster Book page 1F. Have children help you identify each part of the computer. Point to the keyboard, and explain that it contains all the letters of the alphabet. Tell children that the letters are not in the order of the alphabet. The letters are in a different order to make typing quicker and easier. Call out different letters and help children find them on the keyboard.

● If you have a computer show children how to turn it on. Help them practice pressing keys and reading the letters as they appear on the monitor display.

● Show children how to type capital letters. Then have a few volunteers demonstrate typing the alphabet and their names. Show children how to print out their work.

 INFORMAL ASSESSMENT (*See* Activity Masters Plus p. 46)

 MEETING INDIVIDUAL NEEDS (*See* p. 44)

 FOR STUDENTS ACQUIRING ENGLISH

As you point out the parts of a book, say aloud the words for each part. Have children repeat after you. Show children in which direction we read a book and the lines of print in English; keep in mind that other languages display different directionality in both.

Poster Book p. 1F

I See Letters!

monitor

keyboard

mouse

Poster Book p. 1G

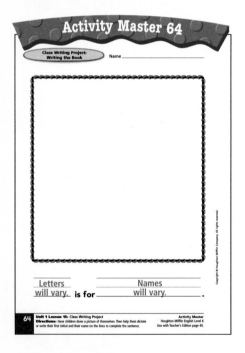

FOR STUDENTS ACQUIRING ENGLISH

Make sure all of the children acquiring English can write their own names. For the Poster Book, help children understand all the picturable nouns chosen by referring to a picture dictionary or providing realia, art, or photos. Write and say the words and have children repeat them.

15 Our Big Book of Names

Lesson Objectives

Children will:
- help plan a Name Big Book
- write letters and their names for a page in the Big Book
- illustrate a page in the Big Book

Materials

Poster Book p. 1G, Activity Masters 64–65, drawing paper, crayons, markers

Focus on Instruction

Remind children that they helped you make a Name Book, using your friends' names. Explain that now they will make a class *Name Big Book* using letters of the alphabet in order and the children's own names. Tell children that each of them will make one or two pages for this book; when all the pages are done, you will put them together to make one class Big Book that will help them remember every person's name and the letters of the alphabet.

Planning the Book Poster Book p. 1G

- Explain that before writing the book, they need to plan what they will say.
- Display Poster Book page 1G. Remind children that the letters of the alphabet follow a pattern and each letter has its own name. Read the alphabet together. Point to each letter as the children say it.
- Then model for children what they will do on their own letter/name pages, writing the letter of your first name and your name in the spaces provided in the sentence at the bottom of the Poster Book page. Say: *Every name begins with a capital letter. My name begins with (letter). I will write the letter and my name on these lines.*

Writing the Book Activity Master 64

- Then hand out Activity Master 64 to each child, saying each letter of the alphabet and having children whose name begins with that letter come up and get the paper.
- Tell children to draw a picture of themselves inside the frame on the Activity Master. Then help them write the first letter of their names. Have them dictate or write their names on the lines provided.
- Finally, collect the pages by having children bring them up in alphabetical order. Ask children to paste their pages on large sheets of paper.

NOTE: If there is more than one child whose name begins with a particular letter, have both children create their own pages. When assembling the book, explain that there really are not two Gs in the alphabet, but in your class name book you need two Gs to show both names. Similarly, if there are letters that are not represented among your students, tell children that the class name book has only the letters that match the beginning letter of their names.

Sharing the Book

- Remind children that a book has a title that helps readers know what the book is about. Together, decide on a title for the Name Big Book. Have volunteers make a cover.

- Ask children to share their pages with the class. Have each child "read" his or her page. Encourage children to begin by pointing to their letter and then "read" their sentence, for example, "A is for Alicia."

- Bind the pages together. Then read the book together as a group, beginning with the title. As you turn each page, point to the letter, and then read the sentence.

- Praise children for creating a Name Big Book about their own class. Place the Big Book in your Reading and Listening Center.

 SCHOOL-HOME CONNECTION Activity Master 65

Have children take home a copy of "The Alphabet Song" to sing with family members. Have each child find the capital letter that begins his or her first name and circle it. Children may wish to circle letters for their family members' first initials as well.

Activity Master 65

School-Home Connection   Name _____

The Alphabet Song

A B C D E F G

H I J K L M N O P

Q R S and T U V

W and X Y Z.

Now you've heard my ABC's.

Next time won't you sing with me?

Unit 1 Lesson 15: Class Writing Project
Directions: Have children sing the song with family members. Then they can circle their initial and the initials of other family members.
Activity Master **65**
Houghton Mifflin English Level K
Use with Teacher's Edition page 41.

Meeting Individual Needs

Lesson 3 Focus Skill   Oral Language: Making Introductions

RETEACHING ALTERNATIVE STRATEGY

Tell children to pretend you are at a party meeting each other for the first time. Introduce yourself to a child, telling your name and something about yourself. Ask: *What is your name? What can you tell me about yourself?* Give children a chance to introduce themselves and to introduce two people to each other. Prompt children with questions if necessary.

CHALLENGE

Have children pretend to be story characters, such as Goldilocks or the Big Bad Wolf, and introduce themselves to the class as those characters. Children may also enjoy playing favorite characters as they introduce themselves to each other, making up what characters such as Goldilocks and Little Red Riding Hood might say if they met.

FOR STUDENTS ACQUIRING ENGLISH

Allow children to watch several introductions between more proficient classmates. Provide a simpler model as needed, such as: *Hello. My name is _____ What is your name?* Allow children ample opportunity to practice introducing themselves and asking classmates' names. Provide prompts as needed.

Lesson 4 Focus Skill   Oral Language: Following Directions

RETEACHING ALTERNATIVE STRATEGY

Play a variation of Follow the Leader in which you give one-step oral directions and children follow them. Say: *Stand up. Pat your head. Sit down.* Continue by saying simple two-step directions. Say: *Raise your hand and put it down.* Ask volunteers to take turns being the leader and giving first one-step and then two-step oral directions.

CHALLENGE

Play Two-Step Mother May I in which the child who is "Mother" gives two-step directions to the other players in turn. (Example: *Mother, may I take a baby step? You may take one baby step and two giant steps.*) The other players must ask: *Mother, may I?* before following the direction.

FOR STUDENTS ACQUIRING ENGLISH

Before you begin the game of Follow the Leader, allow children acquiring English to watch as more proficient classmates perform some simple one-step commands. Encourage them to join in when they feel ready. Use commands, such as: *Stand up. Touch your nose. Jump up and down. Point to me.* Call attention to the missing "you" in the commands.

Lesson 5 Focus Skill   Viewing: Nonverbal Clues

RETEACHING ALTERNATIVE STRATEGY

Stretching your arms overhead and then yawning with your eyelids closed, ask: *How do I feel if I do this?* (sleepy, tired) *How do you know?* Then put your finger to your pursed mouth and ask: *What do I mean if I do this?* (Be quiet.) Then whisper feelings or gestures for children to act out and their classmates to identify. (Examples: laughing, crying, waving hello)

CHALLENGE

Have children work in pairs to develop gestures and facial expressions for situations such as: "I'm tired." "Come with me." "I don't like this food." "I'm cold." Have each pair share the gestures and expressions they created for others to guess.

FOR STUDENTS ACQUIRING ENGLISH

Keep in mind that nonverbal cues and meanings of gestures vary considerably among cultures. As volunteers share expressive gestures, say the corresponding words in English. Have children acquiring English repeat the words and make the faces or gestures with you. Do this several times for each word.

Lesson 6 Focus Skill   Viewing: Same and Different

RETEACHING ALTERNATIVE STRATEGY
Assemble a group of letters, including some duplicate letter shapes. Select two identical uppercase letters and ask: *Are these letters the same or different?* Then select two different letters and ask the question. Use the letters to explain the terms *same* and *different.* Repeat with other selections.

CHALLENGE
Have children play Memory with letter cards. Provide children with two sets of alphabet cards. Have children mix up the cards and place them face down in rows. Players take turns turning over two cards at a time. If the letters are the same, the player keeps the pair and takes another turn. If the letters are different, the player turns the cards back over. The player with the most cards wins the game.

FOR STUDENTS ACQUIRING ENGLISH
Use the blocks, math counters, or other objects you have chosen to introduce or review shape and color words and words used for comparing. Then have children work in groups to arrange two or more items together according to sameness or difference; for example, same color, same shape; different materials.

Lesson 7 Focus Skill   Grammar: Nouns

RETEACHING ALTERNATIVE STRATEGY
Make a chart of naming words for kinds of people and places at school. Add drawings to help children remember these words. List people on the left and places on the right. Focus on common nouns rather than proper nouns for individuals. Begin the list with *teacher, boy, girl* on the left and *classroom* on the right. Then have children suggest naming words for people in the cafeteria, library, principal's office, and so on.

CHALLENGE
Show children how to fold a page of construction paper in half to make a four-page booklet. Have them draw pictures of the people and places they see in their school or neighborhood, putting one person and place on each page. Help children label each person and place with common nouns.

FOR STUDENTS ACQUIRING ENGLISH
Use Poster Book p. 1D to teach or review naming words for people and places. Have children repeat the naming words after you. Children can also ask questions using the naming words; for example, *Where is the doctor?*

Lesson 8 Focus Skill   Grammar: Special Nouns and *I*

RETEACHING ALTERNATIVE STRATEGY
Help children make posters of themselves. First print this sentence frame on the board: *My name is _____. I live in _____.* Print your own name and city or town to complete the sentences, pointing out the capital letters. Then give children the sentence frame printed on drawing paper. Have children dictate or write the missing words and draw a picture.

CHALLENGE
Have children make a bulletin board display of favorite storybook characters. Children can find and copy the names of their favorite characters to complete the sentence frame *My name is _____. I live in _____.* Then they can draw pictures of the characters to illustrate their sentences.

FOR STUDENTS ACQUIRING ENGLISH
Be prepared to help children acquiring English practice the names of storybook characters shown for the Challenge activity. Build background as necessary. Ask children to name story characters from their own cultures and use them to help children complete the sentence frames as shown above.

Meeting Individual Needs

Lesson 9 Focus Skill Vocabulary: Words for Feelings

RETEACHING ALTERNATIVE STRATEGY
Tell children you are very happy today. Ask: *How can my face show my feelings?* (It can smile.) Act out several facial expressions that show different feelings, and have children name the feeling and act it out themselves. Then suggest different situations, and ask volunteers to name and act out how they might feel. Examples: You get a pony for your birthday. Your best friend moves away. You win a race.

CHALLENGE
Divide children into groups of two or three. Secretly give each group a word for a feeling, and have them make up a skit that shows characters experiencing the feeling. Ask others to identify the feeling being dramatized.

FOR STUDENTS ACQUIRING ENGLISH

Children acquiring English will need help with many of the words for feelings. As classmates dramatize feelings, ask choice questions, such as: *Is _____ happy? Is _____ silly or serious?* Use some opposites and some unrelated pairs. After a response is given, have all the children repeat it.

Lesson 10 Focus Skill Vocabulary: Positional Words

RETEACHING ALTERNATIVE STRATEGY
Ask a volunteer to point to the top, middle, and bottom of the board. Then draw write-on lines on the board, and have a volunteer point to the top, middle, and bottom rules. Give children a copy of your school's handwriting model, lined paper, and pencils or crayons. Have them follow the model to write letters that touch the top, middle, and bottom rules.

CHALLENGE
While others close their eyes, have two children strike a pose. Ask classmates to open their eyes and observe. Then, as others close their eyes again, have the two change their pose slightly. When classmates open their eyes, ask them to tell the new position of the pose.

FOR STUDENTS ACQUIRING ENGLISH

Ask volunteers to point to the top, middle, and bottom of several classroom objects as you say the words. Have children acquiring English repeat after you. Then move on to full phrases, such as *the bottom of the page.* Check for correct pronunciation of *bottom.*

Lesson 11 Focus Skill Writing: Writing the Alphabet

RETEACHING ALTERNATIVE STRATEGY
Make a flat, damp surface for writing the alphabet in the sand table. Use a yardstick to press write-on rules into the sand. Give children a sample of your school's handwriting model. Then have pairs of children take turns writing letters of the alphabet, and checking the letters against the handwriting model.

CHALLENGE
Have children create their own pages for a picture dictionary. First have them write the capital and lowercase letters from the handwriting model. Then children can illustrate the page with pictures of animals and other objects beginning with the letter for that page.

FOR STUDENTS ACQUIRING ENGLISH

Make sure that children acquiring English can see the complete alphabet and that they understand you are going to practice writing these same letters in the sand. Show the children exactly how to form each letter. Demonstrate precisely where to begin, how to make and connect the elements in each letter, and where to end.

Lesson 12 Focus Skill Writing: Writing Names

RETEACHING ALTERNATIVE STRATEGY
Children can make tactile glitter name cards. Remind them that first and last names begin with capital letters, and help them write their full names with a squeeze bottle of white glue on construction paper. Then have children sprinkle glitter over the letters and let them dry. Children can trace the letters with their fingers as they name the letters.

CHALLENGE
Explain the importance of children's knowing their full name, complete address, parents' names, and their home and work telephone numbers. Help children find out and dictate or write this information on adhesive labels. Point out that part of writing this information so it is easy to understand is the correct use of capital letters. Have children put these labels on the insides of backpacks, lunch boxes, and notebooks.

FOR STUDENTS ACQUIRING ENGLISH

Before children acquiring English make their names in glue and glitter, allow them to practice writing their names using several different media, including crayons, markers, and chalk. Make sure the children write from left to right and that they know where to use capital letters.

Lesson 13 Focus Skill Study Skills: Parts of a Book

RETEACHING ALTERNATIVE STRATEGY
Take the children to the school library for a Book Search. Display a library book and ask: *What does the cover tell us about the book?* Point out the title page and table of contents and ask children what information they provide. Then have pairs of children find and tag other examples of book parts in library books. Ask the pairs to show the class different book parts and tell what information they provide.

CHALLENGE
Have children design covers and write or dictate title pages and tables of contents for a book about themselves. Suggest they use books from the school library as models.

FOR STUDENTS ACQUIRING ENGLISH

As you point out the parts of a book, say the words and have the children repeat them after you. Show children in which direction a book is read in English and also the directionality of lines of print. Keep in mind that other languages display different directionality in both.

Lesson 14 Focus Skill Study Skills: Letters on a Keyboard

RETEACHING ALTERNATIVE STRATEGY
Children can have a Letter Hunt using the computer keyboard. Give each pair of children a set of capital alphabet cards. Show children how to type capital letters on the computer keyboard. Then have pairs take turns picking a card, saying the letter name aloud, and typing the matching letter on the computer, while the other checks for typing accuracy.

CHALLENGE
Pairs of children can have an Alphabet Contest. Have each child type the alphabet, print it out, and trade printouts with a partner. Partners can check each other's work for errors. Have partners continue typing and checking, working toward no errors. Give a round of applause to the first pair who type the alphabet with no errors.

FOR STUDENTS ACQUIRING ENGLISH

As children acquiring English work with the capital alphabet cards, make sure they can see a complete alphabet with capital and lowercase letters. Make sure children understand that the order on the computer is not the order of the alphabet. Encourage the children to refer to each letter by its name.

Unit 2
Words We Know

In this unit, children learn about common groups of words. By listening to and discussing a counting book, they are introduced to number words, color words, animal names, and rhyming words and their use in creating a language pattern. Children participate in the modeled writing of a counting book about animals and then work together with you to create a counting Big Book. Unit skills develop language and relate to the published model and/or the unit focus.

What You Will Find in This Unit . . .

Unit 2 Planning Guide

Words We Know

	Poster Book	Transparency	Activity Masters Plus
DAILY COMMUNICATION LINKS			
Daily Routines *(50–51)*			
The oral language activities provide daily opportunities for children to develop their understanding of number, color, animal, and rhyming words. • **Interactive Bulletin Board:** Number Wheel, Color Wheel, Daily Message • **Daily Discussion Activity:** "Five Little Chickadees" *See also* Additional Resources *(229–233)*			
Center Activities *(52–53)*			
• Reading and Listening Center • Creative Arts Center • Math Center • Writing Center • Science Center			54
A Published Model ⏱ *1 day, 20 minutes* **Lesson 1** Listening to a Counting Book *(54–55)* *One Gray Mouse*			
Modeled Writing ⏱ *about 2 days, 20 minutes each day* **Lesson 2** Making a Counting Book *(56–57)*	2A, 2B	2–1, 2–2	66–68
Focus Skills ⏱ *6 days, 2 lessons a day, 20 minutes each day*			
Lesson 3 Oral Language: Listening for Rhyme *(58)*			69
Lesson 4 Oral Language: Using the Telephone *(58)*			70
Lesson 5 Viewing: Recognizing Signs *(59)*	2C		
Lesson 6 Viewing: Same and Different *(59)*			71
Lesson 7 Grammar: Nouns: Animals and Things *(60)*	2D		
Lesson 8 Grammar: Adjectives: Numbers and Colors *(60)*	2D		72
Lesson 9 Vocabulary: Rhyming Words *(61)*			
Lesson 10 Vocabulary: Color, Size, and Shape *(61)*			73
Lesson 11 Writing: Writing Poems *(62)*			
Lesson 12 Writing: Writing Lists *(62)*			
Lesson 13 Study Skills: Numbers on a Keyboard *(63)*	1F, 2E		
Lesson 14 Study Skills: Categorizing/Classifying *(63)*			
Class Writing Project ⏱ *about 2 days, 20 minutes each day* **Lesson 15** A Counting Big Book *(64–65)*	2F		74–76

 MEETING INDIVIDUAL NEEDS *(66–69)*

Activities for Special Needs/Inclusion, for Students Acquiring English, for Reteaching, and for Enrichment/Challenge

Meeting Individual Needs

▶ **FOR SPECIAL NEEDS/INCLUSION:** *Houghton Mifflin English* Audiotape ; *See also* Reteaching.

▶ **FOR STUDENTS ACQUIRING ENGLISH:**
- Notes and activities are included in this Teacher's Edition throughout the unit to help you adapt or use lessons with students acquiring English.
- Students can listen to the published model *One Gray Mouse* on audiotape.

▶ **RETEACHING**
- Activities for reteaching the focus skills are included on pages 66–69.

▶ **ENRICHMENT/CHALLENGE**
- Activities for challenge/enrichment that are correlated to focus skill lessons are included on pages 66–69.

 All audiotape recordings are also available on CD.

Additional Resources

Audiotapes

 Technology Tools
CD-ROM: Curious George® Paint & Print Studio
Paint, Write & Play! (published by The Learning Company)
*Type to Learn Jr.™

*©Sunburst Technology Corporation, a Houghton Mifflin Company. All rights reserved.

INTERNET: http://www.eduplace.com/rdg/hme/
Visit Education Place for these additional support materials and activities:
- author biographies
- patterns for shape booklets

 Informal Assessment
Activity Masters Plus, Assessment Checklists, pages 45–47

Keeping a Journal

In kindergarten, journals can be blank notebooks or folders filled with paper. As children draw and write about school activities, important events, and special thoughts, they can watch their writing growth as the year progresses.

School-Home Connection

Suggestions for informing or involving family members in learning related to this unit are included in the Teacher's Edition throughout the unit.

Daily Routines

The oral language activities suggested here provide daily opportunities for children to develop their understanding of number, color, animal, and rhyming words. Refer to the **Interactive Bulletin Board** and **Daily Discussion** ideas on pages 10–13 and 20–21 for help in establishing Daily Routines for your classroom.

Interactive Bulletin Board

Number Wheel

Ask volunteers to spin the spinner and say the number it lands on. Make a paper clip chain using the corresponding number of clips and post it next to the Number Wheel.

Color Wheel

Review the color words on the Color Wheel. Then have volunteers spin the spinner and name the color the arrow lands on. Ask children wearing that color to raise their hands. Together, count to find the total number. Help children generate an oral sentence to describe each result.

Daily Message

Each day record one sentence children have generated while using the Color Wheel. Model the conventions of using a capital letter at the beginning of the sentence and a period at the end. Have children repeat the sentence as you point to each word.

Number Wheel

Color Wheel

Daily Message

9
Nine children are wearing
something red.

Daily Discussion

Using the text below, sing **"Five Little Chickadees."** Count down with your fingers as each chickadee flies away. (*See* Additional Resources page 231 for the music.) Then recite the song again, emphasizing the rhyming word pairs *door/four, tree/three, you/two,* and *sun/one.* Tell children that these words rhyme, or sound alike at the end. Have children sing and act out the song with you. After performing the song a few times, use the Think and Discuss questions below.

Think and Discuss

- What number words did you hear?
- Are the numbers in an order? What is the order?
- What rhyming words did you hear?
- Did you hear any words that name colors or animals? What are they?

Follow a similar procedure daily, using different songs, poems, chants, or finger plays that include color, number, animal, and/or rhyming words. (*See* Additional Resources pages 229–233.)

RHYMING WORDS As children listen to the different selections you share, ask them to identify rhyming word pairs. Have them suggest additional words that rhyme with each pair. Print their suggestions on the board and reread each list of words, emphasizing the matching ending sounds.

CATEGORIES OF WORDS Keep a chart of number, color, and animal words used in the selections. Children can illustrate the words during transitional times.

 INFORMAL ASSESSMENT (*See* Activity Masters Plus pp. 46, 48)

Number Words	Color Words	Animal Words
one		chickadee
two		
three		
four		
five		

Daily Discussion Activity

Five Little Chickadees
American Counting Song

 Five little chickadees peeping at the door,
One flew away and then there were four;
Chorus Chickadee, chickadee, happy and gay,
Chickadee, chickadee, fly away.

 Four little chickadees sitting on a tree,
One flew away and then there were three;
Chorus

 Three little chickadees looking at you,
One flew away and then there were two;
Chorus

 Two little chickadees sitting in the sun,
One flew away and then there was one;
Chorus

 One little chickadee left all alone,
It flew away and then there were none;
Chorus

Center Activities

Center Activities provide additional daily opportunities for children to develop their understanding of numbers and number words, colors and color words, animal names, and rhyming words.

Reading and Listening Center

PUBLISHED MODEL Children can listen to *One Gray Mouse* on audiotape as they follow along in the book. **Listening**

RHYMING WORDS Have children work in pairs. One child says a word. The partner names a rhyming word. The children continue back and forth naming words until they can think of no more that rhyme. Children take turns choosing the first word. **Listening/Speaking**

Writing Center

WRITING COLOR LISTS Have children label the top of a piece of paper with a color "splotch" of their choice. Then have them list, using pictures and/or words, things they know of or see that are that color.

FORMING NUMERALS Post written models of the numerals 1 to 10. Place a shallow layer of cornmeal or salt in a flat pan. Then have children use a finger to write each numeral in the pan. Shake the pan gently to erase.

MAKING NUMBER LABELS Have children make labels that identify the quantity of various objects in the classroom. For example, a child might write *4* on a self-stick note and post it on a window with four panes, or the child might write *10* and post it on a block construction that uses ten blocks.

 JOURNAL Have children represent their favorite number, color, and animal in their journals with pictures and writing.

Creative Arts Center

STORY RETELLING Prepare finger puppets from old latex gloves for the groups of animals named in *One Gray Mouse*. (*See* Teacher's Resource Master 54 for instructions.) Have children use the puppets to retell the story, or have them retell the story as a finger play, raising the correct number of fingers for each animal. **Speaking**

MAKING PHONE CALLS Write several phone numbers on index cards. Have children choose a card when at the center and use the number as their "phone number." Using two old telephones, children can take turns calling and talking to one another. **Listening/Speaking**

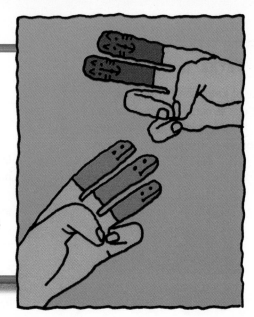

Math Center

PLAYING A COLOR-NUMBER GAME Make ten number cards (numerals and words for 1 to 10) and five picture-word cards for five different colors. Provide a set of ten colored counters to match each of the five colors on the cards. One child chooses a number and a color card, names the color and number, and then sets out the matching number of colored counters. A partner checks the results. Children alternate roles. **Speaking/Viewing**

Science Center

MAKING COLORS Set out red, blue, and yellow food coloring; clear plastic cups filled with water; and stirrers. Let children experiment by mixing different numbers of drops and colors of food coloring in the glasses of water. Have them share information about the numbers of drops and colors they used as well as describe the new colors and shades that result. **Speaking/Viewing**

① Listening to a Counting Book

About the Author

Katherine Burton

Some of Katherine Burton's stories start out as bedtime stories for her two daughters. With each retelling, she develops the stories a little more.

Bibliography

You may also wish to read aloud these counting books.

- *Let's Go Visiting* by Sue Williams
- *Ten Red Apples* by Pat Hutchins
- *Roar! A Noisy Counting Book* by Pamela Duncan Edwards

FOR STUDENTS ACQUIRING ENGLISH

In addition to reviewing the numbers, teach colors and animals. Next, point to objects in the room and ask: *What color is that?* Then teach animal sounds for the animals in the book.

Lesson Objectives

Children will:

- listen for and identify a language pattern in a published model
- evaluate the relationship of visuals and text
- identify the medium used for illustrations
- respond personally and critically to the selection

Materials

One Gray Mouse

Optional Materials

tag board, crayons or markers

Reading the Model

The counting book *One Gray Mouse* uses number, color, animal, and rhyming words in a repeating language pattern for the numbers 1 through 10.

Building Background

Review the numbers 1 through 10 by leading children in specific movements, such as touching their toes three times. Have children count aloud as they complete each movement, emphasizing the final number, "1, 2, 3." Repeat, varying the numbers and the movements.

Introducing Vocabulary

- Discuss with children the meaning of each key vocabulary word: *lake, wig, log,* and *pail.* As you review each word, display a picture card you have made for the word, or point to the corresponding illustration in *One Gray Mouse.*

- Ask a volunteer to use each word in a sentence. (Sample answer: *The clown is wearing a red wig.*) Hold up the matching illustration or picture card as the word is mentioned.

Predicting and Purpose Setting

PICTURE WALK Display *One Gray Mouse* and read aloud the title. Identify the author (Katherine Burton) and the illustrator (Kim Fernandes). Preview the first six pages, having children describe what they see on each page. Then ask volunteers to predict what they think will come next in the book and to explain why. If necessary, help them see the pattern of ascending numbers and the matching number of animals.

Explain that in some books words are used over and over in the same way to make a pattern that repeats. Tell children that animal names are one kind of word the author of *One Gray Mouse* uses over and over. Have children listen for animal names as you read the book aloud.

 This selection is also available on audiotape.

Listening As a Writer

Think About Language

ANIMAL NAMES Ask children to recall the animal names they heard. Then review all the animals by paging through the illustrations and having children name each kind of animal.

NUMBER AND COLOR WORDS Display pages 4–5, pointing to and naming the numeral one. Explain that there is one mouse. Ask: *What color is the mouse?* (gray) *What color is his house?* (black) Have children predict what number will come next. Turn the page and have them check their predictions. Review all the number and color words in this way by having children read the numerals, count the animals, and answer your questions about the colors.

RHYMING WORDS Explain that rhyming words have the same ending sounds. Reread page 4, emphasizing the words *mouse* and *house*. Tell children that these two words rhyme. Reread each remaining page, asking children to listen for and name the pair of rhyming words. (*cat/mat, snake/lake, fish/dish, pigs/wigs, bee/tree, frog/log, bear/chair, duck/truck, snail/pail*)

LANGUAGE PATTERN To help children hear the language pattern, have them clap out the rhythm of the text for the number 1 with you as you read the words aloud. Repeat for the numbers 2 and 3. Have children share the repeating language pattern they discovered. Review with them the use and placement of number, color, animal, and rhyming words. If necessary, help them see that each animal is the same color as the object they saw with the previous animal.

NOTE If children are discussing and responding to *One Gray Mouse* on a day following your initial reading, reread the selection.

Think About the Pictures

- Ask children to tell how the pictures help make the meaning of the story clear. Help them see that the number of the animals, the locations, the objects, and the colors match the words in the story.

- Let children look at several illustrations. Ask them how they think the pictures for this book were made. If necessary, explain that the images were made from clay and then photographed. Have children compare these illustrations with others they know that were painted or drawn. How are they the same? How are they different?

Responding

- **Personal Response** Assign each child a number from 1 to 10. Children can dictate or write what they liked or disliked about the part of the story that goes with their number. Did they like the animal? the colors? the illustrations? Why or why not?

- **Critical Thinking** Have children tell what number would come next if the book were to continue. (eleven) What color would that animal have to be? (gray)

Poster Book p. 2A

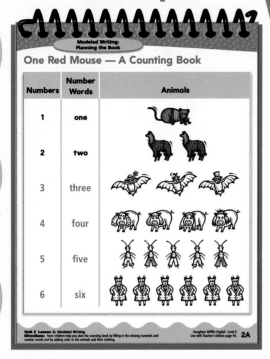

Poster Book p. 2B

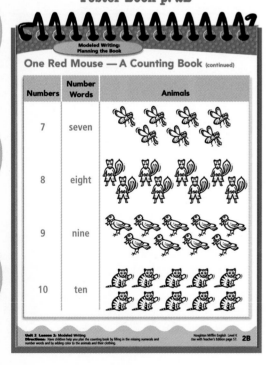

② Making a Counting Book

Lesson Objectives

Children will:
- help plan and draft a counting book
- recognize and use number, color, animal, and rhyming words

Materials

Poster Book pp. 2A–2B, dry erase markers, Transparencies 2–1 and 2–2 or chart paper, large drawing paper, crayons or colored markers, Activity Masters 66–68

Focus on Instruction

Recall with children that *One Gray Mouse* is a counting book that includes number words, color words, animal names, and rhyming words. Explain that now you are going to work together to write your own class counting book that uses these same kinds of words.

Planning the Book Poster Book pp. 2A–2B

- Tell children that first you must plan what you are going to write and decide who will read the counting book. Display Poster Book page 2A and read the title aloud.

- Point out the numeral 1 and the number word *one*. Explain that one red mouse is wearing one blue blouse. Ask children to name the words you said that rhyme. (*mouse/blouse*)

- Repeat this procedure for the number 2, pointing out the purple pajamas on the blue llamas. Have children identify the rhyming words *llamas* and *pajamas*.

- For the remaining rows of the chart, ask children to help you fill in the missing numerals (3–6) and number words. Together, select a color for the animals in each group and a color for the article of clothing the animals are wearing. Have volunteers help you color the animals and the clothing with the chosen colors. (Example: purple bats wearing pink hats)

- Continue this procedure, completing the next chart (numbers 7–10) on Poster Book page 2B.

Writing the Book Transparencies 2–1 and 2–2

Explain to children that now you are ready to write your counting book. Display Transparency 2–1, or copy the text onto chart paper. Read the title aloud. Point out that the title tells what your book will be about.

MODELING THE LANGUAGE PATTERN Read aloud the first two sentences on Transparency 2–1, having children repeat after you. Help children identify the language pattern by comparing the two sentences. Ask: *How are these two sentences alike? How are they different?*

DRAFTING THE TEXT Ask children to help you draft the remaining text, using the information on Poster Book pages 2A and 2B as your guide.

- Read the third sentence aloud. Ask volunteers to name the colors of the bats and their hats, as shown on Poster Book page 2A. Write the missing color words. Then have children name the number of hats. Fill in the missing numeral *3*. Have children "read" with you the completed sentence.

- Continue this procedure for each remaining sentence frame on Transparencies 2–1 and 2–2. Occasionally ask a volunteer to help draft the text by writing a familiar letter or word.

MODELING CONCEPTS OF PRINT Help children become familiar with concepts of print by occasionally modeling as you write.

- Point out that you are moving from **left to right** as you record letters and words. As you read a sentence aloud, follow the text with your finger, using a sweeping motion from left to right.

- Reinforce the **concept of a word** by explaining that the group of letters you have written stands for a word. Name the word. Point out that you have left a space before and after it.

- Reinforce **sound-symbol relationships**. Pause occasionally and name the letter and its sound at the beginning of a word before you record it. Have children repeat the letter sound with you.

Sharing the Book

- Read the completed text together chorally. Praise children for their help in planning and writing. Explain that now you are going to work together to make your writing into a book.

- Print each line of text at the bottom of a large piece of drawing paper. Or, if you used chart paper, cut the text into strips, with each numeral and its text on a separate strip. Glue each strip onto a piece of large drawing paper.

- Have one child or a small group illustrate each page. (Display Poster Book pages 2A–2B for reference.) Ask another child or group to make a cover.

- Assemble the pages, asking children to help you put them in counting order. Then bind the pages. Place the book in your Reading and Listening Center.

SCHOOL-HOME CONNECTION Activity Masters 66–68

Children can make their own counting books to take home. Have them color the illustrations on Activity Masters 66–68 and then add colors and trace the numerals to complete the matching text. Then ask children to cut the pages on the dashed lines. Help them staple the pages together.

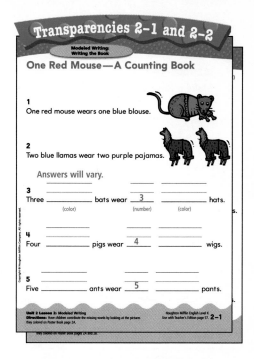

 FOR STUDENTS ACQUIRING ENGLISH

To help children identify the words that rhyme on Transparency 2–1, say each sentence aloud and then have children repeat in chorus. Challenge children to name the words that rhyme. Then as you write, sound out each word and ask the children to repeat after you.

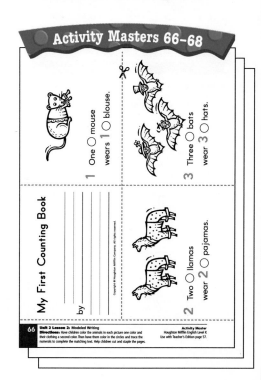

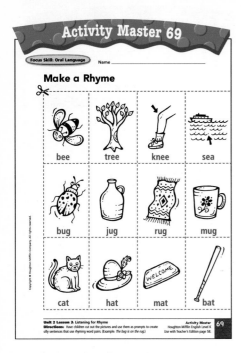

Activity Master 69

Focus Skill: Oral Language   Name _____

Make a Rhyme

bee	tree	knee	sea
bug	jug	rug	mug
cat	hat	mat	bat

Unit 2 Lesson 3: Listening for Rhyme
Directions: Have children cut out the pictures and use them as prompts to create silly sentences that use rhyming word pairs. (Example: *The bug is on the rug.*)

Activity Master
69
Houghton Mifflin English Level K
Use with Teacher's Edition page 58.

 FOR STUDENTS ACQUIRING ENGLISH

Children may be unfamiliar with songs like "Twinkle, Twinkle, Little Star." Take time to teach it to them with actions. Then have them raise their hands when they hear rhymes. Finally, have them work in pairs or small groups to make silly sentences on Activity Master 69.

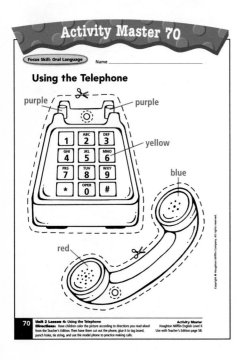

Activity Master 70

Focus Skill: Oral Language   Name _____

Using the Telephone

purple   purple

yellow

blue

red

70 Unit 2 Lesson 4: Using the Telephone
Directions: Have children color the picture according to directions you read aloud from the Teacher's Edition. Then have them mount the page on tag board, cut out the phone, tie string, and use the model phone to practice making calls.

Activity Master
Houghton Mifflin English Level K
Use with Teacher's Edition page 58.

---

③ Listening for Rhyme

Lesson Objectives

Children will:
- identify rhyming words
- substitute words in a rhyming pattern

Materials

One Gray Mouse, Activity Master 69, Additional Resources p. 234

- Remind children that rhyming words are words that end with the same sounds. Reread page 8 of *One Gray Mouse*, emphasizing *snake* and *lake*. Have children name the rhyming words.

- Tell children to listen for rhyming words as you read aloud a familiar rhyme or song, such as "Twinkle, Twinkle Little Star." (*See* Additional Resources page 234.) Pause after each couplet, and ask children to identify the rhyming words. (*star/are, high/sky*) Then reread the rhyme, having children supply the second rhyming word in each couplet.

- Have children cut out the pictures on Activity Master 69 and use them as prompts to make up silly sentences. Have them substitute rhyming words in sentence frames, such as: *The _____bee_____ is on my _____knee_____.*

④ Using the Telephone

Lesson Objectives

Children will:
- identify parts of a telephone
- learn how to make a telephone call

Materials

One Gray Mouse, real or model telephone, Activity Master 70, crayons, scissors, tag board, glue, hole-punch, string

- Have children recall that they learned about numbers in *One Gray Mouse*. Explain that people use numbers when they make a phone call.

- Show a telephone. Explain the purpose of each part. Then have children follow your directions to complete Activity Master 70. Say: *1. Find the parts of the phone used to punch in the telephone number. Color them yellow. 2. Find the part used for speaking. Color it red. 3. Find the part used for listening. Color it blue. 4. Find the parts used to hang up. Color them purple.*

- Have children mount the page on tag board and cut out the entire phone. Help them punch holes and string the receiver to the body of the phone.

- Demonstrate how to answer the phone. Have pairs model polite ways to begin and end phone conversations using their cutout phones.

 INFORMAL ASSESSMENT (*See* Activity Masters Plus pp. 45–47)

 MEETING INDIVIDUAL NEEDS (*See* p. 66)

Focus Skill **Viewing**

⑤ Recognizing Signs

Lesson Objective

Children will:
• recognize and understand common signs

Materials

Poster Book p. 2C

• Discuss ways people communicate, such as talking, writing, or using hand signals. Ask volunteers to demonstrate an example of each way you discuss.

• Explain that signs are another way to communicate. Display Poster Book page 2C and discuss each sign. Where would children see the sign? What does it mean? Why is it important? Have children point out distinguishing features of each sign, such as color or shape.

• Point to different signs on the page. Ask children to act out or describe what they would do if they saw the sign. For example, point to the stop sign and say: *You are riding your bike, and you see this sign. What do you do?*

⑥ Same and Different

Lesson Objective

Children will:
• identify attributes that are the same and those that are different

Materials

One Gray Mouse, three books (two identical books and one that is different), Activity Master 71, crayons

• Show the illustration of the snails from *One Gray Mouse*. Point to different snails and have children describe them. Then discuss ways that all the snails are the same. (They are all snails. They all have red shells, brown bodies, and two eyes.) Direct children's attention to the snails' patterns, and explain how the patterns on the snails are different.

• Display two books that are the same. Ask children to identify all the details, such as size, shape, and color, that make the books identical. Guide children to use the word *same* in their responses. (Sample answer: The books are the same size.)

• Next, display two books that are different. Have children tell how the books are different. Guide them to use the word *different* in their responses.

• Distribute Activity Master 71. Have children color the two pictures in each row that are the same and mark an X on the one that is different.

 INFORMAL ASSESSMENT (*See* Activity Masters Plus pp. 45–47)

 MEETING INDIVIDUAL NEEDS (*See* pp. 66–67)

Poster Book p. 2C

Focus Skill: Viewing
Signs We Know

Unit 2 Lesson 5: Recognizing Signs
Directions: Help children identify the signs and discuss their meanings, purposes, and features.
Houghton Mifflin English Level K
Use with Teacher's Edition page 59. **2C**

 FOR STUDENTS ACQUIRING ENGLISH

Have children form pairs and together make a set of stop and go signs. Then teach children to play a version of Red Light, Green Light. One child holds the signs and tells the partner when to stop and go as he or she moves forward.

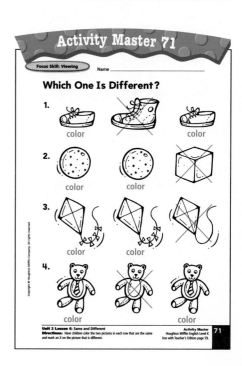

Activity Master 71

Focus Skill: Viewing Name _____

Which One Is Different?

Unit 2 Lesson 6: Same and Different
Directions: Have children color the two pictures in each row that are the same and mark an X on the picture that is different.
Activity Master **71**
Houghton Mifflin English Level K
Use with Teacher's Edition page 59.

Focus Skill **Grammar**

Poster Book p. 2D

Focus Skill: Grammar
Animals, Things, Numbers, and Colors

Untitled H. Pippin, 1945. Hirshhorn Collection, D.C. Superstock

Unit 2 Lessons 7 and 8: Nouns and Adjectives
Directions: Have children identify and name the pictured animals and things. Then have them identify the number and color of various items.

Houghton Mifflin English Level K
Use with Teacher's Edition page 60. **2D**

7 Nouns

Lesson Objective	Materials
Children will: • identify nouns for animals and things	*One Gray Mouse*, chart paper, markers, Poster Book p. 2D

ANIMALS AND THINGS Remind children that they already learned that naming words can name people or places. Explain that other naming words name animals or things. Review that naming words are also called nouns.

- Display several pages of *One Gray Mouse*, and have children identify the pictured animals. Record each animal name in a list on chart paper.

- Next, ask volunteers to point out and name words for things that are shown in the illustrations. (Sample answers: *mat, basket, log, sink, dish, chair*) Record these words on a second piece of chart paper.

- Discuss the fine art on Poster Book page 2D. Ask children to point out and name the animals and the things they see. Add these words to your word lists.

- Have children suggest other nouns they know for animals and things. Then ask volunteers to add illustrations to the lists. Post them on your Word Wall.

8 Adjectives

Activity Master 72

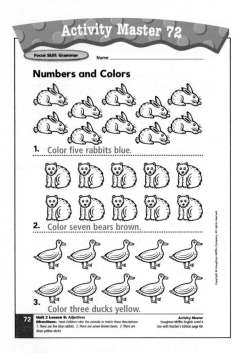

Focus Skill: Grammar Name _____

Numbers and Colors

1. Color five rabbits blue.

2. Color seven bears brown.

3. Color three ducks yellow.

72 Unit 2 Lesson 8: Adjectives
Directions: Have children color the animals to match these descriptions.
1. There are five blue rabbits. 2. There are seven brown bears. 3. There are three yellow ducks.

Activity Master
Houghton Mifflin English Level K
Use with Teacher's Edition page 60.

Lesson Objective	Materials
Children will: • identify adjectives for number and color	*One Gray Mouse*, Poster Book p. 2D, Activity Master 72

NUMBERS AND COLORS Tell children that some words describe things. Point out that number words can describe how many and that color words describe how something looks. Explain that describing words are also called adjectives.

- Use the illustrations in *One Gray Mouse* to review number and color words. Ask volunteers to name the number and color of various animals and things you point to in the book. Repeat the procedure, using Poster Book page 2D.

- Distribute Activity Master 72. Have children color the animals to match these descriptions that you read aloud. Say: *1. There are five blue rabbits. 2. There are seven brown bears. 3. There are three yellow ducks.*

 INFORMAL ASSESSMENT (*See* Activity Masters Plus pp. 46–48)

 MEETING INDIVIDUAL NEEDS (*See* p. 67)

 FOR STUDENTS ACQUIRING ENGLISH

After children complete Activity Master 72, have volunteers describe the pictures using numbers and colors. For example, they might say: *There are seven brown bears. There are five blue rabbits.* As they do so, correct as needed and have the class repeat what is said.

Focus Skill   Vocabulary

⑨ Rhyming Words

Lesson Objective	**Materials**
Children will:	*One Gray Mouse*
• identify and generate rhyming words	

- Display pages 10–11 of *One Gray Mouse*. Say: *fish, pink,* and *dish*. Ask children to tell which two words rhyme. (*fish/dish*) Explain that these words rhyme because they have the same ending sounds.

- Name animals from *One Gray Mouse*, such as *cat* and *snake*, and ask volunteers to think of and name real words that rhyme, such as *mat* and *lake*. Display the appropriate illustrations as necessary.

- Have children generate other rhymes for these words: *hay, spoon,* and *pie*. (Sample answers: *day, moon, fly*)

 FOR STUDENTS ACQUIRING ENGLISH

Children acquiring English will need help finding rhymes for the words. Say the given words, then say three other words slowly. Have children raise their hands when they recognize the rhyme. For example, say: *dog, boy, girl, hog*. Children should raise their hands when you say *hog*.

⑩ Color, Size, and Shape

Lesson Objectives	**Materials**
Children will:	precut construction paper rectangles, triangles, squares, and circles in three colors (red, blue, yellow) and two sizes (large, small); crayons; Activity Master 73
• identify colors and sizes	
• identify circles, triangles, rectangles, and squares	

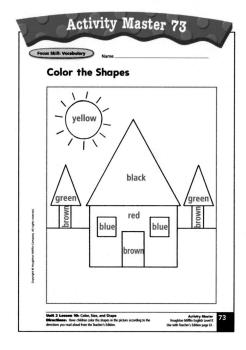

- Gather children in a floor area and display a set of paper shapes. Point out that they can be large or small; red, yellow, or blue; and a circle, triangle, square, or rectangle.

- Then hold up a paper shape, and ask a volunteer to name its color, shape, and size. Repeat with different shapes, giving all children the opportunity to describe a shape.

- Distribute Activity Master 73. Have children describe the picture. Then tell them to use their crayons to follow the directions you read aloud. Say: *1. Color the circle yellow. 2. Color the large triangle black. 3. Color the squares blue. 4. Color the large rectangle red. 5 Color the small rectangles brown. 6. Color the small triangles green.*

 INFORMAL ASSESSMENT (*See* Activity Masters Plus pp. 45–47)

 MEETING INDIVIDUAL NEEDS (*See* p. 68)

FOR STUDENTS ACQUIRING ENGLISH

As you read "1, 2, Buckle My Shoe," teach children actions to accompany each line. Pantomime buckling a shoe, closing a door, and so on. As the class generates the new poem, have them think of actions to go with each of the new lines so children acquiring English can learn the new words.

Sample Rhymes

One, two,
  Make a stew.
Three, four,
  Touch the floor.
Five, six,
  Do some tricks.

Focus Skill **Writing**

⑪ Writing Poems

Lesson Objectives	Materials
Children will:	markers, chart paper,
• listen to a model poem	Additional Resources p. 229
• dictate words to complete a rhyming pattern	

- Remind children that they learned about words that rhyme. Ask volunteers to share pairs of rhyming words.

- Explain that writers often use rhyming words to make their poems fun to read and listen to. Read "One, Two, Buckle My Shoe" on page 229 of Additional Resources. Reread it. Have children chime in on the rhyming words.

- Help children generate new lines to replace the second line in each rhyming couplet. Write the new class-generated nursery rhyme on chart paper. Read the new poem aloud. Have children chime in on the rhyming words.

⑫ Writing Lists

Lesson Objectives	Materials
Children will:	*One Gray Mouse*, magazines,
• create picture lists	supermarket advertisements,
• use dictation, scribble writing, or temporary spelling to label lists	construction paper, glue, scissors, crayons or markers

- Explain to children that lists usually include numbers and/or words written one after another. Have volunteers discuss different kinds of lists they know about. (Examples: shopping lists, guest lists, packing lists) Explain that some people write lists to keep track of things, such as what they need to buy at a store or what they need to bring somewhere.

- Tell children that you would like to invite one of each type of animal from *One Gray Mouse* to a pretend party. Have children recall the animals from the story as you record them in a numbered list on the board. Tell them that you can use your list to make and send the correct number of invitations.

- Provide old magazines and supermarket advertisements. Ask children to help you create a shopping list for the party. Have them cut and paste in a list pictures of food. Encourage them to number their lists and to label the pictures with writing. Volunteers can share their lists with the class.

 INFORMAL ASSESSMENT (*See* Activity Masters Plus pp. 45–47)

 MEETING INDIVIDUAL NEEDS (*See* pp. 68–69)

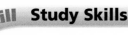 **Study Skills**

⑬ Numbers on a Keyboard

Lesson Objective
Children will:
• locate numbers on a computer keyboard and on a calculator keypad

Materials
Poster Book pp. 1F and 2E, dry erase markers, calculators

Optional Materials
computer, word processing software

• Display Poster Book page 1F. Show children the two sets of numbers on the keyboard. Ask volunteers to locate specific numbers in both places.

• If possible, have children input numbers on a computer, using a word processing program. Have them read the numbers that appear on screen.

• Next, display Poster Book page 2E. Ask volunteers to color the number keys according to the color code. After coloring a number key, have them record the number in the display area. Then pretend to press the CLEAR key and erase the number. Repeat until all number keys are colored.

• Have pairs of children take turns pressing number keys on real calculators and reading the numbers on the displays.

⑭ Categorizing/Classifying

Lesson Objective
Children will:
• categorize objects by color, size, and shape

Materials
sorting circles or shoelaces tied to form rings; sets of attribute blocks or precut construction paper rectangles, triangles, squares, and circles in three colors (red, blue, yellow) and two sizes (large, small)

• Gather children in a floor area with a set of attribute blocks and two sorting circles. Ask children to pick one detail that describes some of the blocks. For example, some are large. Then ask volunteers to help put all the large blocks into one sorting circle and all the other blocks in the other. Repeat, using a different attribute. Ask a volunteer to describe the sort.

• Then have pairs take turns sorting blocks. Have one child choose an attribute and sort the blocks into two groups. The other child describes the sort.

 INFORMAL ASSESSMENT (*See* Activity Masters Plus pp.45–47)

 MEETING INDIVIDUAL NEEDS (*See* p. 69)

Poster Book p. 1F

Poster Book p. 2E

 FOR STUDENTS ACQUIRING ENGLISH
After working with Poster Book page 1F, allow children to examine the picture of the keyboard. Guide them by saying: *Point to the numbers. Find the number ___.* Repeat with the letters.

Poster Book p. 2F

Planning Our Counting Book

red	pink	orange	yellow	green	blue
purple	black	white	brown	gray	

1	one	
2	two	
3	three	
4	four	
5	five	
6	six	
7	seven	
8	eight	
9	nine	
10	ten	

Unit 2 Lesson 15: Class Writing Project
Directions: Have children suggest how to represent each number in their counting book. Use key words and/or drawings to record their ideas.

Houghton Mifflin English Level K
Use with Teacher's Edition page 64. **2F**

FOR STUDENTS ACQUIRING ENGLISH

Help children understand all the words chosen by referring to a picture dictionary or providing realia, art, or photos. Write and say words and have children repeat them. You may want to use the word pairs given in the text to provide children with a rhyme for their counting page.

Class Writing Project

⑮ A Counting Big Book

Lesson Objectives

Children will:
- help choose a topic for a counting book
- help plan a counting book
- write and illustrate a page for a counting book

Materials

Poster Book p. 2F, dry erase markers, large drawing paper, crayons or colored markers, Activity Masters 74–76

Focus on Instruction

Tell children that now you are going to work together to write a counting big book for the class. Recall with them the counting book of animals they wrote. Explain that they can write about animals again, or they can choose another topic. You might read aloud some of the books in the Bibliography on page 54 to help spark topic ideas.

Planning the Book Poster Book p. 2F

- Tell children that for this book, each child will work alone or with a partner to make one page for the book. Explain that when all the pages are done, you will put them together to make one class Big Book.

- Help children think about the kind of number book they want to write. Do they want to use rhyming words? Do they want to represent each number with animals? people? places? and/or things? Together, decide which kind of nouns to use. You may want to help children narrow their choice. For example, "naming words for things" might be narrowed further to "things to eat."

- Display Poster Book page 2F. Ask volunteers to name the numerals and the colors shown. Together, plan what to write for each number. Use pictures and/or key words to record children's suggestions for naming words and colors.

- If children are stuck for an idea, or if you prefer to provide them with a topic and a language pattern, you might use one of the ideas below.

Animals and Food
1 One blue seal eats white oatmeal.
2 ____ ____ apes eat ____ grapes.
Rhyming Word Pairs
seal/oatmeal, poodles/noodles, apes/grapes, snakes/cakes, clams/jams, fleas/peas, flies/pies, goats/oats, bears/pears, parrots/carrots

Animals and Transportation
1 I see one white sheep on one green jeep.
2 I see ____ ____ goats on ___ ____ boats.
Rhyming Word Pairs
sheep/jeep, chimps/blimps, goats/boats, dragons/wagons, raccoons/balloons, crabs/cabs, ducks/trucks, bugs/tugs, cranes/planes, eels/wheels

Writing the Book

- Review with children the planning you did on Poster Book page 2F. If you decided to use a particular sentence pattern, review that pattern as well.

- Remind children that they will work alone or with a partner to make one page for the book. Assign children a number from 1 to 10, or have them make their own selection.

- Distribute large drawing paper. Ask children to dictate or write the sentence for their page and to illustrate their text.

Sharing the Book

- Remind children that books have a title and that the title helps readers know what the book will be about. Together, decide on a title for the book. Have volunteers make a cover.

- Ask children to share their pages with the class. Have them "read" their text and talk about their illustrations. Ask them to count aloud the number of items they pictured and to explain their color choices.

- Have children help you put the pages in counting order, asking the class to say the numbers aloud with you.

- Bind the pages. Then read the book together chorally, beginning with the title. Praise children for their contributions. Place the completed Big Book in your Reading and Listening Center.

 SCHOOL-HOME CONNECTION Activity Masters 74–76

Children can make their own counting books to take home and share with family members. Have them color the illustrations on Activity Masters 74–76 and then add colors and trace the numerals to complete the matching text. Ask children to cut the pages on the dashed lines. Help them staple the pages together to complete the book.

 INFORMAL ASSESSMENT (*See* Activity Masters Plus pp. 45–47)

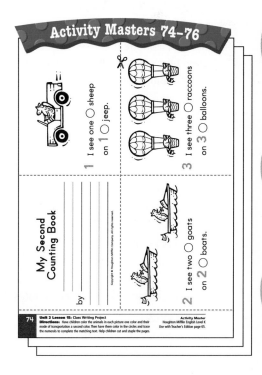

Meeting Individual Needs

Lesson 3 Focus Skill   Oral Language: Listening for Rhyme

RETEACHING ALTERNATIVE STRATEGY
Remind children that rhyming words have the same ending sounds. Have children name the rhyming ending sound for each rhyming pair in the book *One Gray Mouse*.

CHALLENGE
Have children help you write and illustrate the rhyming word pairs from *One Gray Mouse* on oaktag strips. Then cut them apart to make matching puzzle pieces. Children can pair rhyming words by matching up the puzzle pieces. Afterwards they can make their own rhyming word puzzle and exchange them with partners.

FOR STUDENTS ACQUIRING ENGLISH
Use the pictures from the book or make flashcards with the children. Then together name the animals and objects. Either display the flashcards or allow children to use their books to work in pairs, asking each other to identify the words. Encourage children to use complete telling or asking sentences.

Lesson 4 Focus Skill   Oral Language: Using the Telephone

RETEACHING ALTERNATIVE STRATEGY
Review the parts of a phone, using model phones. Ask volunteers to touch each part as you describe it. Have children show how they hold the receiver when using the phone. Model how to input a phone number and use polite language to make a call. Have children practice inputting telephone numbers and calling a family member using model phones.

CHALLENGE
Write telephone numbers on several index cards. Have children practice inputting the telephone numbers on their cutout phones as they act out different roles, such as a family

member, a friend, or a teacher. Have children switch roles and index cards as they make several phone calls.

FOR STUDENTS ACQUIRING ENGLISH
Ask children about the parts of a real telephone. Say, for example: *Where are the numbers? Point to the receiver. Show me how to hold the receiver.* Have partners use the telephones they made to practice. Slowly dictate telephone numbers as the children punch the numbers. Help children find the numbers on the telephone as needed.

Lesson 5 Focus Skill   Viewing: Recognizing Signs

RETEACHING ALTERNATIVE STRATEGY
Take children on a sign hunt in and around the school building. When they spot a sign, help them tell what it means, why it is in that particular location, and what they should do or keep in mind when they see it. Upon returning to the classroom, have children draw pictures of the signs they saw and share them with their classmates.

CHALLENGE
Have children draw accurate versions of signs they have seen in the neighborhood, as well as the signs shown on Poster

Book page 2C. Then discuss which signs could be posted in the classroom. Let children post the signs in appropriate places.

FOR STUDENTS ACQUIRING ENGLISH
As children participate in the sign hunt, be sure they understand what each sign means. Ask about shapes and colors, and help children use each sign's location to figure out what it means. Then return to the classroom and make a map of your school on mural paper. Assign each child a sign that he/she must add.

Lesson 6 Focus Skill   Viewing: Same and Different

RETEACHING ALTERNATIVE STRATEGY

Ask children to look around the room to find some objects to compare. Explain that when they compare two objects, such as pencils, crayons, pictures, or toys, they need to look at size, shape, color, or other features. Ask a child to hold up two objects and have the class tell how the things are the same or different.

CHALLENGE

Show pictures of two animals with some similar characteristics. Ask children to think about how the animals are alike and how they are different. Have them discuss details, such as size, color, and special features. Have volunteers summarize the major likenesses and differences.

FOR STUDENTS ACQUIRING ENGLISH

Review common words people use when they compare things, such as *bigger, smaller, lighter, heavier*. Then present children with a number of objects to compare to a familiar object such as a crayon. Model language: *This book is bigger than the crayon. This penny is smaller than the crayon.* Finally, have each child find and present an object that the class can compare to the piece of paper.

Lesson 7 Focus Skill   Grammar: Nouns

RETEACHING ALTERNATIVE STRATEGY

Explain that naming words, or nouns, can name people, animals, or things. Make a two-column chart with a cat drawn at the top of one column to stand for animals and a chair at the top of the other to stand for things. Then have children cut out pictures of animals and things from magazines and catalogs, glue each picture in the correct column, and dictate its name for you to write on the chart.

CHALLENGE

Have two teams of children go on an animals-and-things scavenger hunt in the classroom. Ask children to share the results of their hunt, and make two lists on chart paper. Write the names for animals and things they found. Read the two lists.

FOR STUDENTS ACQUIRING ENGLISH

Play Animals and Things Charades. Form two teams. Have one member of each team come to you and secretly look at a picture of an animal or a thing, or whisper a word. The two then return to their teams to give silent clues for the animal or item until the team guesses correctly.

Lesson 8 Focus Skill   Grammar: Adjectives

RETEACHING ALTERNATIVE STRATEGY

Provide children with color cards and counters. Display an illustration from *One Gray Mouse*. Point to and name a color on the page. Have children hold up the matching color card. Say: *Color words describe how something looks.* Together, count the animals on the page and have children use counters to show the same number. Say: *Number words describe how many.* Help them use color and number words to correctly describe other illustrations.

CHALLENGE

Use your Color and Number Wheels to help children compose sentences with adjectives for numbers and colors. Model the activity by spinning each arrow and using that combination of color and number words to compose an oral sentence. Record the sentences.

FOR STUDENTS ACQUIRING ENGLISH

Have a number and color scavenger hunt. Have children form pairs, then ask each pair to find a certain number and color of items. The first pair to do so dictates the next items on the hunt. Say: *Find three red things. Find one blue pencil.* Continue until all pairs have had a turn.

Meeting Individual Needs

Lesson 9 Focus Skill   Vocabulary: Rhyming Words

RETEACHING ALTERNATIVE STRATEGY
Remind children that rhyming words have the same ending sounds, for example, *cat/hat*. Tell children to listen to pairs of words and raise their hands when they hear rhyming words. Use these word pairs: *dot/pot, wait/walk, band/hand, sit/kit, deer/pen, bell/tell, bend/send, less/pet, kick/pick, will/kind, kit/sit, goat/coat, job/doll*, and *book/look*. Then help children think of more rhyming words for the rhyming pairs.

CHALLENGE
Have teams of children play a rhyming game. First you say a word, then the team says a rhyming word. You say another rhyming word, and so on until one of you has to say a non-sense word. Then the next team gets a turn. Use one-syllable words with many rhymes, such as *pot, bat, sit, fun, dog, pen*, and so on.

FOR STUDENTS ACQUIRING ENGLISH

Encourage children to make their own rhymes. Write the alphabet on the board and give children a word. Have them find rhyming words for their word by changing the beginning letter until they recognize a real word. For example, *pot: mot* – "No"; *cot* – "Yes, that's a word!"

Lesson 10 Focus Skill   Vocabulary: Color, Size, and Shape

RETEACHING ALTERNATIVE STRATEGY
Use the construction paper cutouts of shapes suggested on page 61. Name all the shapes, colors, and sizes for children. Then have them sort the cutouts into four piles by shape. Have volunteers present a shape to the group, explaining the different colors and sizes.

CHALLENGE
Share books such as *Color Zoo* by Lois Ehlert to show children how much fun shapes and colors can be. Have children use colored shapes of construction paper to make shape animals of their own. Then have them present their creations to the class, saying every color, size, and shape word as they describe their animals.

FOR STUDENTS ACQUIRING ENGLISH

Help children participate in the activity by reviewing the shapes and colors. Hold up shapes and crayons, name each, and have children repeat after you. Then pass them out to the children. Ask, for example: *Where's the circle?* The child with the circle holds it and says, "Here it is!"

Lesson 11 Focus Skill   Writing: Writing Poems

RETEACHING ALTERNATIVE STRATEGY
Remind children that poems are a kind of writing that sometimes uses rhyming words. On the board, write the following poem: *Rain, rain, go away, Come again some other day.* Recite the poem. Then help children think of words that rhyme with *away* and *day*. (Examples: *bay/lay/May/pay/play*) Work together to think of a different second line. (Example: *'Till the merry month of May.*) Have children illustrate the poem and dictate or write the rhyming words.

CHALLENGE
Have children choose a rhyming pair from the book *One Gray Mouse*, such as *pig/wig*. Challenge them to think of a third rhyming word, such as *jig*, and make up a two-line jingle using all three rhyming words, for example:
I saw a pig that danced a jig. It wore a curly yellow wig.

FOR STUDENTS ACQUIRING ENGLISH

Children acquiring English will need help generating word lists for their poems. Encourage each child to choose a topic. Then have pairs name words that they can use. Finally, model sounding out words and trying the letters in the alphabet to find rhyming words.

Lesson 12 Focus Skill Writing: Writing Lists

RETEACHING ALTERNATIVE STRATEGY
Tell children that lists usually show numbers and words written down to help people remember things. Display the writing materials you provide in the Writing Center. Ask children to make a list of the items, drawing pictures, numbering them, and dictating or writing labels.

CHALLENGE
Have children write lists on topics that require imagination, such as Things I Would Need in Outer Space or Undersea Places I Want to Visit. Ask children to draw a picture of each item and dictate or write a label. Then have volunteers share their lists with the class.

FOR STUDENTS ACQUIRING ENGLISH

Children may need help reviewing names of foods found in a supermarket. Have pairs look for pictures of their favorite foods in magazines. Hold up the pictures they find, name each type of food, and have children repeat after you. Pass the pictures back to the pairs and ask, for example: *Where's the apple?* The pair with the picture stands up and says "Here!"

Lesson 13 Focus Skill Study Skill: Numbers on a Keyboard

RETEACHING ALTERNATIVE STRATEGY
Tape paper over the non-number keys on a computer keyboard and a calculator to reduce distractors for children. Hold up a number card, say the number, and have children press the corresponding key on both the keyboard and the calculator. Then have pairs of children take turns as one child holds up number cards and the other presses the corresponding keys.

CHALLENGE
Invite children to create and input simple number patterns using a computer keyboard. (Example: 123123123) Have

them print out their patterns and challenge classmates to extend their patterns.

FOR STUDENTS ACQUIRING ENGLISH

Before attempting the activity, have the children review the numbers 1–10. Teach zero. Then play a counting game by asking questions such as: *How many books are on that table? How many girls are in this class?* Encourage volunteers to say and then write the numbers for their responses.

Lesson 14 Focus Skill Study Skill: Categorizing and Classifying

RETEACHING ALTERNATIVE STRATEGY
Tell children that when they sort things into groups, they must look at a detail that is the same for all items. Help children sort a collection of dress-up clothes into two groups. Place all the clothes on a table. Have children discuss the details they could use to sort the clothes into two groups, one group with the detail, and one without. (Example: buttons, no buttons) Ask children to put the clothes into the groups accordingly.

CHALLENGE
Have groups of three children sort collections of common objects, such as buttons or marbles. Have the first child in

each group sort the objects into two groups by one attribute. Ask the second child to tell how the items within each group are the same and the third child to tell what rule or guideline was used to sort the objects into two groups.

FOR STUDENTS ACQUIRING ENGLISH

Form small groups of mixed proficiencies. Give each group a handful of coins. Have the children sort the coins by denomination. Then ask a question of each child: *How many (nickels, quarters…) do you have?* Repeat the activity with other objects of different colors and sizes.

Unit 3
Sentences for Us

In this unit, children learn about different types of sentences. By listening to and discussing a question-answer book, they are introduced to kinds of sentences and their use in creating a language pattern. Children participate in the modeled writing of a question-answer book about animals and then work together with you to create a question-answer Big Book. Unit skills develop language and relate to the published model and/or the unit focus.

What You Will Find in This Unit . . .

Unit 3 Planning Guide

Sentences for Us

	Poster Book	Transparency	Activity Masters Plus
DAILY COMMUNICATION LINKS **Daily Routines** *(74–75)* The oral language activities provide daily opportunities for children to develop their understanding of sentences. • **Interactive Bulletin Board:** Calendar and Weather Chart, Where Is the Bear?, Daily Message • **Daily Discussion Activity:** Investigating Objects *See also* Additional Resources *(234)* **Center Activities** *(76–77)* • Reading and Listening Center • Writing Center • Block Center • Creative Arts Center • Science Center			
A Published Model 🕐 *1 day, 20 minutes* **Lesson 1** Listening to a Question-Answer Book *(78–79)* *Do Pigs Have Stripes?*			
Modeled Writing 🕐 *about 2 days, 20 minutes each day* **Lesson 2** Making a Question-Answer Book *(80–81)*	3A, 3B	3–1	77–79
Focus Skills 🕐 *about 6 days, 2 lessons a day, 20 minutes each day* **Lesson 3** Oral Language: Listening to Sentences *(82)*			80
Lesson 4 Oral Language: Asking and Answering Questions *(82)*	3C		
Lesson 5 Viewing: Compare and Contrast *(83)*	3D		
Lesson 6 Viewing: Cause and Effect *(83)*	3E		
Lesson 7 Grammar/Mechanics: Verbs *(84)*			
Lesson 8 Grammar/Mechanics: Kinds of Sentences *(84)*	3F		81
Lesson 9 Vocabulary: Parts of the Body *(85)*			
Lesson 10 Vocabulary: Positional Words: *Left* and *Right* *(85)*			82
Lesson 11 Writing: Recording Information *(86)*			
Lesson 12 Writing: Writing Notes *(86)*	3G		
Lesson 13 Study Skills: Reading a Picture Graph *(87)*			83
Lesson 14 Study Skills: Categorizing/Classifying *(87)*			84
Class Writing Project 🕐 *about 2–3 days, 20 minutes each day* **Lesson 15** A Question-Answer Big Book *(88–89)*	3H		85–87

 MEETING INDIVIDUAL NEEDS *(90–93)*

Activities for Special Needs/Inclusion, for Students Acquiring English, for Reteaching, and for Enrichment/Challenge

Meeting Individual Needs

▶ **FOR SPECIAL NEEDS/INCLUSION:** *Houghton Mifflin English* Audiotape ; *See also* Reteaching.

▶ **FOR STUDENTS ACQUIRING ENGLISH:**
- Notes and activities are included in this Teacher's Edition throughout the unit to help you adapt or use lessons with students acquiring English.
- Students can listen to the published model *Do Pigs Have Stripes?* on audiotape.

▶ **RETEACHING**
- Activities for reteaching the focus skills are included on pages 90–93.

▶ **ENRICHMENT/CHALLENGE**
- Activities for challenge/enrichment that are correlated to focus skill lessons are included on pages 90–93.

All audiotape recordings are also available on CD.

Additional Resources

Audiotapes

 Technology Tools
CD-ROM: Curious George® Paint & Print Studio
Paint, Write & Play! (published by The Learning Company)
*Type to Learn Jr.™

*©Sunburst Technology Corporation, a Houghton Mifflin Company. All rights reserved.

INTERNET: http://www.eduplace.com/rdg/hme/
Visit Education Place for these additional support materials and activities:
- author biographies
- patterns for shape booklets

 Informal Assessment
Activity Masters Plus, Assessment Checklists, pages 45–47

 ### Keeping a Journal
In kindergarten, journals can be blank notebooks or folders filled with paper. As children draw and write about school activities, important events, and special thoughts, they can watch their writing growth as the year progresses.

 ### School-Home Connection
Suggestions for informing or involving family members in learning related to this unit are included in the Teacher's Edition throughout the unit.

Daily Routines

The oral language activities suggested here provide daily opportunities for children to develop their understanding of sentences. Refer to the **Interactive Bulletin Board** and **Daily Discussion** ideas on pages 10–13 and 20–21 for help in establishing Daily Routines for your classroom.

Interactive Bulletin Board

CALENDAR

November

SUNDAY	MONDAY	TUESDAY	WEDNESDAY	THURSDAY	FRIDAY	SATURDAY
		1	2	3	4	5
6	7	8	9			

YESTERDAY — Tuesday
TODAY — Wednesday
TOMORROW — Thursday
DAYS OF THE WEEK — Friday, Saturday, Sunday, Monday

Where Is the Bear?

Have a volunteer hide Claire the Bear in the classroom each day. Have other children ask the volunteer yes/no questions to find out where Claire is. Prompt children to use complete sentences. (Example: Is Claire in the Science Center? No, Claire is not in the Science Center.)

The Calendar and Weather Chart

As you update the calendar and weather chart together, have children take turns asking and answering questions about the day and the weather. Prompt them to answer in complete sentences. (Examples: What day was it yesterday? Yesterday was Tuesday. What is the weather today? Today it is cloudy and cool.)

Daily Message

What will we make in the Art Center?
We made an animal mobile.

Daily Message

Preview some of the day's activities. Have a volunteer ask a question about one of the activities. Record the question on the bulletin board. The following day, have a child answer the question in a complete statement. Record the statement beneath the question. Point out the capital letter at the beginning of each sentence and the end marks.

Daily Discussion

Each day bring in an object to spark children's curiosity. (See the suggestions below.) Allow children to examine the object. Then prompt them to talk about it, using the Think and Discuss questions. Model using complete sentences. Then have children think of other things they would like to know about the object. Record their questions. Place the object in the Science Center so that children can explore it. At the end of the day, revisit the questions and have children generate telling sentences to answer their questions.

Think and Discuss

- How does the object look? feel? sound? smell?
- How do you think it is used? Who uses it?
- What is it called?

QUESTION WORDS Display a list of question words (*who, what, where, when, why,* and *how*). Help children understand the kinds of questions each word suggests. For example, explain that *who* asks about a person and *where* asks about a place. Post the list with helpful illustrations, such as a clock next to the word *when* or a map next to the word *where*. Help children use these words correctly as they generate questions about the daily object.

CAUSE AND EFFECT Help children generate cause-and-effect questions and answers about the daily object. (Example: What does a magnet do to a paper clip that is near it? The magnet pulls the paper clip toward it.)

 INFORMAL ASSESSMENT (*See* Activity Masters Plus pp. 45, 47)

Daily Discussion Activity

Suggestions for Daily Objects

prisms

mirrors

magnets

kitchen gadgets

binoculars

unfamiliar tools and hardware

a variety of fabric, vinyl, and fake fur swatches

sandpaper

What sticks to these? What does not stick? How can you find out?

What happens when you look at something far away? What do you see when you look at something close to you? Where would be a good place to use these?

Center Activities

Center Activities provide additional daily opportunities for children to develop their understanding of different kinds of sentences.

Reading and Listening Center

PUBLISHED MODEL Children can listen to the audiotape of *Do Pigs Have Stripes?* as they follow along in the book. **Listening**

COMIC DIALOGUE Provide cartoon strips from newspapers, and have partners look at the strips together, paying attention to the actions of the characters and where the actions take place. Ask children to create dialogue for the characters that includes asking and telling sentences related to what the children understood from their careful viewing. **Viewing/Speaking**

QUESTION-AND-ANSWER CHAIN Record a question on a tape recorder and then rewind the tape to the beginning. Have one child listen to the question and record an answer. That child then thinks of and records another question for the next person. Have children continue the chain until everyone has had a chance to contribute. Then play the entire tape for the class. **Listening/Speaking**

Writing Center

TEXT INNOVATION Provide children with question and answer frames. Write the frames on large pieces of paper that the children use as they draw or write the missing parts. (Example: Does a dog have a shell? No, but a turtle does.) Then have pairs of children take turns saying each question and its answer.

CLASSROOM RIDDLES Have children dictate or write riddles about classroom objects by looking carefully at each object's characteristics and describing the objects without naming them. (Example: These come in many different colors. I use them to draw. What are they? (crayons) **Viewing/Speaking**

 JOURNAL Children can record pictures or words that remind them of questions they have about things they have seen or done. Have them dictate or write their questions near their drawings.

Does a dog have a shell?
No, but a turtle does.

Creative Arts Center

INTERVIEWS Have children work with a partner. Tell them to choose a favorite story character. One partner pretends to be the character while the other acts as a newspaper or television reporter who asks questions during an interview. Children then choose another story character and switch roles. **Listening/Speaking**

WHICH ANIMAL AM I? Have volunteers take turns pantomiming a specific animal's movement. After each pantomime, the audience asks questions about what they saw to help them guess the animal. The actor answers the questions in complete sentences. (Example: Does this animal have a trunk? No, it does not have a trunk.) **Viewing/Listening/Speaking**

HIDDEN ANIMALS Have children work in pairs. Tell each child to draw or choose a picture of an animal from a magazine without showing it to his or her partner. Then have one partner cover up parts of the animal picture as the other child uses the visual clues of the uncovered parts and asks questions to guess the animal. (Example: Is it an elephant? No, elephants do not have stripes.) **Viewing/Listening/Speaking**

 ## Science Center

SINK OR FLOAT? Set up a water tank or tub. Provide objects of varying size, weight, and density. Challenge partners to predict and test which objects will sink or float. Have one partner choose an object and ask the other child whether he or she thinks the object will sink or float and why. (Example: Do you think this orange will float? Why do you think so?) The other child must give his or her prediction in a complete sentence, test it, and then state the results. (Example: I think the orange will sink because it feels heavy. I was wrong. The orange did not sink.) Have children switch roles and continue until they have tested all the objects. **Viewing/Listening/Speaking**

 ## Block Center

As partners work in the block center, have them take turns asking one another questions about their constructions. (Examples: What are you building? How tall will you make your tower?) Help children respond in complete sentences.

About the Author

Melanie Walsh

Melanie Walsh has written and illustrated several children's books. She lives in London, England.

Bibliography

You may also wish to read aloud these question-answer books.

- **What Does the Rabbit Say?** by Jacque Hall
- **Brown Bear, Brown Bear, What Do You See?** by Bill Martin Jr
- **Do Monkeys Tweet?** by Melanie Walsh
- **From Head to Toe** by Eric Carle

A Published Model

① Listening to a Question-Answer Book

Lesson Objectives

Children will:
- listen for and identify a language pattern in a published model
- evaluate the relationship of visuals and text
- respond personally and critically to the selection

Materials

Do Pigs Have Stripes?

Reading the Model

The book *Do Pigs Have Stripes?* uses asking and telling sentences in a repeating language pattern to describe features of different animals.

Building Background

Have children think about how different animals look. Display pictures of familiar animals, such as a duck or a horse. Then ask questions such as *Do ducks have feathers? Do ducks have two legs? Do ducks have big claws?* When children respond no, ask: *What animals do have big claws?*

Introducing Vocabulary

- Discuss the meaning of each key vocabulary word: *spiky, crocodile, porcupine, coat, anteater,* and *antlers*. First, open to the illustration on pages 8–11. Run your finger along the spikes. Explain that a spiky tail is one with sharp points. Discuss what a crocodile is and where it lives.

- Next, explain that some words can have different meanings. Tell children that *coat* can mean "something you wear over your clothes" but that it can also mean "an animal's hair, fur, or wool." Discuss what a porcupine's coat is like. (has long, sharp quills)

- Finally, tell children that an anteater is an animal that has a long nose and a long, sticky tongue that it uses to catch ants and other insects. Then, using the illustration on pages 26 and 27, review how deer use their antlers.

Predicting and Purpose Setting

PICTURE WALK Display *Do Pigs Have Stripes?* Read aloud the title and the names of the author and illustrator. Then point out the nose of the animal on page 5. Have children predict what animal they will see on the next page. Continue the picture walk for several pages, having children check their predictions.

Reread the title and point out the question mark. Explain to children that a group of words that asks something is called an asking sentence or a question. Have children listen for asking sentences as you read the book aloud.

 This selection is also available on audiotape.

FOR STUDENTS ACQUIRING ENGLISH

Before asking about the animal attributes, take a picture walk and ask children to name animals and their body parts. Also, discuss the changes the illustrator has made to the animals.

Listening As a Writer

Think About Language

ASKING SENTENCES Ask a volunteer to tell what all of the asking sentences, or questions, were about. (animals) Reread some of the questions to confirm the answer. Reinforce that these are called asking sentences because they *ask* something. Point out that each ends with a question mark.

TELLING SENTENCES Explain to children that a group of words that *tells* something is called a telling sentence. Reread some of the telling sentences from the book. Ask children whether these are asking or telling sentences. (telling sentences) Note that each telling sentence ends with a period.

LANGUAGE PATTERN Reread the first question, *Does a bird have a big, wet nose?* Ask: *What kind of sentence is this?* (an asking sentence) *How do you know?* (Sample answers: It is a group of words that asks about an animal. It ends with a question mark.) *Do you think this is a good question or a silly question? Why?* (Sample answer: It is silly because birds don't have noses. They have beaks.) Turn the page and read the next sentence. Ask: *What kind of sentence is this?* (a telling sentence) *How do you know?* (Sample answers: It is a group of words that tells something. It ends with a period.) Continue this way for the next two questions and answers. Confirm the question-answer pattern by paging through a few more questions and answers. Then ask why it makes the book fun to read. (Sample answer: You want to turn the pages to see if you can guess the right animal.) Discuss how the pattern changes at the end of the book. Point out the exclamation mark. Explain that this mark tells readers to say the word(s) with strong feeling.

Think About the Pictures

Have children talk about how the illustrations helped them guess the answers to the questions by providing them with clues. Ask volunteers to point out which pictures were most helpful and to explain why. Have them tell if any pictures surprised them.

NOTE If children are discussing and responding to *Do Pigs Have Stripes?* on a day following your initial reading, reread the book.

FOR STUDENTS ACQUIRING ENGLISH

Review the asking and telling sentences by rereading *Do Pigs Have Stripes?* As you read, pause after each sentence and have children tell if the sentence is asking or telling. At that point, children will be familiar with the questions and pictures and can point to their favorites.

Responding

- **Personal Response** Have children recall a real animal they have seen. The animal might be a pet, a farm or zoo animal, or a wild animal. Have them draw the animal and then tell, dictate, or write something about what it looked like.

- **Critical Thinking** Tell children that you would like to add a page to this book that has a picture of a bird's feet. Have children tell, dictate, or write a silly question about the picture. (Example: Does a kangaroo have feet like this?) Then have children tell what would be on the next page.

Poster Book p. 3A

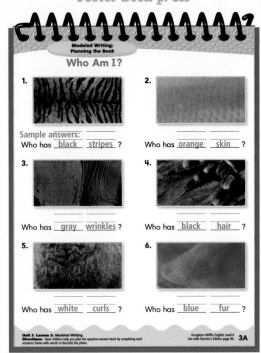

Poster Book p. 3B

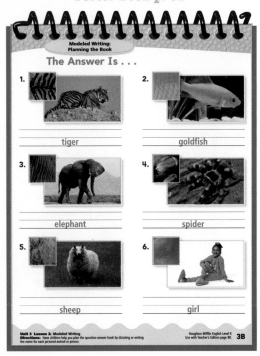

 FOR STUDENTS ACQUIRING ENGLISH

Help children formulate questions for Poster Book page 3A. Point to the part of each animal shown and guide children to describe the color, shape, or pattern.

② Making a Question-Answer Book

Lesson Objectives

Children will:
- help plan and draft a question-answer book
- recognize and use asking and telling sentences

Materials

Poster Book pp. 3A–3B, dry erase marker, Transparency 3–1 or chart paper, large drawing paper, crayons or colored markers, Activity Masters 77–79

Focus on Instruction

Recall that *Do Pigs Have Stripes?* is a book about animals. Remind children that the writing follows a pattern of a question, or asking sentence, followed by an answer, or telling sentence. Explain that you are going to work together to write a question-answer book about animals to share with other kindergarten children.

Planning the Book Poster Book pp. 3A–3B

- Tell children that first you must plan what you are going to write. Display Poster Book page 3A and read the title aloud.

- Point out that each picture has the beginning of a question below it. Read the sentence frame aloud. Then tell children that they will complete each question with words that describe what is shown in the picture. (Examples: Who has black stripes? Who has orange skin?) Have children guess the answer to each question. You may wish to record children's predictions on the board.

- Next, display Poster Book page 3B. Write the answer below each picture as children dictate. Ask whether they were surprised by any of the answers. Point out that the final photograph is of a girl, not an animal. Ask: *Why will this make a good ending for our book?* (Sample answer: It will be a surprise. The readers will expect the answer to be an animal, but instead they'll find out it is a person.)

Writing the Book Transparency 3–1

Explain to children that now you are ready to write your question-answer book. Display Transparency 3–1 or copy the text onto chart paper. Read the title aloud. Point out that the title tells what your book will be about.

MODELING THE LANGUAGE PATTERN Read aloud the first four sentences on Transparency 3–1. Pause after each sentence to ask whether it is an asking or a telling sentence. Point out that the asking sentences begin with *Who* and that your voice goes up at the end. Have children see that the question and answer connect to the related pictures on Poster Book pages 3A and 3B. Explain that you will continue this asking sentence and telling sentence pattern as you write the remaining text.

DRAFTING THE TEXT Ask children to help you draft the remaining text, using Poster Book pages 3A and 3B for reference.

- Point to the first sentence frame. Ask volunteers to recall a photograph on Poster Book page 3A to help complete the question. Write the missing words, such as *gray wrinkles*. Then point to the next sentence frame and to the full photograph of the animal on Poster Book page 3B. Ask children to name the animal. Fill in the missing word *elephant* and trace over the final period. Together read the completed sentences.

- Continue for the next two pairs of frames. When you get to the last pair of sentence frames, remind children that this is where you planned to change the pattern to make it a surprise ending.

- Have volunteers help you complete the sentences. Trace the exclamation point, and tell children that this mark tells the reader to say this answer with strong feeling. Together, read the completed sentences, emphasizing the answers.

MODELING CONCEPTS OF PRINT Help children become familiar with concepts of print by occasionally modeling as you write.

- Point out that you are moving from **left to right** as you record letters and words. As you read a sentence aloud, follow the text with your finger, using a sweeping motion from left to right.

- Reinforce **word spacing** by explaining that the group of letters you have written stands for a word. Read the word. Point out that you left a space before and after it. You may wish to show the spaces between words by having volunteers put a finger in the spaces.

- Reinforce **capitalizing the first word in a sentence**. As you are writing, note that each sentence must begin with a capital letter.

- Reinforce **end punctuation**. As you are writing, ask volunteers to tell how you should end each sentence. Trace over the end marks on the transparency.

Sharing the Book

- Read the completed text together and praise children for their help in planning and writing. Explain that now you are going to work together to make your writing into a question-answer book and share it with another class.

- Print each sentence at the bottom of a large piece of drawing paper. Or, if you used chart paper, cut the questions and answers into strips. Glue each strip onto a piece of large drawing paper.

- Have one child, a pair, or a small group illustrate each page. (Display Poster Book pages 3A–3B.) Ask another child or group to make a cover.

- Assemble the pages, asking children to help you put them in order. Then bind the pages. Place the book in your Reading and Listening Center.

 SCHOOL-HOME CONNECTION Activity Masters 77–79

Children can use Activity Masters 77–79 to make their own question-answer books to take home and "read" with family members. Have children underline the first letter of each sentence and write the appropriate end mark in each box. Then have them color the illustrations and complete the animal drawings. Help children cut the pages on the dashed lines and staple the pages together.

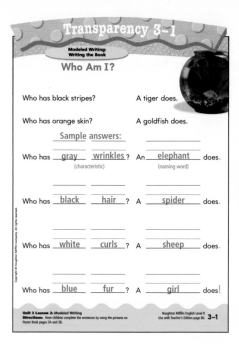

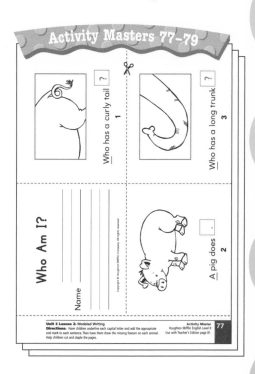

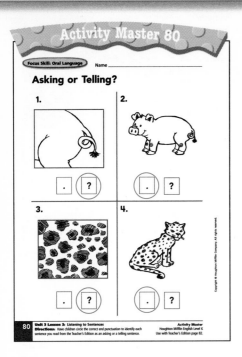

Activity Master 80

Focus Skill: Oral Language Name _____

Asking or Telling?

1.

2.

3.

4.

80 **Unit 3 Lesson 3: Listening to Sentences**
Directions: Have children circle the correct end punctuation to identify each sentence you read from the Teacher's Edition as an asking or a telling sentence.
Activity Master
Houghton Mifflin English Level K
Use with Teacher's Edition page 82.

Poster Book p. 3C

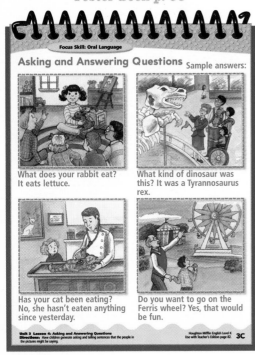

Focus Skill: Oral Language

Asking and Answering Questions Sample answers:

What does your rabbit eat? It eats lettuce.

What kind of dinosaur was this? It was a Tyrannosaurus rex.

Has your cat been eating? No, she hasn't eaten anything since yesterday.

Do you want to go on the Ferris wheel? Yes, that would be fun.

Unit 3 Lesson 4: Asking and Answering Questions
Directions: Have children generate asking and telling sentences that the people in the pictures might be saying.
Houghton Mifflin English Level K
Use with Teacher's Edition page 82. **3C**

 FOR STUDENTS ACQUIRING ENGLISH

Page through *Do Pigs Have Stripes?* and encourage children to complete sentences you begin, for example, *The giraffe is ___. (tall, skinny, spotted...)*

---

③ Listening to Sentences

Lesson Objectives

Children will:
- listen for telling sentences and asking sentences
- identify appropriate end punctuation

Materials

Do Pigs Have Stripes?, index cards, Activity Master 80

Review that a telling sentence is a group of words that tells something. Say a few telling sentences about the animals in *Do Pigs Have Stripes?* (Examples: The crocodile is green. The deer has antlers.) Then review that an asking sentence, or question, is a group of words that asks something. Again, give a few examples. (Examples: Why does the crocodile have a spiky tail? What does an elephant eat?) Tell children to listen to your voice as you say a question. Ask what they hear. (Your voice goes up at the end.)

- Give each child two index cards, one with a period written on it and one with a question mark. Identify the marks and when they are used. Then randomly say asking and telling sentences. Have children listen carefully to your voice, identify the type of sentence, and hold up the correct card.

- Distribute Activity Master 80. Have children circle the correct end punctuation box to identify each sentence you read as an asking or a telling sentence. Say: 1. *Does this tail belong to a cat?* 2. *This tail belongs to a pig.* 3. *Do hippos have spots?* 4. *A leopard has spots.*

④ Asking and Answering Questions

Lesson Objective

Children will:
- generate asking and telling sentences

Materials

Poster Book p. 3C, chart paper, marker

Display Poster Book page 3C. Discuss what is happening in each picture. Ask: *Who might be asking something in the picture? What might this person be asking? How would the other person answer the question?* Guide volunteers to suggest asking and telling sentences. Record their sentences on chart paper. Then help partners generate additional asking and telling sentences for these pictures.

 INFORMAL ASSESSMENT (*See* Activity Masters Plus p. 45)

 MEETING INDIVIDUAL NEEDS (*See* p. 90)

Focus Skill Viewing

⑤ Compare and Contrast

Lesson Objective

Children will:
• compare and contrast animals and things

Materials

Do Pigs Have Stripes?, Poster Book p. 3D, pairs of common classroom items

Alternately display the pictures of the dog (pages 6–7) and the elephant (pages 14–15) from *Do Pigs Have Stripes?* Have children compare and contrast the noses of these two animals. Discuss the size, color, and shape of each nose.

• Then display Poster Book page 3D and point to the first row. Ask children to compare and contrast the cats by telling how they are alike and different.

• Repeat with the remaining rows of items.

• Provide partners with pairs of common classroom objects, such as two crayons, two books, or two jars of paint. Have the partners work together to compare and contrast the objects and then report their findings to the class.

⑥ Cause and Effect

Lesson Objective

Children will:
• identify causes and effects

Materials

Do Pigs Have Stripes?, Poster Book p. 3E

Display the dog on pages 6–7 of *Do Pigs Have Stripes?* Ask: *Why might this dog bark?* (Sample answers: It wants to go outside. A stranger is at the door.) Explain that *why* something happens is a cause; *what happens* is the effect. Tell children that the word *because* is often used to tell about a cause and effect.

• Display Poster Book page 3E. Have children look at the two pictures on the page and discuss the situation.

• Then have a volunteer tell what caused the tear in the picture.

• Help children make up an oral question and an answer to go with the pictures. (Example: Why is the paper torn? The paper is torn because the rabbit ate it.)

• Have children work in small groups to determine possible causes for these effects: a lost lunch box, a broken toy, a smiling mom, trampled flowers.

 INFORMAL ASSESSMENT (*See* Activity Masters Plus p. 45)

 MEETING INDIVIDUAL NEEDS (*See* pp. 90–91)

Poster Book p. 3D

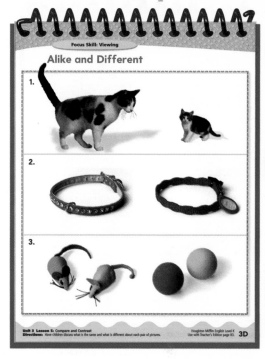

Focus Skill: Viewing
Alike and Different

1.

2.

3.

Unit 3 Lesson 5: Compare and Contrast
Directions: Have children discuss what is the same and what is different about each pair of pictures.
Houghton Mifflin English Level K
Use with Teacher's Edition page 83. **3D**

 FOR STUDENTS ACQUIRING ENGLISH

Help children name the attributes of the different animals and objects by asking questions, such as *How many legs does the elephant have? How many does the dog have? How are their legs different?*

Poster Book p. 3E

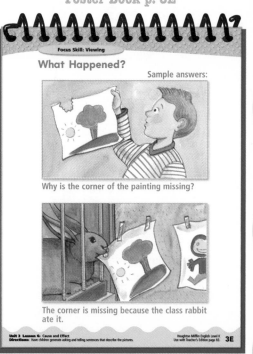

Focus Skill: Viewing
What Happened?

Sample answers:

Why is the corner of the painting missing?

The corner is missing because the class rabbit ate it.

Unit 3 Lesson 6: Cause and Effect
Directions: Have children generate asking and telling sentences that describe the pictures.
Houghton Mifflin English Level K
Use with Teacher's Edition page 83. **3E**

Poster Book p. 3F

Focus Skill: Grammar
Telling and Asking

Activity Master 81

Focus Skill: Grammar   Name _____

Telling and Asking

Unit 3 Lesson 8: Kinds of Sentences
Directions: Have children color and cut out the figures, glue them to craft sticks, and make up asking and telling sentences for their puppets to say. Then ask them to dictate or write one asking and one telling sentence they used.

Activity Master
81
Houghton Mifflin English Level K
Use with Teacher's Edition page 84.

FOR STUDENTS ACQUIRING ENGLISH

To help children participate in the puppet skits, model a dialog between your puppet and a volunteer's. Then have children repeat possible questions and statements they can use. Finally, allow children ample time to practice and perform in small groups before performing for the class.

 Focus Skill **Grammar/Mechanics**

⑦ Verbs

Lesson Objective	**Materials**
Children will:	*Do Pigs Have Stripes?*,
• listen for and identify verbs	Additional Resources p. 234

Display the illustration of the cow on pages 18–19 of *Do Pigs Have Stripes?* Ask children to name and pantomime things a cow can do. (Sample answers: walk, chew, moo, eat) Repeat with other pictures and animals from the book. Explain that the words they named are called action words, or verbs.

● Read aloud the poem "Animals." (*See* Additional Resources page 234) Tell children to listen carefully for words that name actions or the things animals can do. Then ask volunteers to say the action words as they perform or imitate the actions. (*hop, jump, walk, run, swim*)

● Recite the poem together. After you say each question, have children say the answer.

⑧ Kinds of Sentences

Lesson Objective	**Materials**
Children will:	Poster Book p. 3F, dry erase
• generate telling and asking sentences	marker, Activity Master 81,
	craft sticks

Remind children that they have been learning about telling and asking sentences. Ask or prompt a volunteer to give an example of each.

● Display Poster Book page 3F. Have children use telling sentences to describe the first picture. Allow every child to generate a sentence. If a child suggests an incomplete sentence, restate the response as a complete statement.

● Record two of the suggested sentences. As you write, reinforce that a telling sentence begins with a capital letter and ends with a period.

● Next, have children generate asking sentences for the bottom picture. Record two of the sentences. Note the capital letter at the beginning of each sentence and the question mark at the end.

● Then distribute Activity Master 81. Guide children as they cut out, assemble, and decorate the stick puppets. Have them make up telling and asking sentences for the puppets to say and then use them in a skit. Afterward, ask children to tell, dictate, or write one telling and one asking sentence they used.

✓ **INFORMAL ASSESSMENT** (*See* Activity Masters Plus p. 46)

 MEETING INDIVIDUAL NEEDS (*See* p. 91)

Focus Skill Vocabulary

⑨ Parts of the Body

Lesson Objective

Children will:
• identify and name parts of the body

Materials

Do Pigs Have Stripes?, Additional Resources p. 234, drawing paper, crayons

Display the deer picture on pages 26–27 of *Do Pigs Have Stripes?* Point to body parts and ask volunteers to name them. Repeat with other animal pictures. As children identify parts of the body, highlight vocabulary words used to name the same part on different animals. (Examples: *paws, feet, hooves; nose, trunk, snout*)

• Ask children to listen carefully and to point to each body part as you read "Here Are My Ears." (*See* Additional Resources page 234)

• Then have children draw imaginary creatures and label the body parts. Give children the option of dictating or writing their labels.

⑩ Positional Words

Lesson Objective

Children will:
• understand the terms *left* and *right*

Materials

Do Pigs Have Stripes?, Activity Master 82, yarn, crayons or markers

LEFT AND RIGHT Help children distinguish left and right. Make yarn bracelets for children to put on their left wrists. Tell children that the bracelet is on their *left* wrist. Play a brief game of Simon Says, using left/right instructions. (Example: Shake your <u>right</u> foot. Raise your <u>left</u> hand.)

• After the game, display pages 8–11 from *Do Pigs Have Stripes?* Name different parts of the crocodile, and ask volunteers to tell whether the part is pictured on the left page or on the right page. Remind children to look at their bracelet to locate left. Explain that when we read books, we always begin on the left and go to the right.

• Distribute Activity Master 82. Show children how to form an *L* with their left thumb and forefinger. Then have children follow these directions to complete the page: *Draw a cloud on the <u>left</u>. Draw a sun on the <u>right</u>. Draw a tree on the <u>left</u>. Draw yourself on the <u>right</u>.*

 INFORMAL ASSESSMENT (*See* Activity Masters Plus p. 47)

 MEETING INDIVIDUAL NEEDS (*See* p. 92)

 FOR STUDENTS ACQUIRING ENGLISH

Before completing Lessons 9 and 10, review parts of the body and left and right. Then play a version of Simon Says in which the object is not to eliminate children from the game, but to have all children succeed in completing the given gesture. (Example: Simon says, "Touch your right ear! Turn left!")

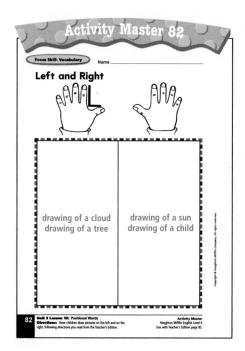

Activity Master 82

Focus Skill: Vocabulary Name _____

Left and Right

| drawing of a cloud drawing of a tree | drawing of a sun drawing of a child |

82 | **Unit 3 Lesson 10:** Positional Words
Directions: Have children draw pictures on the left and on the right, following directions you read from the Teacher's Edition.
Activity Master
Houghton Mifflin English Level K
Use with Teacher's Edition page 85.

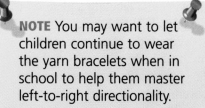

NOTE You may want to let children continue to wear the yarn bracelets when in school to help them master left-to-right directionality.

This is the class
rabbit. His name is
Harry. He has floppy
ears and a pink nose.

Poster Book p. 3G

Focus Skill: Writing

Notes

Dear Maria,
I hope you have
a Happy Birthday.
Your friend,
Sarah

Mom,
Dad called.
Should he buy
apples?
Love,
Alex

Jamal,
Can you come to my house
today? Tell me at recess.
Your pal,
Michael

Dear __Answers will vary.__

Thank you for _____

It was _____

Your friends,

Unit 3 Lesson 12: Writing Notes
Directions: Have children contribute text to complete the thank-you note.

Houghton Mifflin English Level K
Use with Teacher's Edition page 86. **3G**

FOR STUDENTS ACQUIRING ENGLISH

For Lesson 11 give children acquiring English the specific task of
drawing and labeling a picture of
an animal. Then have children
share with the class, naming the
animal's body parts and attributes.
For Lesson 12, show examples of
several notes and then brainstorm
possible sentences to use in notes.

Focus Skill Writing

11 Recording Information

Lesson Objectives

Children will:
- record information by using pictures
- use captions or labels to describe pictures

Materials

chart paper, drawing paper,
markers, crayons

- Recall with children that *Do Pigs Have Stripes?* showed how different animals
  look. Have children describe an animal they all have seen, such as a class pet
  or a squirrel or bird they can observe from the classroom. Ask: *What would
  you show in a picture to give information about the animal?* Draw a picture
  of the animal, using children's suggestions. Then ask volunteers to dictate one
  or two caption sentences, and record them under the picture.

- Have children use the captioned drawing as a model to draw and label their
  own pictures that show something they have seen or experienced. Help them
  dictate or write sentences.

12 Writing Notes

Lesson Objectives

Children will:
- recognize the different purposes of written notes
- write or dictate notes

Materials

Poster Book p. 3G, dry erase
marker, drawing paper, crayons,
glue, glitter

Explain that a good way to leave an important message for someone is to write
a note. Point out that when people write notes, they use different types of sentences, depending on the message.

- Display Poster Book page 3G. Read and discuss the notes that are shown.
  Help children identify the end marks and tell whether the sentences are asking or telling and why someone would write each message. Point out the
  greeting (*Dear…*) and the closings (*Your friend, Your pal, Love*).

- Then use the frame at the bottom of the poster to compose a thank-you note
  to someone special who has helped the class. (Examples: principal, classroom
  visitor, parent) You may want to copy the note onto notepaper and mail it.

- Have children use the models on Poster Book page 3G to help them dictate
  or write their own notes. Suggest that children write a note to thank someone, to give a message to a friend, or to wish someone happy birthday. Allow
  children to decorate their notes. If possible, have family members or parent
  volunteers help children mail or deliver their notes.

 INFORMAL ASSESSMENT (*See* Activity Masters Plus p. 46)

 MEETING INDIVIDUAL NEEDS (*See* pp. 92–93)

Focus Skill | **Study Skills**

13 Reading a Picture Graph

Lesson Objective

Children will:
- make and read a picture graph

Materials

drawing paper, crayons or markers, masking tape, Activity Master 83

Review how the pictures in *Do Pigs Have Stripes?* provided information about animals. Explain that a picture graph also uses pictures to provide information.

- Ask children to draw a picture of their favorite animal, selecting from dogs, cats, or rabbits. Tell children that they will make a picture graph with the pictures. As children draw, use masking tape to create a three-row grid on the floor. Label the rows *cat, dog, rabbit.*

- Have each child place his or her picture in the appropriate row. Then have children use the graph to answer questions such as *Which animal is the favorite? Do more children like cats or dogs? How many children like rabbits?*

- Help children read the picture graph to complete Activity Master 83.

14 Categorizing/Classifying

Lesson Objectives

Children will:
- sort objects into categories
- identify which objects and pictures do not belong

Materials

classroom objects, Activity Master 84, scissors, glue, paper, pencils

- Assemble a group of like objects, such as writing implements. Then add an object that does not belong. (Example: ball) Ask children which object does not belong and how the other objects are alike. Then ask them to name the group, or classify like objects. (Example: writing tools) Repeat with other objects and categories, such as round objects, red objects, pointed objects, etc.

- Have children color and cut apart the pictures on Activity Master 84. Discuss possible sorting categories, and have children practice sorting the pictures different ways. (Examples: fur/no fur, large/small, feathers/no feathers) Then ask children to choose favorite categories, sort the pictures, and paste them onto paper. Help them label each category.

 INFORMAL ASSESSMENT (*See* Activity Masters Plus p. 46)

 MEETING INDIVIDUAL NEEDS (*See* p. 93)

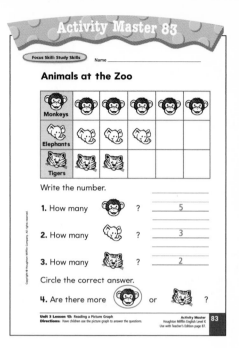

Activity Master 83

Activity Master 84

FOR STUDENTS ACQUIRING ENGLISH

For Lesson 13, be sure children understand all the steps. First, explain all the steps slowly. Then repeat the steps one at a time as children complete each step. Before asking children to do the activity in Lesson 14, have them name and describe the animals in the pictures.

15 A Question-Answer Big Book

Lesson Objectives

Children will:
- help choose a topic for a question-answer book
- help plan a question-answer book
- write and illustrate two pages for a question-answer book

Materials

Poster Book p. 3H, dry erase markers, large drawing paper, crayons or colored markers, Activity Masters 85–87

Focus on Instruction

Tell children that they are now going to work together to write another question-answer book for the class. Remind them that earlier in the unit they wrote a question-answer book about animals. Tell children that this time they will choose a different topic to write about.

Planning the Book Poster Book p. 3H

- Explain to children that for this Big Book, they each will make two pages, a question page and an answer page. Tell them that when all the pages are done, you will put them together to make one class Big Book.

- Help children think about possible topics for their question-answer book. Do they want to ask and answer questions about dinosaurs? about plants? about their community? You may wish to read aloud some of the books in the Bibliography on page 78 to spark topic ideas.

- Choose a topic as a class and record it on Poster Book page 3H. If children cannot decide on a topic, or if you prefer to provide one for them, you might use an idea from the chart below.

Poster Book p. 3H

Class Writing Project:
A Question-Answer Big Book

Planning Our Question-Answer Big Book

Our Topic Answers will vary.

Questions	Answers

Unit 3 Lesson 15: Class Writing Project
Directions: Have children help you plan the question-answer book by suggesting questions and answers for their topic.

Houghton Mifflin English Level K
Use with Teacher's Edition page 88. **3H**

Big Book Ideas		
Animal Noises	**Nursery Rhymes**	**Transportation**
What moos?	Who lost her sheep?	What flies?
What quacks?	Who had a little lamb?	What is long and yellow?
What baas?	Who lived in a shoe?	What has two wheels?
What tweets?	Who sat on a tuffet?	What has four wheels?
What honks?		

- Explain to children that now you will work together to plan what you will write. Have children decide if they want their sentences to follow a pattern. (Example: Who _____? A _____ does.) Then use Poster Book page 3H to record children's suggestions for questions and anwers. Record the complete questions on the left. Use pictures and/or key words to record the answers on the right.

Writing the Book

- Review with children the Big Book planning you did on Poster Book page 3H. If you decide to use a particular sentence pattern, review that pattern as well.

- Then remind children that they will each create two pages for the book—a question page and an answer page. They can either choose or be assigned a question.

- Distribute large drawing paper. Have children dictate or write the question and then the answer on different papers. Display Poster Book page 3H for their reference. Remind children that each question and answer should be a complete sentence. Encourage them to check that each sentence begins with a capital letter and has the correct end mark.

- Distribute drawing materials and have children illustrate their pages.

What is long and yellow?

Sharing the Book

- Remind children that books have titles and that the title helps readers know what the book will be about. Together, decide on a title for the book. Have volunteers make a cover.

- Ask children to share their pages with the class. Have each child "read" his or her pages. Encourage children to discuss their illustrations and how they support each sentence.

- Bind the pages. Then read the book together chorally, beginning with the title. As you read each sentence, point out the end marks. Place the completed Big Book in your Reading and Listening Center.

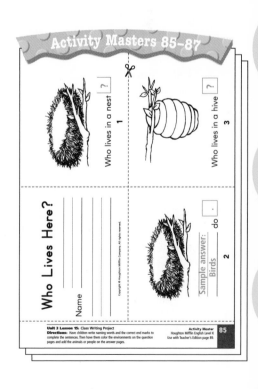

 SCHOOL-HOME CONNECTION Activity Masters 85–87

Children can make their own question-answer book to take home to "read" with family members. Have children write the appropriate punctuation at the end of each sentence and dictate or write a plural noun to answer each question. Finally, have children color the illustrations on the question pages and draw the missing animals or people on the answer pages.

 INFORMAL ASSESSMENT (*See* Activity Masters Plus p. 46)

Meeting Individual Needs

Lesson 3 Focus Skill   Oral Language: Listening to Sentences

RETEACHING ALTERNATIVE STRATEGY

Model both telling and asking sentences. Then read aloud a book that has asking and telling sentences, such as *What Can You Do with a Shoe?* by Beatrice Schenk De Regniers or *What Do You Do, Dear?* by Sesyle Joslin. Have children raise their hands when they hear an asking sentence and put their hands on their heads when they hear a telling sentence. Exaggerate the intonations for questions and statements as you read to help children aurally identify each kind of sentence.

CHALLENGE

Have partners look at magazine pictures or picture books and take turns generating asking sentences and telling sentences about the pictures. Ask them to identify each kind of sentence.

FOR STUDENTS ACQUIRING ENGLISH

Children acquiring English will be able to participate in the Reteaching activity if you help by slightly exaggerating the intonation of questions and statements. Also, model responding to the first few by shouting out "Asking!" or "Telling!"

Lesson 4 Focus Skill   Oral Language: Asking and Answering Questions

RETEACHING ALTERNATIVE STRATEGY

Have a child tell you one thing that happened yesterday. Restate the sentence, pointing out that this is a telling sentence because it is a group of words that tells something. Have other children tell what they learned from this sentence. Then ask the first child a question about what he or she said. Explain that this is an asking sentence because it asks something. Have other children tell what you want to find out from your question. Continue with other examples.

CHALLENGE

Help pairs generate questions and answers about things that happen each day at school or at home. One child asks a question and the other responds with a statement. (Example: What did you eat for breakfast? I ate juice and cereal.)

FOR STUDENTS ACQUIRING ENGLISH

Help each child find a book from the reading section of your classroom or the school library. Show them how to "read" the book, looking for question marks and periods. Then encourage children to share what they have found by pointing to the sentences and repeating them as you read.

Lesson 5 Focus Skill   Viewing: Compare and Contrast

RETEACHING ALTERNATIVE STRATEGY

Display two objects. Explain ways in which they are alike and different. Then show other pairs of objects. Say true and false statements about the ways they are alike and different. Ask children to give a thumbs up if they agree with a statement and a thumbs down if they don't. Encourage children to compare and contrast the two objects in additional ways.

CHALLENGE

Have children compare and contrast two characters from picture books. Suggest that they use the books as props to tell the class how the characters are alike and how they are different.

FOR STUDENTS ACQUIRING ENGLISH

Help children participate in the Reteaching activity by modeling with a volunteer the thumbs up and thumbs down responses. Then be sure to include simple statements that review familiar adjectives. Repeat the activity several times for reinforcement.

Lesson 6 Focus Skill Viewing: Cause and Effect

RETEACHING ALTERNATIVE STRATEGY

Use common classroom events and items to dramatize some cause-effect relationships. (Example: Put something in the wrong spot in the room and then pretend you can't find it.) Ask questions about your dramatizations to help children understand the cause and effect relationship. (Example: Why couldn't I find my notebook? It was not in the right place.) Discuss how the two actions are connected. Then have children perform simple cause-effect dramatizations.

CHALLENGE
Read aloud a book that describes cause-effect relationships, such as *If You Give a Mouse a Cookie* by Laura Joffe Numeroff. Have small groups dictate or write a short cause-effect story, using the book you read as a model.

FOR STUDENTS ACQUIRING ENGLISH

Play a cause-and-effect game such as Telephone! Have all the children sit in a circle; whisper a simple sentence into the first child's ear. After the children whisper the message around, note the effect of repeating it. Experiment with simpler and harder sentences to demonstrate the effect.

Lesson 7 Focus Skill Grammar: Verbs

RETEACHING ALTERNATIVE STRATEGY

Demonstrate an action word, such as *jump*. Then play a movement game to help children identify verbs. Say common nouns and verbs in random order. Have children act out each verb they hear but freeze when they hear a word that is not a verb. Use these as well as other nouns and verbs: *hop*, *pencil*, *book*, *skip*, *crayon*, *walk*, *cat*, *sing*, *computer*, *cup*, and *clap*.

CHALLENGE
Have children make "My Day" posters that describe a typical day. Have them dictate or write three or four actions they do each day. (Example: I play with my puppy.)Then have them draw pictures to illustrate the actions.

FOR STUDENTS ACQUIRING ENGLISH

Help children participate in a variation of the Challenge activity by working in groups of mixed proficiency. Have the intermediate and advanced children draw the images and then act them out. Once the beginners are familiar with the exercise, encourage them to join in.

Lesson 8 Focus Skill Grammar and Mechanics: Kinds of Sentences

RETEACHING ALTERNATIVE STRATEGY

Model asking and telling sentences. Then have partners ask each other questions about what they can do. Partners take turns saying and acting out the answers. Then one child dictates one of the questions and the other dictates the answer. (Example: Can you hop? I can hop.) Record the sentences, allowing the children to write the capital letter at the beginning of each sentence and the end punctuation.

CHALLENGE
Have partners work together to dictate or write and illustrate their own animal riddles. The riddles should include both telling and asking sentences. (Example: I have black and white stripes. I look a like a horse. What am I? I am a zebra.)

FOR STUDENTS ACQUIRING ENGLISH

Have children form pairs. Pass out old magazines. Ask the pairs to cut out different types of sentences from the headings. Remind them to look for the end marks. Then have a class sharing in which the pairs paste their sentences on chart paper in the correct column.

Meeting Individual Needs

Lesson 9 Focus Skill   Vocabulary: Parts of the Body

RETEACHING ALTERNATIVE STRATEGY

Teach children the song "Head, Shoulders, Knees, and Toes" while touching each body part mentioned. Then, as children follow along with each repetition, begin omitting words and touching only the body part.
• Head, shoulders, knees and toes, knees and toes.
• Head, shoulders, knees and toes, knees and toes.
• Eyes and ears and mouth and nose.
• Head, shoulders, knees and toes.

CHALLENGE

Have children draw pictures of themselves, labeling each body part. Then have them write or dictate sentences that tell the purpose of each body part. (Example: I use my eyes to see.)

FOR STUDENTS ACQUIRING ENGLISH

Teach children the song from the Reteaching activity, but before doing so, ask them to help you name the body parts. Be sure children understand and are articulating correctly when they sing the words in the song.

Lesson 10 Focus Skill   Vocabulary: Positional Words

RETEACHING ALTERNATIVE STRATEGY

Trace an outline of your hands on the board, and have children identify them as left and right. Label them. Then have children trace their own hands on paper. Help them label the hands with the words *left* and *right*.

CHALLENGE

Have children fold a piece of paper in half, and then unfold it. Tell children to make a "blob" painting on the left side. Then have them fold the paper again, pressing it so that the paint transfers to the right side. After they unfold it, have them label the sides *left* and *right*.

FOR STUDENTS ACQUIRING ENGLISH

Have children play a version of Follow the Leader in small groups. The child at the front of the line shouts the direction (left, right) and his or her group follows. Once all children have led, add the instruction that the leaders also shout a verb. (Example: Hop left!)

Lesson 11 Focus Skill   Writing: Recording Information

RETEACHING ALTERNATIVE STRATEGY

Draw a picture of something you like to do, such as gardening. Then model labeling your picture to record information. Have partners ask each other what they like to do. Then have them draw pictures of their favorite activity. After they dictate or write labels for the picture, they can share their pictures and labels with each other.

CHALLENGE

Ask pairs to share information about special activities. One child tells about an activity, such as a trip to the beach or a school project, without naming the activity. The other child draws a picture and writes a caption that shows what he or she thinks the activity is.

FOR STUDENTS ACQUIRING ENGLISH

Hand out paper and explain that children will be drawing what you say. Dictate a drawing for them. For example, say: *Draw a sun at the top. Draw grass at the bottom and a boy and girl in the middle.* Be sure to give children time to draw between instructions.

Lesson 12 Focus Skill   Writing: Writing Notes

RETEACHING ALTERNATIVE STRATEGY

Remind children that notes are helpful ways to give information. Use Poster Book page 3G to review the parts and form for a thank-you note. Then guide children in writing a thank-you note to a parent or a grandparent.

CHALLENGE
Have partners write notes, such as thank-you notes, holiday cards, or friendship notes to their classmates. Help them dictate or write messages in their notes and cards. Suggest that they add illustrations. Have classroom mail delivery time so children can share their notes.

FOR STUDENTS ACQUIRING ENGLISH

Have children form small groups. Pass out magazine pictures of people experiencing emergencies or everyday life. Then ask children to name objects in the pictures. Finally, have the groups compose messages for each picture and share them with the class.

Lesson 13 Focus Skill   Study Skills: Reading a Picture Graph

RETEACHING ALTERNATIVE STRATEGY

On chart paper prepare a two-row grid comparing numbers of squirrels and birds. Model how to read it by asking questions such as *Are there more squirrels or birds? How do you know?* Then distribute two-row grids and groups of objects to pairs of children. Help children place their objects, such as pencils and paintbrushes, on their grids. Then have them ask and answer questions about their concrete graphs.

CHALLENGE
Have children work in small groups of two or three. Assign each group a different classroom object, such as chairs or

toy trucks. Children should count the objects and record them on a class picture graph.

FOR STUDENTS ACQUIRING ENGLISH

Help children acquiring English participate in both the Reteaching and Challenge activities as the official counters. Form groups of mixed proficiencies for each of the activities and have the beginning students count the objects throughout the activity.

Lesson 14 Focus Skill   Study Skills: Categorizing/Classifying

RETEACHING ALTERNATIVE STRATEGY

Group classroom objects, such as crayons, markers, and buttons, to model how to categorize and classify objects. Point out that like objects are together. Children can practice categorizing and classifying by dividing themselves based on colors in their clothing. They can also use such categories as sneakers/shoes or bus riders/walkers.

CHALLENGE
Have children review the animals named in *Do Pigs Have Stripes?* Ask partners or small groups to identify categories of animals. Help children write their categories and list the ani-

mals in each group. (Example: Pets—dog, cat, bird; Wild Animals—crocodile, elephant, anteater)

FOR STUDENTS ACQUIRING ENGLISH

Help children join in the Reteaching activity by first reviewing names of clothing and colors. Point to different clothing items and ask a variety of questions such as *What's that? Is _____ wearing a blue shirt or a red shirt? What color is my sweater?* For additional practice, children can take turns asking the questions.

Unit 4
Personal Narrative

In this unit, children are introduced to narrative writing and learn that a personal narrative is a true story about something that happened to the author. Children listen to a book about preparing for a party and participate in the modeled writing of a personal narrative about a surprise party. Then children work together with you to write about a shared class experience, using the writing process. Unit skills develop language as well as relate to and support narrative writing.

What You Will Find in This Unit . . .

Unit 4 Planning Guide
Personal Narrative

	Poster Book	Transparency	Activity Masters Plus
DAILY COMMUNICATION LINKS			
Daily Routines (98–99)			
The oral language activities provide daily opportunities for children to develop the basic concepts and skills needed to compose personal narratives.			
• **Interactive Bulletin Board**: Calendar, Daily Message			
• **Daily Discussion Activity**: Telling Personal Stories			
Center Activities (100–101)		4–1	
• Reading and Listening Center • Writing Center			
• Creative Arts Center • Social Studies Center			
A Published Model ⏱ *1 day, 20 minutes*			
Lesson 1 Listening to a Personal Narrative (102–103) *The Coconut Flan*			
Modeled Writing ⏱ *about 2-3 days, 20 minutes each day*			
Lesson 2 Personal Narrative (104–106)	4A	4–2	88
Focus Skills ⏱ *about 6 days, 20 minutes each day*			
Lesson 3 Oral Language: Using Polite Language (107)			
Lesson 4 Viewing: Main Idea and Details (108)	4B		
Lesson 5 Grammar: Nouns (109)	4C		89
Lesson 6 Grammar/Mechanics: Kinds of Sentences (110)	4D		90
Lesson 7 Vocabulary: Exact Nouns (111)	4E		91
Lesson 8 Writing: Using Details (112)	4F		92
Shared Writing ⏱ *about 2–3 days, 20 minutes each day*			
Lesson 9 Personal Narrative (113–115)	4G	4–3	
Independent Writing ⏱ *about 1–3 days, 20 minutes each day*			
Lesson 10 Personal Narrative (116-117)			
☑ **Writing Prompts** (195)			93
MEETING INDIVIDUAL NEEDS (118-119)			
Activities for Special Needs/Inclusion, for Students Acquiring English, for Reteaching, and for Enrichment/Challenge			

Meeting Individual Needs

▶ **FOR SPECIAL NEEDS/INCLUSION:** *Houghton Mifflin English* Audiotape ; *See also* Reteaching.

▶ **FOR STUDENTS ACQUIRING ENGLISH:**
- Notes and activities are included in this Teacher's Edition throughout the unit to help you adapt or use lessons with students acquiring English.
- Students can listen to the published model *The Coconut Flan* on audiotape.

▶ **RETEACHING**
- Activities for reteaching the focus skills are included on pages 118–119.

▶ **ENRICHMENT/CHALLENGE**
- Activities for challenge/enrichment that are correlated to focus skill lessons are included on pages 118–119.

 All audiotape recordings are also available on CD.

Additional Resources

Audiotapes

 Technology Tools
CD-ROM: Curious George® Paint & Print Studio
Paint, Write & Play! (published by The Learning Company)
*Type to Learn Jr.™

*©Sunburst Technology Corporation, a Houghton Mifflin Company. All rights reserved.

INTERNET: http://www.eduplace.com/rdg/hme/
Visit Education Place for these additional support materials and activities:
- author biographies
- patterns for shape booklets
- writing prompts

 Informal Assessment
Activity Masters Plus, Assessment Checklists, pages 45–47

Keeping a Journal
In kindergarten, journals can be blank notebooks or folders filled with paper. As children draw and write about school activities, important events, and special thoughts, they can watch their writing growth as the year progresses.

 School-Home Connection
Suggestions for informing or involving family members in learning related to this unit are included in the Teacher's Edition throughout the unit.

Daily Routines

The oral language activities suggested here provide daily opportunities for children to develop basic concepts and skills they will need to write personal narratives. Refer to the **Interactive Bulletin Board** and **Daily Discussion** ideas on pages 12–13 for help in establishing Daily Routines for your classroom.

Interactive Bulletin Board

The Calendar

Each day, as you work with the *yesterday*, *today*, and *tomorrow* pockets, have volunteers compose oral sentences about personal experiences. Ask them to begin their sentences with the words *yesterday*, *today*, and *tomorrow*. (Examples: Yesterday I visited Grandma and Grandpa. Today I will fingerpaint at school. Tomorrow I will play catch with my brother.)

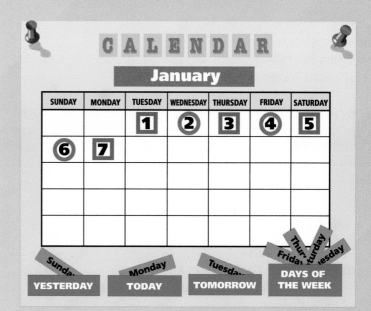

Daily Message

Each day, to reinforce the concept of personal narrative, ask a different volunteer to dictate a telling sentence about something the whole class will do together that day. Write the sentence and then read it aloud. Point out the capital letter at the beginning and the period at the end.

Today we will make masks.

Daily Discussion

Each day, call on a different volunteer to tell a personal narrative about something that really happened to the speaker. Tell children that they will want to add a few details to help classmates picture the story in their minds. Explain that some details tell how something looked, sounded, smelled, tasted, or felt. Also use the suggestions in **Telling Personal Stories**, and follow up with the Think and Discuss questions below.

Think and Discuss

- Was the story about just one thing that really happened to you?

- Who is the *I* or *me* in the story?

- Talk about what happened in the beginning, in the middle, and at the end. Did the story answer the questions *who, what, when,* and *where*?

- Did you picture what happened in your mind? What words helped you see what happened?

- What was interesting about the beginning? What did the ending tell about how you felt or how things worked out in your story?

TIME WORDS As children listen to each other's personal narratives, have them note words that tell about times of the day, days of the week, months of the year, and the seasons. Create a word web for each category. Draw blank word webs on chart paper to fill in as children tell their narratives.

NOUNS Record the nouns children use in the Daily Discussion. Work together to create a chart titled Nouns: Naming Words. List both proper and common nouns, using the categories People, Animals, Places, and Things. When listing proper nouns, point out that names for special people, animals, places, or things begin with capital letters. Have volunteers add illustrations to the chart.

Daily Discussion Activity

Telling Personal Stories

You may want to tell your own personal narrative. You could invite other teachers, aides, or your principal to tell personal narratives, too.

After you listen to each personal narrative, point out how each story told about things that really happened. Talk about each beginning and the outcome of each story. You may want to tape-record the personal narratives for children to play in the Listening Center.

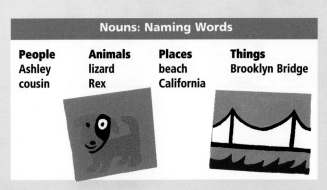

Nouns: Naming Words			
People	**Animals**	**Places**	**Things**
Ashley	lizard	beach	Brooklyn Bridge
cousin	Rex	California	

Center Activities

Center Activities provide additional daily opportunities for children to develop and reinforce concepts and skills that support composing personal narratives.

Reading and Listening Center

PUBLISHED MODEL Children can listen to the audiotape of *The Coconut Flan* as they follow along in the book. **Listening**

ORAL NARRATIVE On a tape, prerecord a simple personal narrative about an experience, such as going to the beach or celebrating a special occasion. After children listen to your narrative, have them draw any people, places, animals, or things that you named. Have them work with partners to compare their picture lists of naming words. **Listening/Speaking**

ASKING ABOUT DETAILS Have children work with partners to tell each other about one thing they did that day or the day before. After children tell a story about themselves, have each partner ask questions relating to the size, color, shape, sound, taste, or feel of things in the story or to what the speaker thought or felt about the experience. **Listening/Speaking**

Creative Arts Center

Transparency 4–1

GROCERY STORE ROLE PLAY Have children recall a particular visit to a grocery store. Then ask volunteers to act out that visit. Use Transparency 4–1 to project the grocery store background like that in *The Coconut Flan* against a white surface. Have children use dialogue appropriate to the situation. They can use polite language when buying or selling groceries. After children have acted out buying items at the grocery store, create a list of children's purchases on the board or on chart paper. Remind children that there is a naming word for everything they find at a grocery store. **Speaking/Viewing**

apples
green beans
bread

Writing Center

MY EXPERIENCE Ask children to tell about one experience. Then have each of them fold an 11" x 17" piece of paper into thirds. Help children label the sections *Beginning*, *Middle*, and *End*. Then they can draw in order what happened, using the appropriate section. **Speaking**

SEASONAL PICTURES Ask children what they enjoy doing during each season. Provide a spinner showing pictures representing the four seasons. Have each child spin a season and draw a picture of one thing that happened to them during that season. Ask children to dictate or write a sentence about the picture. Then have volunteers share their pictures and sentences with the class. The audience of classmates should ask questions to clarify events. **Viewing/Speaking**

JOURNAL Children can record their daily activities in journals and use them as a resource for personal narrative topics. Allow time each day for children to write and draw in their journals. Prompt their writing by asking thoughtful questions. (Examples: What was the most interesting thing you did today? What was the hardest thing? What did you do that was fun?)

Social Studies Center

OUR COMMUNITY Have children draw and label pictures of people and places in their own neighborhoods, such as police officers, dentists, doctors, firefighters, the post office, and the library. Ask children to share their drawings and use them to tell about personal experiences with these people or places in their neighborhoods. **Speaking**

Doctor   Firefighter

A Published Model

About the Author

María Isabel Tierra

María Isabel Tierra remembers wonderful afternoons she spent as a child with her grandmother in Costa Rica. Those memories inspired her to write *The Coconut Flan.* Today she lives in Boston, Massachusetts.

Bibliography

You may also wish to read aloud these personal narratives.

- *My Fire Truck*
  by Michael Rex
- *Under the Table*
  by Marisabina Russo
- *Just Me and My Dad*
  by Mercer Mayer
- *Do Like Kyla*
  by Angela Johnson

NOTE The published model is written in the style of a personal narrative although it is not a true story about a real girl's experiences.

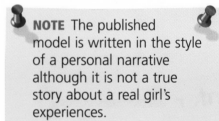

FOR STUDENTS ACQUIRING ENGLISH

During the picture walk, help children focus. Say: *Look at this picture. Where is Ligia? Why might she be there?* As you read, pause frequently to ask: *What is Ligia doing? Why?* At the end of the story, ask children to tell you what Ligia and her aunt did in the beginning, middle, and end of the story.

① Listening to a Personal Narrative

Lesson Objectives

Children will:
- listen to and discuss the characteristics of a published model of a personal narrative
- listen for sequence
- understand the use of dialogue
- evaluate the relationship of visuals and text
- respond personally and critically to the selection

Materials

The Coconut Flan, drawing paper, crayons

Optional Materials

shredded coconut

Reading the Model

The Coconut Flan
by María Isabel Tierra, illustrated by Vivi Escrivá

The Coconut Flan is about a girl who shops for ingredients for a flan that her aunt will bake for a party. It is written in the style of a personal narrative.

Building Background

Have children share what they know about baking. What are their family specialties or ethnic favorites? Have they ever helped bake something? What ingredients did they use? Point out that different ingredients are important. Sugar makes cake taste sweet. Nuts add crunch. What would happen if someone left out something important? (The cake wouldn't be right.)

Introducing Vocabulary

- Discuss key vocabulary words: *tía, aunt, cousins, coconut, flan, shredded.*
- Explain that your aunt is the sister of your mother or father; your aunt's children are your cousins. Then tell children that *tía* is the Spanish word for *aunt.*
- Point out the illustration of a flan on page 22, and explain that flan is a sweet baked custard made from sugar, eggs, and milk.
- If possible, allow children to taste samples of shredded coconut. Explain that the inside of the coconut is shredded, or cut into small strips, and dried. You may want to tear a piece of paper to show the act of shredding.

Predicting and Purpose Setting

PICTURE WALK Display *The Coconut Flan* and read the title aloud. Take a picture walk through the selection. Point out the main characters on page 8: a girl named Ligia (LEE-hee-ah) who tells the story, and her aunt, Tía Chabela (TEE-ah chah-BEHL-ah), who bakes the flan. Prompt children with questions as they look at pages 9–11. Finally, ask children to predict what the book will be about. (Sample answer: A girl goes to the store to buy something.)

Explain that a personal narrative is a true story about something that really happened to the writer. Set a purpose for reading by telling children to listen for what happens at the beginning, in the middle, and at the end of the story.

 This selection is also available on audiotape.

Listening As a Writer

Think About Personal Narrative

I AND ME Reread pages 8 and 9. Emphasize the words *I* and *me*. Point out that *I* is always a capital letter. Ask children what words show that Ligia is telling the story about herself. (*me, I*)

BEGINNING, MIDDLE, END Have children recall the story sequence. If necessary reread pages 5–7, 10–11, and 20–23. Ask children to tell what happened in the beginning, in the middle, and at the end of the story. Ask questions that help children recall the order of events. (Examples: Why did Ligia go to the store? What did she buy instead of shredded coconut?)

A GOOD ENDING Explain that sometimes at the end of a story everything works out and a problem is solved. Reread the story ending on pages 20–23. Have children recall what problem Tía Chabela had. Then ask: How did Ligia say they could solve the problem?

Think About Writer's Craft

DIALOGUE Reread dialogue on pages 20–21, using inflection to emphasize who is speaking. Show the children these passages. Point out that quotation marks show the speaker's exact words. Explain that dialogue helps the reader know exactly what happened.

Ask children to join you in a sing-song of Ligia's song, "Shredded Coconut." Discuss how the words to this song create a happy, carefree mood or feeling. These exact words make the story more real, as if you were there with Ligia.

Think About the Pictures

Remind children that in the middle of the story, Ligia went to the store three times. Reread pages 9–11, and have children tell what they see on each page. Then reread pages 13–15, and have children tell what they see on each page and what items are the same and different. (Ligia goes back to the same store, but she sees different things on the way to the store.) Discuss with children how the pictures tell a story too. They show what changes and what stays the same each time Ligia goes to the store.

 NOTE If children are responding to the selection on a day following your initial reading, reread the book.

Responding

Spaghetti

- **Personal Response** Have children think about how much Ligia's family loved flan. Ask children what special food they might make for a family party. Have them tell, draw, or dictate their responses and then share their work with classmates.

- **Critical Thinking** Ask children to imagine that Ligia bought raisins instead of coconut the first time she went to the store. How might this change the story? (Sample answer: Tía Chabela might make raisin flan.)

MEETING INDIVIDUAL NEEDS **FOR STUDENTS ACQUIRING ENGLISH**

Guide children as necessary in describing their special meal, providing sentence stems such as *I like _____ because it's _____* (*sweet/spicy*, etc.). As children draw, walk about the room, helping them learn specific vocabulary to explain their meal in English.

Modeled Writing

② Personal Narrative

Lesson Objectives

Children will:

- recognize the purpose, use, and characteristics of a personal narrative
- understand purpose and audience
- become familiar with the writing process
- help plan and draft a personal narrative

Materials

Poster Book p. 4A, dry erase markers, Transparency 4–2 or chart paper, Activity Master 88

Focus on Instruction

- Review that *The Coconut Flan* is a model of a well-written story about something that happened to the writer.

- Discuss examples of times when people write or tell about something that really happened to them, such as writing letters or visiting with friends or relatives. Have children give examples of times when they tell about something that really happened.

MODELING PREWRITING

Choose a Topic

Recall with children that *The Coconut Flan* was about events leading up to a party. Tell them that you want to write a real story about something that happened to you at a party and would like their help in writing it. Explain that first you have to decide on your audience, or the people for whom you are writing, and what event you want to write about. (You may want to choose an alternate topic to the one suggested here.)

> ### Alternate Topic Ideas
> - baking my first dessert
> - giving a family party
> - forgetting something at the grocery store
> - celebrating something special
> - cooking with a family member

FOR STUDENTS ACQUIRING ENGLISH

Acting out the beginning and middle of the story enables children acquiring English to participate in the writing process. However, you will need to help them write a script. Use the illustrations of the surprise party as an outline. Act out the part of the teacher to initiate the children's participation.

Think Aloud Once I went to a party that I thought was for a friend, but my friends surprised me. The party turned out to be for me. I want to share with my mother and father what happened leading up to the party and how I felt. I know my parents would like to read about this experience.

Plan the Personal Narrative Poster Book p. 4A

- Remind children that before you begin to write a real story about yourself, you need to plan your story.
- Display Poster Book page 4A. Be sure to use dry erase markers when adding details to the pictures.

Think Aloud Before I start writing I have to remember what happened and in what order I want to tell about what happened. These three pictures show how my friends surprised me with a party. The first picture shows what I will tell about in the beginning of my story. My friend called me to invite me to a party for another friend. The next picture shows me wrapping a gift to take to the party. This is what I will tell in the middle. The last picture shows my story ending. When I got to the surprise party, I found out it was for me!

In the beginning of the story, I want to tell details about me and the room in my house where this story takes place. Could someone color my hair and the red sweater I wore that day? My telephone is on my kitchen table. Please draw the table. In the middle of the story I can tell about the big box I wrapped in blue paper. Could someone add color to the paper in the drawing? Finally, in the end I want to describe the party decorations in the room at my friend's house. Please add orange streamers and blue balloons to the ending drawing.

MODELING DRAFTING   Transparency 4–2

To model drafting, use Transparency 4–2 or copy the frame onto chart paper. As children dictate text, reinforce skills they have learned by pointing out specific capital letters and punctuation marks as you write.

TITLE Display Transparency 4–2 and read the title aloud. Point out that the title tells what the event is.

BEGINNING Tell children that a good beginning starts off a story in an interesting way. Using the picture in the *Beginning* box on Poster Book page 4A as a prompt, have children help you draft a beginning. Model capitalizing the word *I*.

Think Aloud We need to think of a good beginning that will interest the reader. What can we write that will make a reader want to find out what happened?

Poster Book p. 4A

MIDDLE Tell children that you need to write down what happened in order.

Think Aloud I am going to use the Poster Book picture and the details we added when I planned the middle of the story. I didn't know that the party was for me. I want to tell that I bought a present and wrapped it in pretty blue paper. I'll tell how hard it was to keep a secret.

END Using the picture and the details you've added to the *End* box as prompts, model writing sentences for a good ending. Record them on the transparency.

Think Aloud I need a good ending for my story. I think I could tell how everyone shouted, "Surprise!" when I walked into my friend's house. I can tell how happy I felt!

MODELING PUBLISHING

- Praise children for how well they listened as you wrote about the surprise party. Read the personal narrative aloud from beginning to end.

- Tell the children that you plan to make a clean, neat copy to send to your parents.

 SCHOOL-HOME CONNECTION
Activity Master 88

Have a classroom volunteer or assistant print the personal narrative. Reproduce this copy for children to illustrate and take home to share with family members. Hand out Activity Master 88. Tell children that you want them to draw pictures for the beginning, middle, and end of a real story about themselves at a different party.

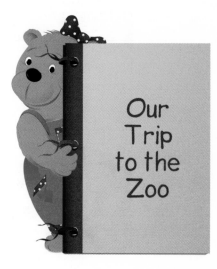

MODELING REFLECTING

To help children think more about their writing experience, model the process of reflection.

Think Aloud I liked remembering what happened at the beginning and at the end of the story. The middle was harder to do. I had to add details and think about what happened in order.

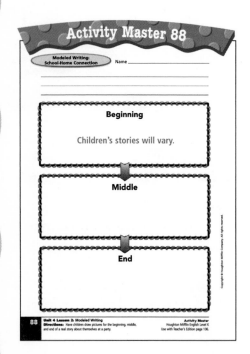

Activity Master 88

Modeled Writing:
School-Home Connection   Name _____

Beginning

Children's stories will vary.

Middle

End

88 Unit 4 Lesson 2: Modeled Writing   Activity Master
   Directions: Have children draw pictures for the beginning, middle,   Houghton Mifflin English Level K
   and end of a real story about themselves at a party.   Use with Teacher's Edition page 106.

Focus Skill — Oral Language

③ Using Polite Language

Lesson Objectives	**Materials**
Children will:	grocery store flyer

- use polite language in different situations
- recognize the difference between formal and informal language

Warm-Up

Reread page 11. Ligia asked, "May I have some milk, please?" Discuss with children times when they use the words *please* and *thank you*.

Teach

- Tell children that people use polite language in grocery stores and other places. Model polite and impolite ways to ask for groceries. (Examples: May I have some bananas, please? Give me some bananas.) Point out that words like *please, may I,* and *thank you* are polite words to use when asking for and receiving things from others.

- Point to items on a grocery store flyer. Then have pairs use polite language as they play the roles of a clerk and a customer purchasing one of the items.

- Discuss the difference between formal and informal language. In some situations, such as at home, we are more relaxed in asking for something. We might say, "More potatoes, please," rather than, "May I have more potatoes, please?" We might answer, "Thanks," instead of "Thank you."

Try It Out

Have pairs of children demonstrate using polite language in three situations: at a birthday party, in a classroom, and at a family dinner. First, discuss each situation; then ask volunteers to act it out, using polite language.

1. A child receives a gift at a birthday party. (Example: Thank you! I like it a lot!) A child leaves a birthday party. (Example: Thank you for inviting me.)

2. A child asks a classmate to share the blocks in a classroom. (Examples: May I use some of the blocks, please? Please hand me the red block. Thank you.)

3. A child asks for a dish at a family dinner. (Example: Please pass the macaroni and cheese. May I have more chicken, please?)

Wrap-Up

Ask children to describe other times when they use polite language. Remind children to say the words *please* when they ask for something and *thank you* when they receive something.

 INFORMAL ASSESSMENT (*See* Activity Masters Plus p. 46)

 MEETING INDIVIDUAL NEEDS (*See* p. 118)

 FOR STUDENTS ACQUIRING ENGLISH

Formal expressions using the words *may I* and *thank you* may be unfamiliar to English language learners. Write some examples on the board of brief, polite dialogue that might be spoken in a store, at a party, or in the classroom. Then read them to the children, modeling how each line might be said. Have children repeat the lines after you. Now they are ready to practice using polite language.

Poster Book p. 4B

Focus Skill: Viewing

A Picture Full of Details

Main Idea Everyone has fun at the park.

Sample answers:
Detail A boy and his grandfather play catch.

Detail Some people have a picnic.

Unit 4 Lesson 4: Main Idea and Details
Directions: Have children identify the main idea and details in the picture.

Houghton Mifflin English Level K
Use with Teacher's Edition page 108. **4B**

FOR STUDENTS ACQUIRING ENGLISH

Be sure children understand that they are drawing something they have done at a park rather than drawing a park in general. Model drawing yourself at a park and telling what happened that day. Before children share their pictures, brainstorm some useful words on the board (*ran, seesawed up and down, fell, climbed, slid*). Use each word in a sentence, and have children repeat sentences. Then have volunteers share their pictures.

Focus Skill Viewing

4 Main Idea and Details

Lesson Objective	**Materials**
Children will:	Poster Book p. 4B, dry erase marker
• identify the main idea and details in a picture	

Warm-Up

Display page 14 from *The Coconut Flan*. Ask children to tell the one big idea that is in the picture. (Sample answer: Ligia sees a woman putting sugar in her coffee.) Then read the sentence at the top of the page, and point out that the picture and words work together to tell the main idea. Then ask volunteers to point out details in the picture. (Sample answer: The woman is sitting in a rocking chair on her porch.)

Teach Poster Book p. 4B

● Display Poster Book page 4B. Ask children to describe what they see in the picture. Have children share their experiences at a park like the one in the picture.

● Tell children that the main idea of a picture can be the one big idea that is shown. Ask children to identify the main idea of the picture. (Sample answer: Everyone has fun at the park.) Write this sentence at the top of the page, and then read it aloud.

● Call attention to the various activities that are going on in the park. Ask volunteers to identify people and activities shown. Explain that all the fun things people are doing in the picture are details. Details are smaller pieces of information that support the main idea. Add detail sentences to the Poster Book.

Try It Out

Have children draw pictures that show a real experience at a park. Tell them to add as many details as possible. Then have them dictate or write a sentence that tells the main idea of their picture.

Wrap-Up

Have children use their pictures to tell about their experiences. Have them state the main idea and talk about interesting details. Tell children that they will be thinking about the main idea and details in a picture when they write and illustrate a story about themselves.

 INFORMAL ASSESSMENT (*See* Activity Masters Plus p. 46)

 MEETING INDIVIDUAL NEEDS (*See* p. 118)

Focus Skill Grammar

⑤ Nouns

Lesson Objective

Children will:

• recognize nouns that name people, animals, places, and things

Materials

Poster Book p. 4C, dry erase marker, Activity Master 89; several pictures of people at work, animals, places, and objects; four sheets of chart paper; scissors; paste; drawing paper, tagboard; and craft sticks

Warm-Up

Open to pages 13–15 in *The Coconut Flan*. Have children name some of the things they see in the pictures, such as the dog, the neighbor, the sugar, and the store. Record children's responses on chart paper or on the board and read them aloud. Remind them that these words are naming words.

Teach Poster Book p. 4C

• Remind children that they already know that naming words, or nouns, can name people, animals, places, or things. Display Poster Book page 4C.

• Ask volunteers to name the people in the picture. Label each person they identify, and then read the labels aloud. Repeat with animals, places, and things.

• Then have children recall their own visits to a mall or store. Ask them to suggest additional naming words for people, animals, places, and things they saw at the mall or store. Record responses under the appropriate heading on the Poster Book.

Try It Out Activity Master 89

Together, name the pictures in the first row and identify them as naming words for people. Then have children cut out the picture and word at the bottom of the page that also names a person and glue it in the appropriate place. Children complete Activity Master 89 by matching pictures to categories.

Wrap-Up

Have children share their work. Then ask them to suggest other naming words that belong in each row. Tell them that they will want to use interesting naming words when they write stories about themselves.

 INFORMAL ASSESSMENT (*See* Activity Masters Plus p. 47)

 MEETING INDIVIDUAL NEEDS (*See* p. 118)

Poster Book p. 4C

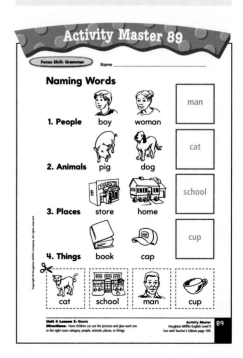

FOR STUDENTS ACQUIRING ENGLISH

Review familiar and new vocabulary. Encourage children to share the nouns they see in the pictures first. This will ensure that these children can state the nouns they know. They could make picture vocabulary sheets, which record all the words they feel confident using in their labeled pictures.

Poster Book p. 4D

FOR STUDENTS ACQUIRING ENGLISH

Read Poster Book page 4D, exaggerating the intonation (how your voice rises and falls) of each sentence. Have children repeat the sentences with the same intonation. This will help children learn how statements, questions, and exclamations are read in English.

Activity Master 90

Focus Skill | **Grammar/Mechanics**

⑥ Kinds of Sentences

Lesson Objectives

Children will:
- identify statements, questions, and exclamations
- use correct end punctuation

Materials

Poster Book p. 4D, dry erase marker, Activity Master 90, index cards

Warm-Up

Read the sentence on page 5 in *The Coconut Flan*. *Today there is a party at Tía Chabela's.* Write it on the board. Then reread it, tracking the print from left to right as you read. Remind children that this is a sentence and that they learned about telling and asking sentences in Unit 3.

Teach Poster Book p. 4D

- Display Poster Book page 4D. Have children describe the large picture at the top of the page. Point out that each sentence begins with a capital letter. Read the first sentence and explain that it is a *telling sentence*. Have children explain that a telling sentence tells what someone or something did and ends with a period. Have a volunteer circle the period.

- Repeat with the remaining sentences. Have children explain that a *question* asks something and ends with a question mark. Have them explain that an *exclaiming sentence* shows strong feeling and ends with an exclamation point.

- Point to picture 1 and have children describe it. Then read the caption with inflection to help children decide what kind of sentence it is. Ask a volunteer to add the correct end punctuation. Repeat with pictures 2 and 3.

Try It Out Activity Master 90

As you read with inflection, children complete Activity Master 90 by writing the correct end punctuation for each sentence. Say:

1. *This cheese is good* (period)
2. *May I have a loaf of bread, please* (question mark)
3. *This is a great prize* (exclamation point)

Wrap-Up

Review the three kinds of sentences and their end marks. Point out to children that when they write stories about themselves, using different kinds of sentences will make their stories more interesting.

 INFORMAL ASSESSMENT (*See* Activity Masters Plus p. 47)

 MEETING INDIVIDUAL NEEDS (*See* p. 119)

Focus Skill Vocabulary

⑦ Exact Nouns

Lesson Objectives

Children will:
- use exact nouns for more general ones
- understand that word choice can shape ideas, feelings, and actions

Materials

Poster Book p. 4E, dry erase marker, Activity Master 91

Warm-Up

Display pages 6–7 of *The Coconut Flan*. Ask: *What word names all of the characters?* (people) Point to a girl and ask: *What word names this character?* (girl) Then point to a boy and ask: *What is a word for this character?* (boy)

Teach Poster Book p. 4E

- Display Poster Book page 4E. Read the first sentence aloud. Help children identify each picture and read the naming words.

- Discuss the exact noun choices to replace the word *store* in the sentence and why each one could fit. Help children understand the difference in meaning of the two words. Have them choose one of the exact nouns pictured. Write the word in the sentence frame to replace *store*, and read the new sentence aloud. Repeat with the remaining items.

- As an extension, have children suggest other exact nouns that would fit in each sentence and record them on Poster Book page 4E.

Try It Out Activity Master 91

Name the pictures in each row together. Then read the following sentences aloud. Have children complete Activity Master 91 by circling the labeled picture that shows the best exact noun to take the place of the general noun in each sentence. Say:

1. *The toy is round.*
2. *This pet can fly.*
3. *The worker cooks.*
4. *I live in a building.*

Wrap-Up

Have children share their answers on Activity Master 91. Ask children to explain how they decided which picture to choose and to name the exact noun. Then remind children that when they tell or write real stories about themselves, they should use exact nouns to give a clearer picture to their audience.

 INFORMAL ASSESSMENT (*See* Activity Masters Plus p. 48)

MEETING INDIVIDUAL NEEDS (*See* p. 119)

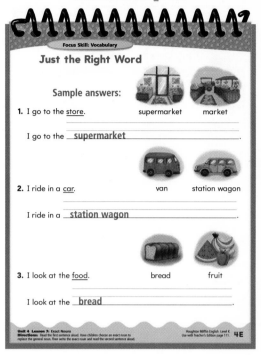

FOR STUDENTS ACQUIRING ENGLISH

Help children acquiring English with the activity on Poster Book page 4E by defining the exact nouns listed (*supermarket, market, van, station wagon, bread, fruit*). Have the children help you draw or describe them. Ask: *What does it look like? How can we draw it? What is the difference between the two?*

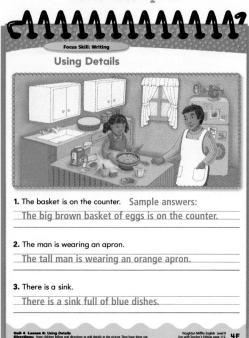

Poster Book p. 4F

Focus Skill: Writing
Using Details

1. The basket is on the counter.   Sample answers:
   The big brown basket of eggs is on the counter.

2. The man is wearing an apron.
   The tall man is wearing an orange apron.

3. There is a sink.
   There is a sink full of blue dishes.

Unit 4 **Lesson 8: Using Details**
Directions: Have children follow oral directions to add details to the picture. Then have them use the details in the picture to add detail words to base sentences.
Houghton Mifflin English Level K
Use with Teacher's Edition page 112.   **4F**

 FOR STUDENTS ACQUIRING ENGLISH

Before completing the Poster Book activity on page 4F, children acquiring English may need to review some vocabulary, such as *basket*, *eggs*, *apron*, *sink*, and *dishes*. To review these, label each item in the Poster Book. Then on the board draw eggs, an apron, and dishes, labeling them and asking the children to repeat the words.

Activity Master 92

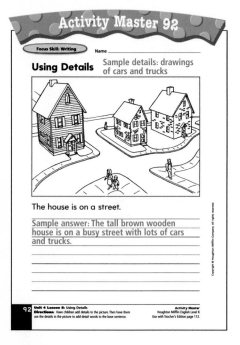

Focus Skill: Writing   Name _____
Using Details   Sample details: drawings of cars and trucks

The house is on a street.

Sample answer: The tall brown wooden house is on a busy street with lots of cars and trucks.

92 Unit 4 **Lesson 8:** Using Details
Directions: Have children add details to the picture. Then have them use the details in the picture to add detail words to the base sentence.
Houghton Mifflin English Level K
Use with Teacher's Edition page 112.
Activity Master

Focus Skill   Writing

⑧ Using Details

Lesson Objectives
Children will:
- create telling sentences describing additional details in pictures
- add details to a drawing and dictate a description

Materials
Poster Book p. 4F, dry erase markers, Activity Master 92, photographs or travel posters

Warm-Up

Display pages 6–7 of *The Coconut Flan*. Ask volunteers to name and describe whom and what they see. Discuss sizes, shapes, colors, and numbers of things. Tell them that these details make the pictures more interesting.

Teach Poster Book p. 4F

- Display Poster Book page 4F. Ask a volunteer to identify the place in the picture. Talk with children about what they see in the kitchen. Then have volunteers follow these directions to add details to the picture. Say:

  1. *Draw eggs in the basket.*

  2. *Color the man's apron orange.*

  3. *Draw blue dishes in the sink.*

- Read aloud the first base sentence on Poster Book page 4F. Then ask a volunteer to point to the picture of the basket. Have children tell what they added to the basket as well as other details about the basket's color, size, and so on. Help children use the details to orally compose an elaborated sentence. Write the elaborated sentence below the base sentence, and read it aloud. Point out that the details they added make both the sentence and the picture more interesting.

- Repeat with the remaining base sentences.

Try It Out Activity Master 92

Children complete Activity Master 92 by using crayons to add details and color to the neighborhood scene. When children have finished, read the base sentence aloud. Help them each dictate or write an elaborated sentence that reflects the details they added to their pictures.

Wrap-Up

Have volunteers share their new sentences and the details they added to Activity Master 92. Remind children that they will add details to sentences when they write stories about themselves.

 INFORMAL ASSESSMENT (*See* Activity Masters Plus p. 47)

 MEETING INDIVIDUAL NEEDS (*See* p. 119)

9 Personal Narrative

Lesson Objectives

Children will:

- choose a topic and an audience for a personal narrative
- contribute to a personal narrative, using the steps of the writing process
- reflect on their writing experience

Materials

Poster Book p. 4G, dry erase markers, Transparency 4–3 or chart paper

Focus on Instruction

Tell children that you are going to work together to write a class story about an event that they all did together. Remind them that good writers usually follow certain steps when they write something that others will read.

PREWRITING

Choose a Topic

- Help children decide what one event to write about and for whom they will write it. Remind children that a class story is a true story about something that happened to them. Point out that their families like to know about things that happen to them, so they could write the story for their families.

- Brainstorm topic ideas with children. Ask: *What fun project did we work on together? What did we do? What field trip did we take that you might like to tell about? Where did we go? What special people have visited our class? What did they tell us about?*

- Decide together on the topic and the audience for the personal narrative.

> Topic Ideas
> - a project
> - a field trip
> - a school fair
> - a special visitor

Plan the Personal Narrative Poster Book p. 4G

- Display Poster Book page 4G. Write the topic as the title for the personal narrative, and read it aloud.

- Discuss the order in which the events took place, using the terms *beginning*, *middle*, and *end* to recall the main events.

- Have children act out what happened. Draw simple pictures or write key words in the three frames on the Poster Book. Then have children retell the events.

- Display Poster Book page 4G for reference when drafting the personal narrative.

FOR STUDENTS ACQUIRING ENGLISH

At the beginning of the writing process, tell children that they will be taking the story home to share with their families. Declaring the purpose and audience early in the process will help keep them motivated and show them the usefulness of writing. To help children give details, review adjectives with them. Ask: *What colors can we use? What sounds or textures can we add?*

Poster Book p. 4G

Shared Writing: Prewriting

Planning Our Personal Narrative

Title ___Answers will vary.___

Beginning

Middle

End

Unit 4 Lesson 9: Shared Writing
Directions: Write the topic as the title. Then have children help you draw pictures and write key words to show which events took place in the beginning, middle, and end.

Houghton Mifflin English: Level K
Use with Teacher's Edition page 113. **4G**

NOTE As you draft, point out the correct use of capital letters and punctuation marks. You may wish to omit details and dialogue so that children can add these elements when they revise their writing.

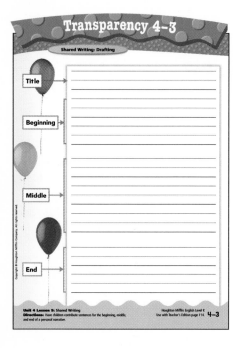

DRAFTING Transparency 4–3, Poster Book p. 4G

- Review with children what makes a great story about themselves.

What Makes a Great Personal Narrative?

- The story tells about one thing that really happened to you.

- *I*, *me*, or *we* shows who is telling the story.

- A good beginning starts the story in an interesting way, and a good ending tells how you felt or how things worked out.

- Details tell what happened in the beginning, middle, and end.

- Then ask volunteers to contribute text ideas for each element of the draft, using the completed graphic organizer on Poster Book page 4G as a guide. Record children's suggestions on Transparency 4–3 or on chart paper. Help children generate the following:

  - a **title** that tells about the one thing that really happened

  - an interesting **beginning sentence** to start the personal narrative

  - **details** to tell what happened in the beginning, middle, and end

  - a good **ending** to tell how the writers felt or how things worked out

- Then read the draft together, checking that their story has all it needs to be a great personal narrative.

REVISING

- Reread the draft aloud. Ask the questions on the chart below. Tell children that these questions will help them think about whether their narrative will be clear and interesting to their families, their audience.

> Questions for Revising
> ✔ Did we tell about one thing that really happened?
> ✔ Did we use the word *we*?
> ✔ Did we use details to tell what happened in the beginning, middle, and end?
> ✔ Do we have an interesting beginning and a good ending?

- Remind children they have learned about adding details and using dialogue. Ask if they would like to add any details or dialogue to the class story.

> big, yellow school
> We took a bus to the aquarium.
> ^

PUBLISHING

Make a clean final copy of the class story, and then make an individual copy for each child. Have children illustrate their own copies.

SCHOOL-HOME CONNECTION Have children take their own copies home to share with family members.

A Visit with Officer García

REFLECTING

Praise children for planning and writing a class story so thoughtfully. Discuss their writing experience. Ask:

- *What was easy to do? What was hard?*
- *What did you like about writing a story about a shared class experience?*
- *What did you learn that will help you the next time you plan and write a story about yourself?*

Independent Writing

⑩ Personal Narrative

Lesson Objectives	**Materials**
Children will:	drawing paper, writing paper,
• tell, dictate, or write a personal narrative	Activity Master 93
• listen and respond to the writing of peers	

Focus on Instruction

Explain to children that they are going to write stories about themselves. Tell them they should choose a topic to write about. They must also keep in mind for whom they are writing. Use these ideas to help children plan, write, and share their personal narratives.

Planning Ideas

THINKING ABOUT TOPICS Help children list possible topics by recalling a special time, such as a holiday party, or a recent event, such as a trip to the park. Children who are having trouble thinking of their own topics can use one of the Writing Prompts on page 117. You might also read books from the Bibliography on page 102 to spark ideas.

ORGANIZING IDEAS Help children develop their topics by recalling exactly what happened. Children can work in pairs to re-enact their experiences and identify the parts in order.

Writing

Allow children to produce their personal narratives in the format that is most appropriate to their own stage of writing development as indicated below.

FOR STUDENTS ACQUIRING ENGLISH

Have pairs of children review their stories and think of more details. Model telling your story while a volunteer acts it out. Encourage the children to do the same. This will enable them to practice retelling their story and seeing the details they may have missed.

Writing Portfolio

If you are collecting samples of children's writing, decide if you want to save this piece.

Student Sample

I im goh to a SaPoWUbT PaeD to PaT and MY fad avcS amahda.

I'm going to a sleepover party tonight and my friend is Amanda.

Late Beginning Writer

Writing Options		
Emergent Writers	**Early Beginning Writers**	**Late Beginning and Transitional Writers**
Have children draw pictures to represent the events of their personal narratives. They can then add pretend or "scribble" writing to describe them and tell their narratives to an adult, or they can dictate their narratives to an adult to record.*	Children can draw pictures to represent the events of their personal narratives. They can then label them with single words or phrases and tell their narratives to an adult, or they can dictate their narratives to an adult to record.*	Children can write their personal narratives using temporary spelling. They can add illustrations to support their text.

*Some children may feel their writing is not valid if an adult rewrites it.

 INFORMAL ASSESSMENT (*See* Activity Masters Plus p. 47)

Ideas for Sharing

Have children share their completed personal narratives by "reading" them aloud or by using one of the suggestions below.

Write It   Children can make picture albums by drawing pictures and using sentences from their narratives as captions.

Say It   Have children retell their personal narratives as they sit in the Author's Chair.

Show It   Ask children to bring in objects, such as postcards or toys, relating to their stories. They can explain what objects they have brought and then tell their stories.

After each child shares his or her work, the listener or listeners should tell the author at least one thing they liked about the personal narrative.

 INTERNET CONNECTION
See www.eduplace.com/rdg/hme/ for printable patterns for making shape-paper booklets.

 FOR STUDENTS ACQUIRING ENGLISH

Another option for sharing is to have partners practice reading and acting out finished products. Allow enough time for each partner to practice reading their story and acting out their partner's version.

Writing Prompts

SOCIAL STUDIES

Special things that people do the same way for a long time are called traditions. In *The Coconut Flan*, Ligia's family has a tradition of eating flan. Does your family have any special traditions? Draw a picture of something special your family does together in the frames on Activity Master 93. Write or tell about what your picture shows.

Activity Master 93

Independent Writing: Writing Prompts

Name _____

My Special Family Tradition

Children's pictures of family traditions will vary.

Children may choose to write about holiday meals, birthday parties, or other family celebrations.

Unit 4 Lesson 10: Independent Writing
Directions: Have children draw a picture of a special family tradition and then dictate or write sentences about the picture.

Houghton Mifflin English Level K
Use with Teacher's Edition page 117.

93

MUSIC

What is your favorite song? Sing the song with a friend. Then think about how you learned it. Do you remember a special time when you sang it? Write or tell about that time.

 INTERNET CONNECTION
See www.eduplace.com/rdg/hme/ for more writing ideas.

Meeting Individual Needs

Lesson 3 Focus Skill Oral Language: Using Polite Language

RETEACHING ALTERNATIVE STRATEGY

Make the skill more concrete by asking partners to use polite language when working together. Show children how to use the words *please* when asking for something and *thank you* when receiving something, such as books, blocks, puzzles, or crayons.

CHALLENGE

Use empty food containers and play money to set up a classroom grocery store. Encourage children to use polite language as they buy and sell groceries. Some children may be able to organize foods by category, take inventory by counting types of foods, make advertisements for daily specials, set prices, and make change.

FOR STUDENTS ACQUIRING ENGLISH

Pretend you'll have a party in class. Show children how to invite each other and accept politely. Say: *Would you like to come to our party? Yes, thank you.* Then line up all the children outside the classroom door. Model how to greet and respond. Say: *Hello, welcome to our party. Hello, thank you for having me.* Then as you welcome each child, have that child welcome the next one.

Lesson 4 Focus Skill Viewing: Main Idea and Details

RETEACHING ALTERNATIVE STRATEGY

Ask children each to draw a picture that shows them doing an activity they really enjoy, such as riding a bike. Tell them to add details by showing what they wear and what special equipment or materials they use. Then ask children to tell about the picture and identify its main idea and details.

CHALLENGE

Provide main idea sentences for children, and have them draw or write details. For example, *Someone special to me is _____.* Ask children to copy the sentence, draw a picture, and draw or write details that tell why that person is special.

FOR STUDENTS ACQUIRING ENGLISH

Find a detailed picture or photograph from a magazine or picture book. Discuss its main idea and details. Ask: *What's happening here? What is the main activity or idea in the picture? What are the special details?* Then ask children to draw their own picture with the same main idea but different details.

Lesson 5 Focus Skill Grammar: Nouns

RETEACHING ALTERNATIVE STRATEGY

Play this game to help children identify nouns. Give children four sheets of paper. Have them draw a stick figure on one to stand for a person, a cat on another to stand for an animal, a house to stand for a place, and a box to stand for a thing. Then read aloud the following words: *cow, table, teacher, gas station, pen, backyard, mother,* and *bird.* Children hold up the appropriate sheet to show whether the noun names a person, animal, place, or thing.

CHALLENGE

Have children name people, places, things, and animals in the classroom. Then help them write labels on self-stick notes and post them around the room. Children can take turns giving each other classroom tours in which they use the labels to point out and name people, animals, places, and things.

FOR STUDENTS ACQUIRING ENGLISH

Make a Box of Nouns. Provide old magazines and scissors, and have children cut out pictures of nouns. Then have several children show and name each noun as they place the pictures in the Box of Nouns. Use the pictures in the box for review by having children take out a few examples and practice naming or categorizing nouns.

Lesson 6 Focus Skill   Grammar/Mechanics: Kinds of Sentences

RETEACHING ALTERNATIVE STRATEGY

Have children draw a period, a question mark, and an exclamation point on index cards. Review which mark is used with which kind of sentence. Then read aloud these sentences, and have children hold up the appropriate punctuation card for each sentence.

1. There is a party at my uncle's house tonight.
2. Will all my cousins be there?
3. My uncle makes vegetable stew.
4. What kinds of vegetables are in the stew?
5. Oh, no, he forgot carrots and potatoes!
6. The stew smells good now!

CHALLENGE

Have partners draw a period, a question mark, and an exclamation point on index cards. Then have them take turns holding up punctuation cards while their partner says oral sentences.

FOR STUDENTS ACQUIRING ENGLISH

Play a game of Sentence Search. Pair the children, and give each pair a piece of paper. Then give them five minutes to tour the room searching for the three types of sentences in books, magazines, and signs. Have children share their sentences.

Lesson 7 Focus Skill   Vocabulary: Exact Nouns

RETEACHING ALTERNATIVE STRATEGY

Ask a volunteer to do a simple action with a person, animal, or toy, such as putting away blocks. Tell what is happening, saying a sentence that uses a general noun. (Example: He is putting things away.) Point out the general noun things. Ask volunteers to suggest an exact noun that could take its place and use it in an oral sentence. (Example answer: He is putting blocks away.) Repeat the activity with different nouns.

CHALLENGE

Provide groups with old catalogs and magazines, paper, scissors, paste, and markers. Give each group a general noun, such as *people*, *animals*, *clothes*, and *food*. Have each group cut out pictures of exact nouns that can replace its general noun and use the pictures to make a small book of exact nouns.

FOR STUDENTS ACQUIRING ENGLISH

Play the clapping game Categories. Have all the children sit cross-legged in a circle. Clap your hands to the rhythm of the chant: "Categories, names for people, doctor." Repeat, having children call out different examples: teacher, boy, girl, and so on. Continue with names for animals, places, and things.

Lesson 8 Focus Skill   Writing: Using Details

RETEACHING ALTERNATIVE STRATEGY

Read the following base sentence: *The child is wearing shoes.* Have children raise their hand if it tells about them. Point out that, without any details, the sentence could tell about any one of them. Then pick a child, and model how to observe details and add them to the base sentence: *The child with red hair is wearing blue and white shoes.* Have children take turns adding details to the base sentence.

CHALLENGE

Post different pictures of the same subject, such as birds or dogs. Give children a base sentence such as *The dog is cute.*

Have children take turns elaborating on the base sentence to describe one of the pictures, and have others identify the picture.

FOR STUDENTS ACQUIRING ENGLISH

Draw an image representing a noun on the board, and have a volunteer come to the board to draw details. Then label all the details, and say sentences about them. Then play a game of I Spy to focus on detail. Spy objects in the room to model first. Say: *I spy a window shade with a long, worn-out string.*

Unit 5
Description

In this unit, children are introduced to descriptive writing. They listen to a book that describes the experiences of a boy and his family and participate in the modeled writing of a description of popcorn. Then children work together with you to create a class description, using the writing process. Unit skills develop language as well as relate to and support descriptive writing.

What You Will Find in This Unit . . .

Unit 5 Planning Guide
Description

	Poster Book	Transparency	Activity Masters Plus
DAILY COMMUNICATION LINKS **Daily Routines** (124–125) The oral language activities provide daily opportunities for children to develop the basic concepts and skills needed to compose descriptions. • **Interactive Bulletin Board:** Weather Chart; Color, Number, Size Wheels; Daily Message • **Daily Discussion Activity:** Using Our Senses *See also* Additional Resources (234–237) **Center Activities** (126–127) • Reading and Listening Center • Creative Arts Center • Writing Center • Science Center		5–1	
A Published Model ⏱ *1 day, 20 minutes* **Lesson 1** Listening to Descriptions (128–129) *Night Sounds, Morning Colors*			
Modeled Writing ⏱ *about 2-3 days, 20 minutes each day* **Lesson 2** Description (130–132)	5A	5–2	94
Focus Skills ⏱ *about 6 days, 20 minutes each day*			
Lesson 3 Oral Language: Sound Words (133)	5B		95
Lesson 4 Viewing: Observation (134)	5C		96
Lesson 5 Grammar: Adjectives: Look and Feel (135)	5D		97
Lesson 6 Grammar: More Adjectives (136)	5E		98
Lesson 7 Vocabulary: Synonyms (137)			99
Lesson 8 Writing: Sensory Details/Similes (138)	5F		100
Shared Writing ⏱ *about 2–3 days, 20 minutes each day* **Lesson 9** Description (140–141)	5G	5–3	
Independent Writing ⏱ *about 1–3 days, 20 minutes each day* **Lesson 10** Description (142–143) ✓ Writing Prompts (143)			

 MEETING INDIVIDUAL NEEDS (144-145)

Activities for Special Needs/Inclusion, for Students Acquiring English, for Reteaching, and for Enrichment/Challenge

Meeting Individual Needs

▶ **FOR SPECIAL NEEDS/INCLUSION:** *Houghton Mifflin English* Audiotape ; *See also* Reaching.

▶ **FOR STUDENTS ACQUIRING ENGLISH:**
- Notes and activities are included in this Teacher's Edition throughout the unit to help you adapt or use lessons with students acquiring English.
- Students can listen to the published model *Night Sounds, Morning Colors* on audiotape.

▶ **RETEACHING**
- Activities for reteaching the focus skills are included on pages 144–145.

▶ **ENRICHMENT/CHALLENGE**
- Activities for challenge/enrichment that are correlated to focus skill lessons are included on pages 144–145.

 All audiotape recordings are also available on CD.

Additional Resources

Audiotapes

 Technology Tools
CD-ROM: Curious George® Paint & Print Studio
Paint, Write & Play! (published by The Learning Company)
*Type to Learn Jr.™

*©Sunburst Technology Corporation, a Houghton Mifflin Company. All rights reserved.

INTERNET: http://www.eduplace.com/rdg/hme/
Visit Education Place for these additional support materials and activities:
- author biographies
- patterns for shape booklets
- writing prompts

 Informal Assessment
Activity Masters Plus, Assessment Checklists, pages 45–47

 Keeping a Journal

In kindergarten, journals can be blank notebooks or folders filled with paper. As children draw and write about school activities, important events, and special thoughts, they can watch their writing growth as the year progresses.

 School-Home Connection

Suggestions for informing or involving family members in learning related to this unit are included in the Teacher's Edition throughout the unit.

Daily Routines

The oral language activities suggested here provide daily opportunities for children to develop basic concepts and skills they will need to compose descriptions. Refer to the **Interactive Bulletin Board** and **Daily Discussion** ideas on pages 10–13 and 20–21 for help in establishing Daily Routines for your classroom.

Interactive Bulletin Board

Weather Chart

	M	T	W	T	F
Sunny					
Rainy					
Cloudy					
Windy					
Snowy					

Color, Number, Size Wheels

Color, Number, Size Wheels

Review the words on the wheels. Have volunteers spin the spinners and name the words the arrows land on. Then ask them to use two or more of the words to describe a personal belonging or something in the classroom. (Examples: I have a small brown puppy. The big blue bookcase has three shelves.)

Weather Chart

Each day as you update the Weather Chart, ask volunteers to compose oral sentences that describe the day's weather. Children can use the weather word(s) marked on the chart as well as sensory words that will help listeners see, feel, hear, or smell the type of weather outside. (Examples: Today is warm and sunny. It is rainy, and the wind is howling.)

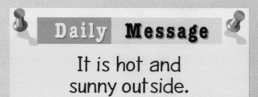

Daily Message

It is hot and sunny outside.

Daily Message

Each day record one sentence children have generated while working with the Weather Chart. Model for them using a capital letter at the beginning of a sentence and a period at the end. Have children read the sentence aloud with you as you point to each word. Ask children to tell which word(s) helps them picture what the weather is like.

Daily Discussion

Review with children what the five senses are. Tell them that when they look at something, they can try to see it not only with their eyes, but also with their ears, nose, mouth, and hands. Explain that word pictures that tell how things look, feel, sound, taste, and smell are called descriptions.

Each day bring in an object, or have a volunteer bring in an object, to place in a Using Our Senses box. Ask a volunteer to describe the object, using words that tell how it looks, feels, sounds, tastes, and/or smells. Have classmates guess what the object is based on the words children use in their descriptions. Then talk about the description, using the Think and Discuss questions below.

Think and Discuss

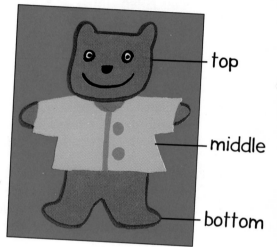

- Which describing words told you how the object looks? feels? sounds? tastes? smells?
- Which describing words did you like best? Why?
- Which describing words helped you most to picture the object in your mind?
- What other words could you use to paint a word picture of this object?

POSITIONAL WORDS As children describe items in the Using Our Senses box, suggest that they use positional words such as *top/middle/bottom* and *left/right* to help make their descriptions clear. (Example: It has two soft, round ears on <u>top</u>.) Ask volunteers to make labeled pictures that show the meanings of these positional words. Post the pictures in your classroom.

ADJECTIVES Have children help make a class chart of sensory words. List the words in categories that tell how things look (color, shape, size), feel, sound, taste, and smell. Record words children use in their oral descriptions as well as other words they may suggest as they work through this unit. Ask volunteers to add illustrations. Post the chart on your Word Wall.

👁	✋	👂	👄	👃
red	soft	loud	sour	smoky
tiny	smooth	squeaky	salty	fresh
square	hard	quiet	juicy	sweet
spotted	bumpy	buzzing	spicy	fishy

 INFORMAL ASSESSMENT (*See* Activity Masters Plus pp. 45, 47)

Center Activities

Center Activities provide additional daily opportunities for children to develop and reinforce concepts and skills that support the composing of descriptions.

Reading and Listening Center

PUBLISHED MODEL Children can listen to *Night Sounds, Morning Colors* on audiotape. **Listening**

DESCRIPTION RIDDLES On a blank tape, prerecord Who Am I? and What Am I? description riddles. For each riddle, use sensory words to describe a person, an animal, or a thing. Children use the sensory word clues to guess what is being described. Some children may want to make up their own riddles for a partner to guess. **Listening/Speaking**

LISTENING TO MUSIC Collect different kinds of music. Have children close their eyes as they listen to each piece. Ask them to describe what picture comes to mind as they listen. Have children write or tell orally a description of what the music makes them think of. **Listening/Speaking**

"I wear a hard hat, a long shiny coat, and tall boots. I'm often in smoky places Who am I?"

Writing Center

DESCRIPTIVE LABELS Ask children to draw a picture of a person, an animal, a place, or a thing that they find interesting. Have them label their drawing with sensory words that describe the item. Compile the drawings into a class book titled "Our Five Senses." Place the book in your Reading and Listening Center.

SENSORY WORD SCRAPBOOK Suggest that children start a sensory word scrapbook. Ask them to collect objects and pictures that have interesting shapes, colors, and/or textures. Have them tape or paste each item into the scrapbook and label it with appropriate adjectives. Tell children that they can use the words from their scrapbooks when they write descriptions.

 JOURNAL Have children use pictures and words to describe things that are particularly meaningful to them, such as an important person, a pet, a favorite toy, or a special place.

Creative Arts Center

MUSICAL SOUNDS Provide a variety of instruments to play, or supply children with materials to make their own. (Examples: a stringed instrument made by stretching rubber bands across a shoebox, percussion instruments made by placing rice or pebbles in plastic containers) Have children listen carefully to the sounds and use adjectives to describe them. They can also compare the sounds to other familiar noises. (Example: The drum is loud and booming. It sounds like thunder.) **Listening/Speaking**

DRAMA Gather kitchen props, such as plates, bowls, and silverware. Have children use the props to act out a breakfast scene similar to the one in *Night Sounds, Morning Colors*. Project Transparency 5–1 onto a white surface to create the background scenery. As children act out eating their breakfast, have them describe each thing they eat. **Speaking**

Science Center

SEE AND SNIFF Partially fill each of several clear plastic cups with a common edible liquid, such as pancake syrup, vinegar, orange juice, or corn oil. Ask children to use their senses of sight and smell to describe each liquid and then to guess what it is. **Viewing/Speaking**

OBSERVATION As children participate in different experiments that you conduct in this center, have them record their observations. They can use pictures and words to describe what they see, feel, hear, taste, and smell. They might record their observations over time or at a particular moment. **Viewing**

A Published Model

① Listening to Descriptions

About the Author

Rosemary Wells

Author-illustrator Rosemary Wells has more than 40 picture books and young adult novels to her credit. She is best known for her books about a rabbit named Max and his sister, Ruby. Max and Ruby are based on the author's own children, Victoria and Beezoo.

 INTERNET CONNECTION
See www.eduplace.com/kids/ for information about Rosemary Wells.

Bibliography

You may also wish to read aloud these books that include descriptions.

- *My Goose Betsy*
  by Trudi Braun
- *Rain Talk*
  by Mary Serfozo
- *Spring Thaw*
  by Steven Schnur
- *Squish! A Wetland Walk*
  by Nancy Luenn

MEETING INDIVIDUAL NEEDS **FOR STUDENTS ACQUIRING ENGLISH**

Children may be unfamiliar with the vocabulary of daily and yearly cycles. Say and act out daily routines. Use pictures, a clock, and a picture calendar to teach times of the day and year.

Lesson Objectives

Children will:
- listen to and discuss the characteristics of a published model that includes descriptions
- listen for sensory details
- understand the use of similes and word choice
- evaluate the relationship of visuals and text
- respond personally and critically to the selection

Materials

Night Sounds, Morning Colors; drawing paper; crayons or markers

Reading the Model

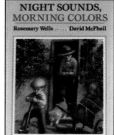

The book *Night Sounds, Morning Colors* includes descriptive text about the sights, sounds, textures, smells, and tastes in the everyday life of a child and his family.

Building Background

Review the parts of a day: morning, afternoon, and night. Have children tell what happens during each. What activities do they do? What meals do they eat? Then review the seasons of the year: spring, summer, fall, and winter. Ask volunteers to describe the changes they notice during each season. What is the weather like? What special activities do they do? Help children see that the times of day and the seasons of the year repeat.

Introducing Vocabulary

Introduce the key vocabulary words by reading aloud the following sentences. Discuss the meaning of each underlined vocabulary word. Use the illustrations in the published model to support children's understanding of these words.

> The <u>mist</u> made it hard to see the tree. (p. 5)
> Ana always puts jam on her <u>biscuit</u>. (p. 6)
> They went into the <u>pagoda</u>. (p. 8)
> We use our best <u>china</u> when company comes. (p. 11)
> Cars must go slowly in a school <u>zone</u>. (p. 18)
> An <u>icicle</u> hung from the roof. (p. 24)

Predicting and Purpose Setting

PICTURE WALK Display *Night Sounds, Morning Colors* and read aloud the title, the author, and the illustrator. Point out that the book has four sections. Read the title of one section at a time. (Example: "When I Wake Up") Then take a picture walk through just those pages, having children describe what they see. Ask volunteers to predict what each section will be about and tell why. If necessary, explain that the book describes different experiences that the boy has.

Tell children that a good description helps readers see, feel, hear, taste, and smell what the author is telling about. Point out that as you read, children should listen carefully for words that tell how things sound and feel. Read the book aloud.

 This selection is also available on audiotape.

Listening As a Writer

Think About the Descriptions

SOUND AND FEEL After listening, ask children to recall things that the boy hears and feels as well as how the author describes them. Then reread pages 11–12. Have volunteers identify the sounds and the sensory words that tell about them. (Sample answer: rain on the leaves—*pattering, popping*) Next, display and reread "Winter Walk" (pages 22–32). At stopping points, ask children to tell how the author describes the way things feel.

LOOK Remind children that the author also describes the way things look. Reread pages 5–8, pausing occasionally to ask children to identify what is being described as well as the words the author uses to explain how it looks.

TASTE AND SMELL Finally, reread the section "In My Kitchen" one page at a time. Discuss the various words and phrases that describe tastes and smells. Have volunteers explain which descriptions are their favorites and why.

Think About Writer's Craft

SIMILES Display and reread page 10. Explain that sometimes writers paint word pictures by telling how one thing is like something else. Ask: *What does the author say Grandpa's voice is like?* (ocean waves) *What does this tell you about how Grandpa's voice sounds?* Next, display and reread page 25. Ask: *What does the author say the pine needles are like?* (a mattress) *How are the needles like a mattress?* (They're spongy and springy.)

WORD CHOICE: MOOD Discuss how sometimes writers paint word pictures by choosing words to create a certain feeling or mood. Explain that authors might use words to make a happy, sad, quiet, sleepy, lively, or mysterious feeling. Read a few passages from the selection, and ask children to tell how the words make them feel. You might begin with the description of gardening on page 7.

Think About the Pictures

Hold up and reread pages 14–15. Ask children to describe the illustration and how it works with the text to create a feeling. Have them tell what information they learned from the picture that they didn't know from hearing the text. (Example: The boy's dog is with him.) Ask children to choose favorite illustrations and to tell how they work with the text to create a feeling. Then ask: *What does the picture tell you that you didn't know from hearing just the words?*

NOTE If children are discussing and responding to *Night Sounds, Morning Colors* on a day following your initial reading, reread the book.

FOR STUDENTS ACQUIRING ENGLISH

On chart paper, draw pictures with labels for each of the senses. (Eyes = sight, ears = sound…) Reread parts of *Night Sounds, Morning Colors*. Pause after each section and ask children to which senses the section appeals. Refer to the labeled drawings. You may want to add sketches to represent the senses that are described in the text.

Responding

- **Personal Response** Ask children to think of a time they had an experience similar to one the boy had. Have them draw a picture of the experience. Ask them to share their work with a partner, describing orally what they saw, heard, felt, smelled, and/or tasted.

- **Critical Thinking** Ask children to imagine that the boy and his brother went on a walk during the summer. Have them describe what the boys might have seen, felt, heard, tasted, and smelled.

Grandpa reads to me.

Modeled Writing

② Description

Lesson Objectives

Children will:
- recognize the purpose, use, and characteristics of a description
- understand purpose and audience
- become familiar with the steps of the writing process
- help plan and draft a description

Materials

Poster Book p. 5A, dry erase marker, Transparency 5–2 or chart paper, Activity Master 94

Optional Materials

popcorn maker, popcorn, butter, salt

Focus on Instruction

- Remind children that *Night Sounds, Morning Colors* includes many descriptions that help readers know just what the boy saw, heard, smelled, felt, and tasted. Ask children to recall a few of the things that the boy describes.

- Explain that a description can paint a word picture of a person, a place, a thing, or an event. Have volunteers name different places where they see or hear descriptions. Discuss each type children mention, including the writer's purpose for writing. If children are unable to think of instances of descriptive writing, use some of these examples to prompt discussion:

> a For Sale poster
>
> a toy catalog
>
> a post card from a friend on vacation
>
> a TV advertisement
>
> a Lost and Found notice
>
> a radio news story

MODELING
PREWRITING

Choose a Topic

Recall with children that in *Night Sounds, Morning Colors,* the author describes different foods. Tell children that you recently went to a movie and had some delicious popcorn. Explain that you want to write a description of the popcorn and would like their help.

Think Aloud The other day, I saw a movie and had some wonderful popcorn at the theater. I am going to write a letter to a friend telling him [her] about the movie, and I want to include a description of the popcorn.

Plan the Description Poster Book p. 5A

- Tell children that before you begin writing the description, you need to plan what you want to say.

Think Aloud Before I write, I have to decide what details I want to include. I need to remember how the popcorn looked, felt, sounded, tasted, and smelled.

- Display Poster Book page 5A. Remind children that a good description helps readers see, feel, hear, taste, and smell the thing being described. Explain that we use our eyes, hands, ears, mouth, and nose to get this information. Then ask volunteers to suggest sensory details that tell about the popcorn. Record each word or phrase in the appropriate list.

HANDS-ON LEARNING
Before showing the Poster Book, you might make some real popcorn with children so that they can describe it from firsthand experience. Have them obtain sensory information by looking at, touching, smelling, listening to, and tasting the popcorn.

Poster Book p. 5A

MODELING DRAFTING Transparency 5–2, Poster Book p. 5A

To model drafting, use Transparency 5–2 or copy the frame from the transparency onto chart paper. As children dictate text, reinforce mechanics skills they have learned by pointing out specific capital letters and punctuation marks as you record them.

TITLE Explain that now you are ready to write your description. Display Transparency 5–2 and read the title aloud. Point out that the title tells the topic of the description.

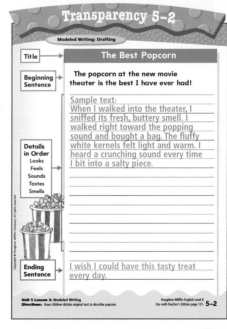

BEGINNING SENTENCE Tell children that the first sentence of a good description names the one thing the description will be about. Read together the beginning sentence on the transparency.

Think Aloud This is a good beginning sentence because it will let my friend know that the description will be about popcorn.

DETAILS Next, ask children to help you draft the main text for the description. Have volunteers suggest sentences that describe the popcorn, using the sensory details you recorded on Poster Book page 5A. Point out that the details need to be in an order that makes sense. Explain that for this description, you could tell what you noticed first, second, third, and so on. Record children's contributions on the transparency.

ENDING SENTENCE Have children help you think of a good ending sentence, and record it on the transparency.

Think Aloud To end my description, I need to write a sentence that tells what I thought or how I felt about the popcorn.

MODELING
PUBLISHING

- Have children echo read the completed description by having them repeat each sentence after you read it. Praise children for how well they helped you complete the piece.

- Tell children that later, when you write your letter to your friend, you will copy the description neatly as part of your letter.

SCHOOL-HOME CONNECTION Activity Master 94

Children can make an advertisement for movie popcorn to take home and share with family members. Have them color the drawing on Activity Master 94 and then dictate or write a descriptive caption to promote the popcorn. Suggest that they use some sensory words from Poster Book page 5A. You may want to attach a copy of the description that the class wrote together.

MODELING
REFLECTING

To help children think more about their writing experience, model the process of reflection.

Think Aloud I liked thinking about all the different details I could use to describe the popcorn. I learned how important it is to use all my senses.

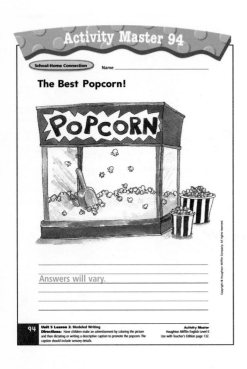

Activity Master 94

School-Home Connection   Name _____

The Best Popcorn!

POPCORN

Answers will vary.

Unit 5 Lesson 2: Modeled Writing
Directions: Have children make an advertisement by coloring the picture and then dictating or writing a descriptive caption to promote the popcorn. The caption should include sensory details.

Houghton Mifflin English Level K
Activity Master
Use with Teacher's Edition page 132.

Focus Skill · Oral Language

③ Sound Words

Lesson Objective

Children will:
• recognize and use onomatopoeia

Materials

Poster Book p. 5B, dry erase marker, Activity Master 95

Warm-Up

Read aloud page 14 of *Night Sounds, Morning Colors*. Ask children to identify the words that name sounds the boy hears. *(whirr, hoot, chuckle, click)* Discuss what is making each sound and how each word sounds like the sound itself. Repeat the activity, reading aloud page 11 *(pattering, popping, clinks)* and page 12 *(tapping, gushes)*.

Teach Poster Book p. 5B

● Explain that words like *hoot*, *pop*, and *tap* that sound like the sounds they name are called sound words.

● Display Poster Book page 5B and have children identify the pictures. Ask children to think of a sound or sounds that each pictured item makes. Have a volunteer make each sound and name a word that imitates the sound.

● Label each picture with an appropriate sound word or words. For each picture, have children complete this sentence frame orally: *A* _____ *says,* "_____." (Sample answer: A *drum* says "*boom*.")

FOR STUDENTS ACQUIRING ENGLISH

Children who have a home language other than English may be unfamiliar with the English sounds for objects. You will need to teach the sounds.

Try It Out Activity Master 95

Have children identify the pictures on Activity Master 95. Then ask them to mark the pictures, following your directions. Say: 1. *Circle something that goes* buzz. *Mark an X on something that goes* ding-dong. 2. *Circle something that goes* creak. *Mark an X on something that goes* honk. 3. *Circle something that says* quack. *Mark an X on something that goes* tick-tock. 4. *Circle something that goes* pop. *Mark an X on something that says* moo.

Wrap-Up

Whisper a sound word to one child. Have the child say the word while pantomiming the action of the object or animal that makes the sound. Classmates guess who the child "is." (Example: Child pantomimes being a lion while saying the word *roar*.) Repeat with other volunteers. Remind children that they can use sound words when they describe something.

 INFORMAL ASSESSMENT (*See* Activity Masters Plus p. 45)

 MEETING INDIVIDUAL NEEDS (*See* p. 144)

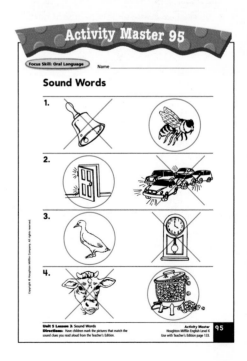

Activity Master 95

Focus Skill **Viewing**

④ Observation

Lesson Objective	Materials
Children will: • use observation to identify details and to make comparisons	selected classroom objects, cloth, Poster Book p. 5C, Activity Master 96

Warm-Up

Play an observation game. Collect several objects, place them on a table, and cover them with a cloth. Explain to children that you are going to remove the cloth for a couple of minutes and that they should look carefully at all the items. Replace the cloth. Ask children to recall what they saw, having them see how many items they can name and describe. Challenge children to remember as many details as they can.

Teach Poster Book p. 5C

- Explain that when we observe something, we pay careful attention to it by using our senses. Remind children that the boy in *Night Sounds, Morning Colors* noticed many details. He was very observant! Reread page 17 of the selection. Ask children what the boy notices about his grandmother's wallet when he holds it. (It's creaky, strong, and worn shiny. It smells like old leather.)

- Display Poster Book page 5C. Ask children to look carefully at the first picture and to describe what they see. Ask: *What do you notice? What colors, shapes, and sizes do you see? What are the people doing? How do they feel?* Tell children that there are two things wrong in the picture. Ask them to look carefully and find the two things. (cake on pie table; balloon man wearing chef's hat)

- Repeat the activity, using the second picture. (clock with letters, not numerals; toy truck in pet store window)

Try It Out Activity Master 96

Tell children that they are going to practice looking carefully. Have them complete Activity Master 96 by finding and coloring the picture in each row that is different.

Wrap-Up

Have volunteers share the pictures they colored on Activity Master 96. Ask them to tell how they decided which picture was different. Remind children that one way we get information is by looking.

✓ **INFORMAL ASSESSMENT** (*See* Activity Masters Plus pp. 45–47)

MEETING INDIVIDUAL NEEDS (*See* p. 144)

Poster Book p. 5C

Activity Master 96

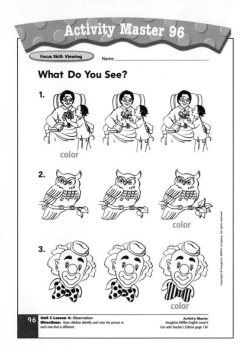

Focus Skill Grammar

⑤ Adjectives

Lesson Objective

Children will:
- identify and use adjectives that describe how things look and feel

Materials

Poster Book p. 5D, dry erase marker, Activity Master 97

Warm-Up

Play a game of I Spy. Think of something in the classroom and describe it for children using adjectives that tell how it looks and feels. (Example: It is <u>round</u> and <u>red</u>. It feels <u>smooth</u>.) Have children guess what you are thinking of. Continue, asking volunteers to think of the objects and give the clues.

Teach Poster Book p. 5D

- Remind children that they already know that some words describe things. Review that describing words are also called adjectives.

- Read aloud page 5 of *Night Sounds, Morning Colors*. Ask children which words describe how things look. *(big, droopy, emerald)* Help them see that these words tell size, shape, and color. Then ask children how the morning mist and the raindrops might feel. *(wet, damp)* Explain that describing words can tell how something looks or feels.

- Display Poster Book page 5D. Point to a few items in the picture and have children describe how they look and feel, using adjectives for color, shape, size, and texture.

- Then say specific adjectives for look or feel. Have volunteers find matching items on the poster and mark them. (Example: Find something that is red. Put an X on it.) Continue naming adjectives such as *big, little, round, square, red, blue, bright, striped, smooth, sharp, slippery, cold, chilly, bumpy, hard, soft, wet, shiny,* and *furry.*

Try It Out Activity Master 97

Ask children to color the picture on Activity Master 97. Then have them dictate or write adjective labels for color, size, shape, and/or texture to describe objects in the picture.

Wrap-Up

Have volunteers share the pictures they colored on Activity Master 97 as well as the words they chose to label their pictures. Remind children that one way to describe something is to tell how it looks and feels.

 INFORMAL ASSESSMENT (*See* Activity Masters Plus p. 46)

 MEETING INDIVIDUAL NEEDS (*See* p. 144)

Poster Book p. 5D

FOR STUDENTS ACQUIRING ENGLISH

Children will need help naming adjectives. Play Categories in which you say a category and children shout out adjectives in that category. For example, say: *Colors* or *Shapes* and have children call out a color or a shape and point out an object that fits each adjective they give.

Poster Book p. 5E

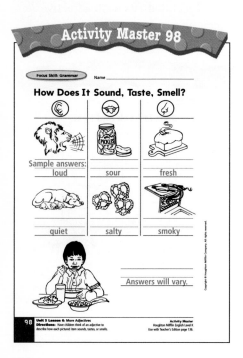

Focus Skill: Grammar

How Does It Sound, Taste, and Smell?

Cat, Mouse, Bacon, and Cheese © 1820 Anonymous The Bridgeman Art Library

Sample answers: quiet, squeaky, salty, fresh

Unit 5 Lesson 6: More Adjectives
Directions: Have children use adjectives to describe how things sound, taste, and smell.

Houghton Mifflin English Level K
Use with Teacher's Edition page 136.   **5E**

FOR STUDENTS ACQUIRING ENGLISH

During the activities, help children with the names of adjectives by offering choices. Ask: *Does a lemon taste sweet or sour? Is a lion's roar loud or soft?* Use realia and pictures to aid comprehension.

Activity Master 98

Focus Skill: Grammar   Name _____

How Does It Sound, Taste, Smell?

Sample answers:
loud   sour   fresh

quiet   salty   smoky

Answers will vary.

98   Unit 5 Lesson 6: More Adjectives
Directions: Have children think of an adjective to describe how each pictured item sounds, tastes, or smells.

Activity Master
Houghton Mifflin English Level K
Use with Teacher's Edition page 136.

Focus Skill   **Grammar**

⑥ More Adjectives

Lesson Objective

Children will:
• identify and use adjectives that describe how things sound, taste, and smell

Materials

Poster Book p. 5E, chart paper, marker, Activity Master 98

Optional Materials

cracker for each child

Warm-Up

Display and reread page 16 of *Night Sounds, Morning Colors*. Ask children to describe the smells and tastes in the bakery. Then have them share information about the smells, tastes, and sounds in a bakery they know. Give each child a cracker, such as a graham cracker or soda cracker. Have them break it and taste it. Ask: *How does it smell and taste?* (sweet, salty, bland) *What sound does it make when you bite or break it?* (crunchy)

Teach   Poster Book p. 5E

• Display Poster Book page 5E. Explain that an artist painted this picture, called *Cat, Mouse, Bacon, and Cheese*, a very long time ago. Ask children to describe what they see and to tell what they think is happening.

• Have children imagine that they are standing beside the table. Ask them to think of adjectives that describe what they would smell and hear as well as what they might taste if they were to sample the foods shown. Record children's suggestions on chart paper. They might include words such as *fresh, sweet, salty, spicy, delicious, smoky, squeaky,* and *hissing*.

• Reread the adjectives to children and have them use each one in an oral sentence to tell about something in the painting. (Examples: The bread smells <u>fresh</u>. The meat is <u>salty</u>.)

Try It Out   Activity Master 98

Help children identify the first six pictures on Activity Master 98. Have them suggest a sensory word to describe each item. Then ask partners to discuss the last picture, thinking of adjectives that describe how things sound, taste, and smell. Have them choose a favorite to dictate or write.

Wrap-Up

Name sensory words for sound, taste, and smell. Have children name as many things as they can to match each word. (Examples: things that sound <u>loud</u>, things that taste <u>sour</u>, things that smell <u>sweet</u>) Remind children that one way to describe something is to tell how it sounds, tastes, or smells.

✓ **INFORMAL ASSESSMENT** (*See* Activity Masters Plus p. 46–47)

MEETING INDIVIDUAL NEEDS (*See* p. 145)

⑦ Synonyms

Lesson Objective

Children will:
- identify and use synonyms

Materials

Activity Master 99

Optional Materials

ice cubes in zip-type plastic bags

Warm-Up

Pass around ice cubes in zip-type plastic bags. Ask children to suggest words that describe their temperature. (Sample answers: *cold, chilly, icy, freezing*) Recall that the boy in *Night Sounds, Morning Colors* took a winter walk. Read this sentence from the book: *A gust of freezing wind blows right through my hair.* Reread the sentence, replacing *freezing* with synonyms children have thought of. Have them pick their favorite version of the sentence.

Teach

- Explain that words like *cold*, *chilly*, *icy*, and *freezing* that have the same or almost the same meaning are called synonyms.

- Tell children that they are going to help you think of some synonyms. Have a volunteer pantomime the action of each sentence below as you read it aloud. Ask children to name other words that have the same or almost the same meaning as the underlined word. Demonstrate how synonyms can be interchangeable by having children repeat each sentence, replacing the underlined word with each synonym they think of. Sample answers:

  1. *We built a big sandcastle.* (huge, enormous, gigantic)
  2. *Kim was happy when she saw the new bike.* (glad, cheerful, delighted)
  3. *Max hit the nails with a hammer.* (tapped, pounded, banged)
  4. *The baby looked scared when it thundered.* (afraid, frightened)

Try It Out Activity Master 99

Ask children to cut apart the picture cards on Activity Master 99. Have them match pairs of pictures that are alike in some way. Then ask partners to think of synonyms to describe each matching pair.

Wrap-Up

Have children share the synonyms they thought of with the class, using complete sentences to describe the pictures they matched. Explain that they can choose just the right synonym to use when they write or tell a description.

 INFORMAL ASSESSMENT (*See* Activity Masters Plus p. 47)

 MEETING INDIVIDUAL NEEDS (*See* p. 145)

 FOR STUDENTS ACQUIRING ENGLISH

Children acquiring English may understand the concept of synonyms but will not be able to generate them. Present choices such as *What are some other words that describe these ice cubes? Can we say* burning, chilly, icy, *or* hot?" Record responses next to picture cues. Repeat this questioning throughout the exercises. Use realia, demonstration, and art or photos.

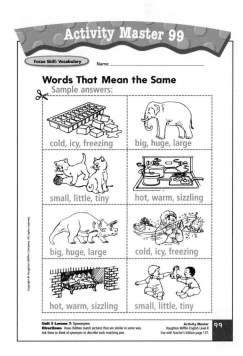

Activity Master 99

Focus Skill: Vocabulary   Name _____

Words That Mean the Same

✂ Sample answers:

cold, icy, freezing	big, huge, large
small, little, tiny	hot, warm, sizzling
big, huge, large	cold, icy, freezing
hot, warm, sizzling	small, little, tiny

Unit 5 Lesson 7: Synonyms
Directions: Have children match pictures that are similar in some way. Ask them to think of synonyms to describe each matching pair.

Houghton Mifflin English Level K
Use with Teacher's Edition page 137.
Activity Master **99**

Poster Book p. 5F

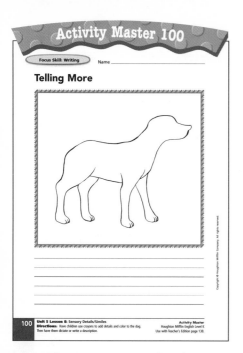

Focus Skill: Writing

Focus Skill   Writing

(8) Sensory Details/Similes

Lesson Objective	**Materials**
Children will: • identify and use sensory details and similes	Poster Book p. 5F, dry erase markers, Activity Master 100

Warm-Up

Display the first illustration in *Night Sounds, Morning Colors*. Point to the spiderweb and say: *This is a spiderweb.* Ask volunteers to think of words to describe the web. Repeat the sentence, adding the adjectives. (Example: This is a big, droopy spiderweb.) Ask children if anything about the web reminds them of something else. Help them generate comparisons. (Examples: It is as soft as a feather. The raindrops look like diamonds.)

Teach   Poster Book p. 5F

- Tell children that you'd like them to help you write some descriptions. Display Poster Book page 5F. Point to the cat, and discuss the kinds of details that would make the picture more interesting and colorful. Decide which details to add, and have volunteers draw them on the cat.

- Read the base sentence aloud: *I have a cat.* Ask children to suggest adjectives that tell about the details they added to the picture. Record two suggestions in the blanks for the first sentence. Read the new sentence aloud. (Sample answer: I have a fluffy orange cat.)

- Explain that another good way to describe the cat is to compare something about it to something else. Have children choose one of the cat's features (*e.g.*, eyes, whiskers) and think of something that these features are like. Complete the simile. (Sample answer: Her eyes are like marbles.)

- Repeat the procedure with the picture of the train. Children might complete the simile by comparing the train to something else that is loud, slow, fast, crowded, or shiny.

Try It Out   Activity Master 100

Ask children to use crayons to add details and color to the dog on Activity Master 100. Then have them dictate or write descriptions of their dogs.

Wrap-Up

Have volunteers share their dog drawings and descriptions. Remind children that they can paint good word pictures by using details and by telling how one thing is like something else.

 INFORMAL ASSESSMENT (*See* Activity Masters Plus pp. 46–47)

 MEETING INDIVIDUAL NEEDS (*See* p. 145)

⑨ Description

Lesson Objectives

Children will:
- choose a topic and audience for a description
- contribute to a description, using the steps of the writing process
- reflect on their writing experience

Materials

Poster Book p. 5G, dry erase markers, Transparency 5–3 or chart paper

Topic Ideas
- a storybook character
- the playground
- a classroom pet
- a treat we made for snack
- a stormy day
- a favorite school event

Focus on Instruction

Explain to children that you are going to work together to write a description. Tell them that they are going to follow the steps that good writers use when writing something that others will read.

PREWRITING

Choose a Topic

- Ask children to think about what they want to describe and for whom they will write their description. Emphasize that they should describe just one person, place, thing, or event. Point out that their topic should be something that will interest the person for whom they are writing.

- Brainstorm topic ideas. List children's ideas on the board or on chart paper, and then discuss them. Ask: *Do we know enough to tell how this looks? feels? tastes? sounds? and smells? Is this something our reader(s) will find interesting?*

- As a group, decide on a topic and an audience.

Plan the Description Poster Book p. 5G

- Display Poster Book page 5G. Record the topic for the description in the center of the graphic organizer and say it aloud.

- Display the actual subject of the description or a picture of it. If this isn't possible, ask children to close their eyes and to picture it in their minds. Help them focus on each sense by asking questions such as *What does it look like? Is it big? little? What color is it? How does it feel when you touch it? Do you smell or taste anything? What sounds do you hear?*

- Record the sensory details children suggest by writing key words or drawing simple pictures in the appropriate circles.

- Together, choose an order for the details in your description. You might describe your subject from top to bottom or from left to right. Or you might tell what you notice first, second, third, and so on. Ask a volunteer to help you number the details in the graphic organizer in an order that makes sense.

Poster Book p. 5G

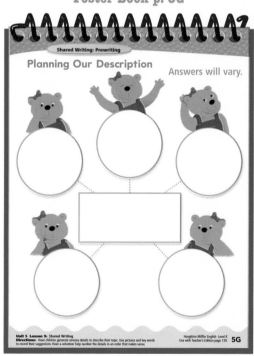

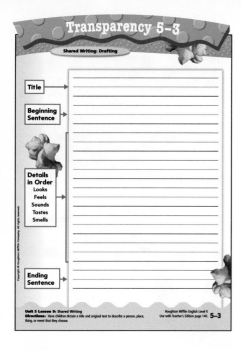

NOTE As you draft, point out the correct use of capital letters and punctuation marks that children have learned. You may also wish to leave one sensory detail incomplete so children can add adjectives or a simile during revising.

DRAFTING   **Transparency 5–3, Poster Book p. 5G**

- Before drafting, review and discuss with children what makes a great description.

What Makes a Great Description?

- A good beginning sentence names the one thing you will describe.

- Details tell how things look, feel, sound, taste, or smell.

- The details are in an order that makes sense.

- A good ending sentence tells what you thought or felt.

- Now, ask volunteers to contribute text ideas for each element of the draft, using the details from the graphic organizer on Poster Book page 5G as a guide. Record children's suggestions on Transparency 5–3 or on chart paper. Help children generate the following text:

- a **title** that tells the topic of the description

- an interesting **beginning sentence** that names the one thing the description will be about

- **details** that tell how things look, feel, sound, taste, and/or smell and that are in an **order that makes sense**

- a good **ending sentence** that tells what children think or feel about the topic

- Read chorally or echo read the draft for your description. Praise children for their contributions.

REVISING

- Together, reread the draft. Then help children evaluate their work by using the Questions for Revising below. Make changes or additions children suggest to improve the description.

> **Questions for Revising**
>
> ✔ Did we tell how things look, feel, sound, taste, or smell?
>
> ✔ Are the details in an order that makes sense?
>
> ✔ Do we have a good beginning and a good ending sentence?

- Discuss with children what they have learned about telling how one thing is like something else. As a group, see if there are similes that could be added to make the description stronger.

The truck was big.
as as an elephant

PUBLISHING

- Make a clean final copy of the description on chart paper. Ask volunteers to add illustrations.

- Help children plan a way to share the description with their intended audience. Afterward, post the finished product or add it to a class Big Book of shared writing.

 SCHOOL-HOME CONNECTION Have a classroom volunteer or assistant type the description and reproduce it for children to illustrate. Children can take home these personalized versions to share with family members.

REFLECTING

Praise children for helping to plan and write the description. Discuss with them their writing experience. Ask:

- *What was easy to describe? What was difficult?*

- *What new describing words did you learn?*

- *How did using your five senses help you? Did you learn any new ways to look at things?*

- *What did you learn that will help you the next time you write a description?*

FOR STUDENTS ACQUIRING ENGLISH

Once children have chosen a topic, encourage them to draw and then act out their ideas. Have them form small groups in which they can show their drawings and then act out their topics. Pantomiming will help them think of new details to include in their pictures. Also, list adjectives, nouns, and verbs they can use.

Writing Portfolio

If you are collecting samples of children's writing, decide if you want to save this piece.

Student Sample

Emergent Writer

Independent Writing

⑩ Description

Lesson Objectives

Children will:
• tell, dictate, or write a description
• listen and respond to the writing of peers

Materials

drawing paper, writing paper, Activity Master 101, Poster Book p. 5E

Focus on Instruction

Tell children that now they will be writing their own descriptions. Explain that first they must decide what they want to describe and for whom they will write their description. Here are some ideas you might use to help children plan, write, and share their work.

Planning Ideas

THINKING ABOUT TOPICS Have pairs or small groups brainstorm topic ideas. Then have each group report their ideas to the class. If individuals are having difficulty thinking of a topic, try reading one of the Writing Prompts on page 143. You might also read aloud some of the books in the Bibliography on page 128 to help spark a topic idea.

ORGANIZING IDEAS Before writing, have children give their description orally to a partner without naming the topic. The partner can ask questions to try to figure out the subject of the description. The questions may give the writer ideas for additional details to include.

Writing

Allow children to produce their descriptions in the format that is most appropriate to their own stage of development, as indicated in the chart below.

Writing Options		
Emergent Writers	**Early Beginning Writers**	**Late Beginning and Transitional Writers**
Have children draw a picture of the person, place, thing, or event they are describing. They can add pretend or "scribble" writing to describe their drawing and then tell their description orally, or children can dictate their description to an adult to record.*	Children can draw a picture to represent the person, place, thing, or event they are describing. Have them label their artwork with descriptive words and/or phrases and then tell their description orally, or they can dictate their complete text to an adult to record.*	Children can write their descriptions using temporary spelling. They can add illustrations to support their text.

*Some children may feel their writing is not valid if an adult rewrites it.

 INFORMAL ASSESSMENT (*See* Activity Masters Plus p. 46)

Ideas for Sharing

Have children share their completed descriptions with the whole class or with a classmate by "reading" their work aloud or by using one of the suggestions below.

Write It Children can write their description on shape paper, making a booklet that is the shape of what they are describing.

Say It Suggest that children record their description, adding sound effects where appropriate. Have them play their taped recording for the class.

Show It Have children display the actual object they are describing or display a photo of it as they "read" their description to the class.

After each child shares, the listener or listeners should tell the author at least one thing they liked about the description. (Examples: Your description paints a good word picture. I liked that you told how things looked and sounded.)

INTERNET CONNECTION
See www.eduplace.com/rdg/hme/ for printable patterns for making shape paper booklets.

Writing Prompts

HEALTH Activity Master 101

Do you have a favorite healthy meal? Draw a picture of it on the plate. Write a word to label each food. Then write a description of the meal. Tell how each food looks, feels, smells, and tastes and why you like it.

FINE ART Poster Book p. 5E

What would you want to touch first in this picture? Write a description of it. Tell how it looks and feels. If it has a sound, a taste, or a smell, tell about that too. If you want, you may write a description of the whole picture.

INTERNET CONNECTION
See www.eduplace.com/rdg/hme/ for more writing ideas.

Activity Master 101

Independent Writing: Writing Prompts   Name _____

A Healthy Meal

Unit 5 Lesson 10: Health Writing Prompt
Directions: Have children draw a favorite healthy meal on the plate. Ask them to label each food and then dictate or write a description of the meal.

Activity Master | **101**
Houghton Mifflin English Level K
Use with Teacher's Edition page 143.

FOR STUDENTS ACQUIRING ENGLISH

Have children work as a group to describe the Poster Book page. Help them with vocabulary by naming the foods. Make labels for the foods and have children place them on the Poster Book. Work with children to use the food names in sentences.

Meeting Individual Needs

Lesson 3 Focus Skill   Oral Language: Sound Words

RETEACHING ALTERNATIVE STRATEGY
Sing a few verses of "Old MacDonald" with children. Point out that the sound that each animal makes is a sound word. Example: "With a moo-moo here and a moo-moo there." Ask children to identify each sound word they sang.

CHALLENGE
Create a sound museum. Have children select objects in the classroom that make sounds. (Examples: toys, musical instruments) Help children label each item with a sound word.

FOR STUDENTS ACQUIRING ENGLISH
Before singing "Old MacDonald," review animal sounds. Begin by naming an animal. Have a volunteer make the animal's sound. Children should use English sound words. (Whisper help to any children who may need it.)

Lesson 4 Focus Skill   Viewing: Observation

RETEACHING ALTERNATIVE STRATEGY
Observe something in the classroom. Model how to describe what you observed. For example, say: *Our guinea pig has soft, brown and white hair. It makes a squeaking sound.* Then ask children to observe something. Remind them to watch carefully to notice all the details they can. After a few minutes, have children describe what they saw to a partner.

CHALLENGE
While others close their eyes, have two children strike a pose. Ask classmates to open their eyes and observe. Then, as others close their eyes again, have the two change their pose slightly. When classmates open their eyes, ask them to tell what is different.

FOR STUDENTS ACQUIRING ENGLISH
Modify the Challenge activity so that children acquiring English can participate. After having the class tell you what has been changed in the poses, have children go to the "statue children" and change them or give them directions to get back to the original pose.

Lesson 5 Focus Skill   Grammar: Adjectives

RETEACHING ALTERNATIVE STRATEGY
Gather objects to sort, such as attribute blocks or buttons. Show children how to sort by one characteristic, such as shape, size, or color. Describe the characteristic: *This is a triangle.* Then have children sort for one and then two characteristics. Each time children finish sorting, ask them to use describing words to explain how they sorted.

CHALLENGE
Put familiar objects into a bag. Partners take turns choosing an item. They pass it back and forth, each saying one sentence that tells how the item looks or feels. Partners see how many sentences they can generate to describe the object.

FOR STUDENTS ACQUIRING ENGLISH
Before having children acquiring English participate in the Reteaching activity, review each object with them. Have them form small groups of mixed proficiency. Hand each group an object and give them time to name it and describe it. Remind children of size, color, and shape words.

Lesson 6 Focus Skill   Grammar: More Adjectives

RETEACHING ALTERNATIVE STRATEGY
Point out objects in the classroom that have a sound, smell, or taste. Then have children draw pictures to represent a sound, a smell, and a taste. Ask them to share their pictures with a partner, using a sense word to describe each one.

CHALLENGE
Have children use toy cooking utensils and dishes to act out making and eating a meal. Ask them to describe how each food tastes and smells and what sounds they would hear while cooking and eating it.

FOR STUDENTS ACQUIRING ENGLISH
Bring in different kinds of finger food including items such as crackers, fruit, and vegetables. Encourage children to describe how each object looks, smells, feels, *and* tastes (if possible)!

Lesson 7 Focus Skill   Vocabulary: Synonyms

RETEACHING ALTERNATIVE STRATEGY
Draw a happy face. Say: *This person is happy*. Explain that other words for *happy* are *glad* and *merry*. Then name a few simple words that have a synonym. (Examples: *big, little, pretty, hot, cold, loud, smart, walk, make*) Ask children to think of one or more synonyms or supply the words for children if they have difficulty. Have them use each synonym in the same oral sentence.

CHALLENGE
Have children make their own mini-thesaurus. Suggest they fold and staple sheets of drawing paper to make a booklet.

Have them draw a picture on each page and label it with two or more synonyms.

FOR STUDENTS ACQUIRING ENGLISH
For extra practice, act out the words listed in the Reteaching activity (*big, little, hot, cold,* and so on) Encourage children to guess what words you're acting out. Your pantomime should elicit many different responses, some of which will be synonyms.

Lesson 8 Focus Skill   Writing: Sensory Details/Similes

RETEACHING ALTERNATIVE STRATEGY
Revisit illustrations of Bingo the puppy in *Night Sounds, Morning Colors*. Help children describe Bingo's size, color, and texture. Ask them to name other things that have either the same color or texture. Help them create similes using the new words. (Example: Bingo is white. Milk is also white. Bingo is as white as milk.)

CHALLENGE
Have children observe classroom objects. Ask them to make up riddles about those objects, using sensory details and similes. (Example: I have long black hands that move around and around. I am round like a dinner plate. What am I?) Transcribe the riddles onto paper and have children illustrate them. Staple the pages together to make a class riddle book.

FOR STUDENTS ACQUIRING ENGLISH
Draw a plain stick figure on the board with colored chalk or on mural paper with crayons. Then have each child come up to add a detail to the drawing. When it is completed, encourage children to name the details. As they do so, repeat the labels, adding similes such as: *The hat is like a tower*.

Unit 6
Story

In this unit, children learn about another type of narrative writing, fictional stories. They listen to a book about a brother and sister and participate in the modeled writing of a story about a brother and sister squirrel. Then children work together with you to create a class story, using the writing process. Unit skills develop language as well as relate to and support narrative writing.

What You Will Find in This Unit . . .

Unit 6 Planning Guide
Story

	Poster Book	Transparency	Activity Masters Plus
DAILY COMMUNICATION LINKS			
Daily Routines *(150–151)*			
The oral language activities provide daily opportunities for children to develop the basic concepts and skills needed to compose stories.			
• **Interactive Bulletin Board:** Attendance List; Daily Message; Color, Number, Size Wheels			
• **Daily Discussion Activity:** Story Read Aloud			
See also Additional Resources *(238–252)*			
Center Activities *(152–153)*		6–1	
• Reading and Listening Center • Math Center • Creative Arts Center			
• Writing Center • Science Center			
A Published Model 🕐 *1 day, 20 minutes*			
Lesson 1 Listening to a Story *(154–155)* *Jamaica Tag-Along*			
Modeled Writing 🕐 *about 2-3 days, 20 minutes each day*			
Lesson 2 Story *(156–158)*	6A	6–2	102
Focus Skills 🕐 *about 6 days, 20 minutes each day*			
Lesson 3 Oral Language: Telling a Story *(159)*			103
Lesson 4 Viewing: Interpreting Pictures *(160)*	6B		104
Lesson 5 Grammar: Singular and Plural Nouns *(161)*	6C		105
Lesson 6 Grammar: Verbs *(162)*	6D		106
Lesson 7 Vocabulary: Opposites *(163)*	6E		107
Lesson 8 Writing: A Good Ending *(164)*	6F		108
Shared Writing 🕐 *about 2–3 days, 20 minutes each day*			
Lesson 9 Story *(165)*	6G	6–3	
Independent Writing 🕐 *about 1–3 days, 20 minutes each day*			
Lesson 10 Story *(168–169)*			109
✓ **Writing Prompts** *(169)*			

MEETING INDIVIDUAL NEEDS *(170–171)*

Activities for Special Needs/Inclusion, for Students Acquiring English, for Reteaching, and for Enrichment/Challenge

Meeting Individual Needs

▶ **FOR SPECIAL NEEDS/INCLUSION:** *Houghton Mifflin English* Audiotape ; *See also* Reteaching.

▶ **FOR STUDENTS ACQUIRING ENGLISH:**
- Notes and activities are included in this Teacher's Edition throughout the unit to help you adapt or use lessons with students acquiring English.
- Students can listen to the published model *Jamaica Tag-Along* on audiotape.

▶ **RETEACHING**
- Activities for reteaching the focus skills are included on pages 170–171.

▶ **ENRICHMENT/CHALLENGE**
- Activities for challenge/enrichment that are correlated to focus skill lessons are included on pages 170–171.

 All audiotape recordings are also available on CD.

Additional Resources

Audiotapes

Technology Tools
CD-ROM: Curious George® Paint & Print Studio
Paint, Write & Play! (published by The Learning Company)
*Type to Learn Jr.™

*©Sunburst Technology Corporation, a Houghton Mifflin Company. All rights reserved.

INTERNET: http://www.eduplace.com/rdg/hme/
Visit Education Place for these additional support materials and activities:
- author biographies
- patterns for shape booklets
- writing prompts

 Keeping a Journal
In kindergarten, journals can be blank notebooks or folders filled with paper. As children draw and write about school activities, important events, and special thoughts, they can watch their writing growth as the year progresses.

Informal Assessment
Activity Masters Plus, Assessment Checklists, pages 45–47

 School-Home Connection
Suggestions for informing or involving family members in learning related to this unit are included in the Teacher's Edition throughout the unit.

Daily Routines

The oral language activities suggested here provide daily opportunities for children to develop basic concepts and skills they will need to compose stories. Refer to the **Interactive Bulletin Board** and **Daily Discussion** ideas on pages 10–13 and 20–21 for help in establishing Daily Routines for your classroom.

Interactive Bulletin Board

Attendance List

As you take attendance each day, ask volunteers to make up fanciful story beginnings about themselves and classmates by completing this sentence frame: *Once upon a time, there was a* [identify character] *named* [child's name] *who lived* [setting]. (Example: Once upon a time, there was a kind princess named Alexa who lived in an enchanted forest.) As a variation, you may wish to have the first child on the attendance list begin a story and have each subsequent child add an oral sentence to continue it.

Attendance List

Anna   Bob   Carlos

Ellen   Fran   Maria

Color, Number, Size Wheels

Color, Number, Size Wheels

Have volunteers spin the wheels and name the color, number, and size words they land on. Then have them use two or more of the words to name and describe an imaginary character (a person or an animal) or an imaginary setting. (Examples: A big boy named John had two blue eyes. John lived in a blue castle that had two big towers.)

Daily Message

Have children choose one sentence from the attendance list activity. Record it as a Daily Message. The sentence can be posted all day as a story starter for children to dramatize in the Creative Arts Center, or to tell or write about in the Writing Center. Children can also use the sentence to start their own stories during free time.

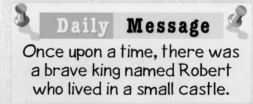

Daily Message

Once upon a time, there was a brave king named Robert who lived in a small castle.

Daily Discussion

Share a fictional story with children each day. Tell a favorite story, read a storybook aloud, read one of the stories on Additional Resources pages 238–250, or play a book on tape. When you read or tell a story, dramatize the tale for children. Dim the lights, and add music for atmosphere. Use props, and put on different hats or shawls for various characters. For different speakers, use distinctive voices, facial expressions, and hand gestures. Make storytelling exciting.

Think and Discuss

- Who are the characters? Are any of the characters like people you know? Explain.

- Where does the story take place?

- What happened in the beginning, the middle, and the end of the story?

- What was the problem? How was it solved, or how did the story turn out?

- Has anything like this ever happened to you? Explain.

GIVING AN OPINION Each day after children have heard and discussed a story, ask them to give an opinion by completing one of the following sentences: *I liked this story because _____. I didn't like this story because _____.* Suggest that children use specific story elements to support their opinions.

SINGULAR OR PLURAL NOUNS After children listen to each story, identify some of the naming words, or nouns, from the story. Ask children to tell you whether each word names one or more than one. Make a word card for each one, and ask volunteers to add illustrations. Put the cards on a chart or word wall.

 INFORMAL ASSESSMENT (*See* Activity Masters Plus pp. 45, 47)

Daily Discussion Activity

Story Read-Aloud

Turn to Additional Resources pages 238–251 for a selection of stories and folktales to read aloud to children.

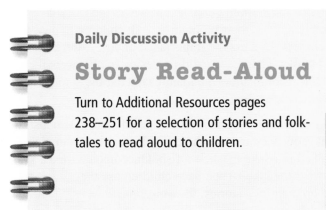

One		More Than One	
1 hen		3 hens	
1 dog		2 dogs	
1 shoe		4 shoes	

Center Activities

Center Activities provide additional daily opportunities to develop and reinforce concepts and skills that support the composing of stories.

Reading and Listening Center

PUBLISHED MODEL Children can listen to *Jamaica Tag-Along* on audio-tape as they follow along in the book. **Listening**

CUMULATIVE STORIES Have children tell cumulative stories, and record them with a tape recorder. Have one child say one or two sentences to begin the story; then rewind the tape to the beginning, and have the next child listen to the tape and continue the story. Repeat the procedure until five or six children have had a chance to contribute. Each day, have the class listen to the taped story and discuss what they like about it. Use new tapes on subsequent days until all the children have participated. **Listening/Speaking**

Writing Center

BOOK COVER PREDICTIONS Display a number of book covers from fiction stories. Ask children to use the covers to make predictions about where the story takes place, who the characters are, and what their problem is. Ask children to pick their favorites and explain their choices. Discuss the importance of cover illustrations in making people want to read books. Then have children design book covers for story ideas they are considering. Tell them to show the main character, the setting, and a hint about the problem. **Viewing/Speaking**

Rebus Stories Provide children with a variety of picture-word cards. Demonstrate how to put them in different sequences and use them to tell stories. (Examples: Once upon a time, a <u>cat</u> walked to a <u>lake</u> to catch a <u>fish</u>. Once upon a time a <u>fish</u> met a <u>cat</u> as it drank water from the <u>lake</u>.) Then have children use the picture-word cards to make up their own stories. **Viewing/Speaking**

JOURNAL Tell children that many story writers include characters and settings like people and places they know in real life. Have children use their journals to draw or make lists of interesting characters and settings based on their own lives. Tell children they can refer to their drawings and notes when they pick characters and settings for writing their stories.

Creative Arts Center

Transparency 6–1

STORY RETELLING Use Transparency 6–1 to project the playground background scenery against a white surface. Ask volunteers to take the parts of Jamaica, Ossie, and Berto and to act out what happens at the basketball court and in the sandlot. **Speaking**

PUPPET SHOW Have small groups of children work together to make puppets and use them to act out favorite stories. Suggest that each group make a different kind of puppet: paper bag puppets, stick puppets, finger puppets, or sock puppets. **Viewing/Speaking**

INKBLOT STORIES Show children how to make inkblot animals by putting a dab of paint on paper, folding the paper in half, and then opening it up. Children can dictate or write stories about the inkblot animal or animals they made. Have children tell their stories to others. The listeners should use the Listening Tips on page 15. **Speaking/Listening**

Math Center

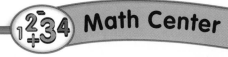

STORIES OF THREE Recall with children stories that include the number three, such as "Three Little Kittens," "The Three Little Pigs," and "The Three Billy Goats Gruff." Have children use plastic animal counters to help them make up and act out their own stories of three. **Speaking**

Science Center

BUILDING WITH SAND Have children experiment with mixing sand and water to build a sandcastle at the sand table. Have them try building with dry sand, very wet sand, and sand of the right dampness. Tell children that after building their sandcastle, they should make up a story about it. Then have children display their sandcastle to the class. Ask: *What happens if the sand is too dry? too wet? just right?* Once children have talked about their observations, have them tell their story about the sandcastle. **Speaking**

A Published Model

About the Author

Juanita Havill

Juanita Havill has written five books about Jamaica as well as other children's books. She lives in Arizona with her family.

 INTERNET CONNECTION

See www.eduplace.com/kids/ for information about Juanita Havill.

Bibliography

You may also wish to read aloud these stories.

- *Whistle for Willie*
  by Ezra Jack Keats
- *Ira Sleeps Over*
  by Bernard Waber
- *Jamaica's Find*
  by Juanita Havill
- *Shy Charles*
  by Rosemary Wells

 FOR STUDENTS ACQUIRING ENGLISH

To illustrate *tag-along* and *follow*, teach the children Follow the Leader. Ask if anyone has a little brother or sister who wants to tag along. During the picture walk, have children describe nouns and verbs they see.

① Listening to a Story

Lesson Objectives

Children will:
- listen to and discuss the characteristics of a published model of a story
- recognize details and exact words in a story
- evaluate the relationship of visuals and text
- respond personally and critically to the selection

Materials

Jamaica Tag-Along

Reading the Model

The book *Jamaica Tag-Along* is a story about a girl who invites a younger child to play after her older brother won't let her tag along with him.

Building Background

- Ask children what they know about basketball. Discuss the object of the game: to throw or shoot the ball into a high basket to make points.
- Ask children whom they play with outside of school. Have they ever asked to play with older children and been told, "You're not old enough"?

Introducing Vocabulary

- Display page 7 of *Jamaica Tag-Along*. Tell children that the boys played basketball, and one player *dribbled*, or bounced, the ball. Next, show pages 12–13. Tell children that basketball is played on a *court*. Say that sometimes when a player shoots the ball, the ball bounces off the *rim* of the basket.
- Point out that Jamaica walked away from the basketball court toward the sandlot. Display pages 16–17, and tell children Jamaica scooped sand into a *mound*. Turn to pages 22–23. Explain that Jamaica and Berto made a sandcastle. Tell children that Jamaica dug a *ditch* around the sandcastle and put water in the ditch to make a *moat*.

Predicting and Purpose Setting

PICTURE WALK Display *Jamaica Tag-Along*. Read the title, the author, and the illustrator aloud. Tell children that to tag along means to follow someone.

- Take a picture walk through *Jamaica Tag-Along*, paging through the book, stopping to talk about the pictures. Stop at pages 8–9 and ask: *What is Jamaica doing in this picture?* (Jamaica is tossing the basketball.) Stop at pages 10–11 and ask: *What is happening here?* (Ossie looks mad. He might be telling Jamaica to go away. Jamaica looks as if her feelings are hurt.) Avoid revealing the ending of the story. Ask children to predict what they think this story will be about.
- Explain that as you read children should listen to find out Jamaica's problem and how she solved it.

  This selection is also available on audiotape.

Listening As a Writer

Think About the Story

PLOT Ask: *What is Jamaica's problem?* (Ossie doesn't want her tagging along.) *How does she solve it?* (She finds a new friend.) Explain that the beginning of a story tells about a problem a character has. The middle of the story tells how the character tries to solve the problem. The ending tells how the problem is solved or worked out. Reread the ending of the story starting on page 24. Have children explain why this is a good ending. Help them understand that the ending shows how Jamaica solved her problem.

SETTING Have children tell where most of the story takes place. (a schoolyard) Read aloud page 6. Ask children which words help them know the setting, or story place. (Sample answers: *sidewalk, school court, school building*)

CHARACTERS Ask children to name the story characters, or people. Point out that what the characters say helps readers know what the characters are like. Read what Jamaica says to Berto on page 23: "You can help me make a bigger castle if you're very careful." Ask children what this tells them about Jamaica.

Think About Writer's Craft

ELABORATION Tell children that details help readers picture exactly what the characters do. Have children compare these sentences about Jamaica: *She parked and crept to the corner. She parked her bike by the bushes and crept to the corner of the school building to watch.* (p. 6) Help children see that the second sentence tells more about where Jamaica parked and why.

WORD CHOICE: EXACT VERBS Point out that the author uses exact action words, or verbs, to describe the characters' actions. Have volunteers act out each of these sentences: *Jamaica <u>went</u> to the edge of the court. Jamaica <u>sneaked</u> to the edge of the court.* (p. 8) Discuss why <u>sneaked</u> tells more clearly how she moved.

Think About the Pictures

Ask volunteers to show how their faces look if they feel bad about something or if someone hurts their feelings. Then display pages 10–11 from *Jamaica Tag-Along* and reread the text. Ask children to look at the picture, tell how each character feels, and explain how they know.

NOTE If children are discussing and responding to *Jamaica Tag-Along* on a day following your initial reading, reread the book.

Responding

- **Personal Response** Ask children to think about a time when they had a problem getting along with someone else and they figured out how to solve the problem peacefully. Have them draw pictures that show how they solved this problem. Then have children share their pictures.

- **Critical Thinking** Ask children to suppose that a different young child wants to play with Jamaica on another day. What do they think she would say to the child? Why? (Answers will vary but should suggest that Jamaica would not reject a younger child because she didn't like having it done to her.)

 FOR STUDENTS ACQUIRING ENGLISH

Have children role-play the dialogue between Jamaica and Ossie, or between Jamaica and Berto. Model sentence stems such as *I feel_____ because you won't let me_____.* Check for correct intonation and encourage children to make up their own sentence stems to express feelings.

② Story

Lesson Objectives

Children will:
- recognize the characteristics of stories
- understand purpose and audience
- become familiar with the steps of the writing process
- help plan and draft a story

Materials

Poster Book p. 6A, dry erase markers, Transparency 6–2 or chart paper, Activity Master 102

Focus on Instruction

- Remind children that *Jamaica Tag-Along* is a well-written story about a character with a problem. Tell children that the author made up this story, even though the characters, setting, and events seem real. Explain that stories have a beginning, a middle, and an end.

- Ask children to name different stories they have heard or read. Mention that some stories, such as *Jamaica Tag-Along*, tell about things that could happen in real life. Other stories, such as fairy tales and talking-animal stories, could not happen in real life.

- Ask children to tell where they could find stories. (Examples: books, movies, videos, TV, cartoons, plays) Tell them that stories can be read, seen, or heard.

MODELING PREWRITING

Choose a Topic

Recall with children that Ossie and Jamaica in *Jamaica Tag-Along* are brother and sister. Tell children that you want to write a story about a brother and sister and would like their help. Explain that first you have to decide for whom you are writing the story and why.

Think Aloud I enjoy making up stories about animals. Animals can be characters in a story too. Sometimes the animals have the same problems that children have. I remember a problem my sister (or brother) had, and I would like to write this story to send to my sister (or brother) to remind her/him of how problems work out.

Plan the Story Poster Book p. 6A

- Remind children that before beginning a story, a writer needs to think about what happens in the beginning, middle, and end.

Think Aloud Before I start writing, I think about the order in which I should tell my story. In the beginning of the story I need to tell who the characters are and the setting. Then in the middle I will tell about the problem. Finally, I will tell what happens at the end.

- Display Poster Book page 6A. Tell children that the first picture shows the beginning of the story. Tell them that a little flying squirrel named Squeak and her older brother Scurry lived in a tall tree. They decided to fly to the next tree to visit their cousins. Scurry knew how to fly. He spread out his legs and glided between the trees.

- Explain that the second picture shows the middle of the story. Ask a volunteer to describe what is happening in the middle of the story. (Sample answer: Squeak tried to fly, but she fell down.)

- Ask children to help you come up with an ending that solves Squeak's problem. Ask: *How do you think Squeak will get to the other tree if she cannot fly?* Draw the story ending. Be sure to use dry erase markers.

Poster Book p. 6A

MODELING DRAFTING   Poster Book p. 6A, Transparency 6–2

To model drafting, use Transparency 6–2, or copy the frame from the transparency onto chart paper. As children dictate text, reinforce mechanics skills they have learned by pointing out specific capital letters and end marks as you record them.

TITLE Explain that now you are ready to write your story. Display Transparency 6–2, and read the title aloud. Point out that the title tells what the story is about.

BEGINNING Explain that the beginning of a good story tells who the characters are and where the story takes place. Display Poster Book page 6A. Using the first picture on the Poster Book, draft the beginning of the story on the transparency. Read the first sentence and tell why it is a good beginning.

Think Aloud The beginning of the story should tell that the main characters are a little flying squirrel named Squeak and her big brother named Scurry. The beginning should also tell that the story takes place in a tall tree!

MIDDLE Have a volunteer identify the problem. Using the pictures on the Poster Book, have volunteers suggest sentences that describe the events in order. Record their suggestions on the transparency.

END Have children help you draft a good ending that tells how the problem was solved or how things worked out. Record it on the transparency.

Think Aloud To end this story, I need to decide how Squeak could solve her problem. What if she built a flying machine? What if she climbed to the next treetop instead of trying to fly again? Could Squeak become a champion climber instead? How else could the story end?

MODELING PUBLISHING

- Read the story aloud. Praise children for how well they helped you complete the story.

- Tell children that you will make a clean copy of the story. Help children plan how they will share their final copy of the story with their chosen audience.

 SCHOOL-HOME CONNECTION **Activity Master 102**

You may want to have a classroom volunteer or assistant print the story. This copy can be reproduced for children to illustrate and take home to share with family members. Children can also complete Activity Master 102 to share with their families.

MODELING REFLECTING

To help children think more about their writing experience, model the process of reflection.

Think Aloud I learned how important it is to include details about the character's problem and to show clearly how the character solves the problem.

The Bird That Could Not Sing

Focus Skill — Oral Language

③ Telling a Story

Lesson Objectives
Children will:
• retell a traditional story, using speaking tips
• use gestures and facial expressions in retelling a story

Materials
Activity Master 103

Warm-Up

Remind children that *Jamaica Tag-Along* is a story. Tell children that they are going to learn how to tell interesting stories to each other.

Teach

• Read a familiar story, such as *Goldilocks and the Three Bears* by Jan Brett, or retell it in your own words. Guide children in identifying the characters, setting, problem, and solution. Help them recall what happens in the beginning, middle, and end of the story.

• Help children prepare to tell the story orally. Tell them to follow these tips:

> **Speaking Tips**
> Look at your audience.
> Speak slowly, clearly, and loudly enough for everyone to hear.
> Use hand movements, facial expressions, and different voices to show how your characters talk, act, and feel.

• Then model how to tell a story by telling the beginning.

• Ask volunteers to tell the middle and end of the story. Have others take turns telling the whole story to the class on subsequent days.

Try It Out Activity Master 103

Help children dramatize "Little Red Riding Hood." First use a storybook version to remind children of the events. Then have children use Activity Master 103 to make stick puppets. Help children color, cut out, and glue the puppets. Then use the puppets to introduce the characters and model retelling the story. Then have children retell the story, prompting them with questions such as, *Whom did Little Red Riding Hood see in her grandmother's bed?*

Wrap-Up

Have children review the tips for storytelling and discuss what was difficult or easy for them. Point out that after writing stories, children can tell them aloud.

 INFORMAL ASSESSMENT (*See* Activity Masters Plus p. 45)

 MEETING INDIVIDUAL NEEDS (*See* p. 170)

INFLUENCE OF MEDIA
Present two versions of *Peter and the Wolf* by Sergei Prokofiev to show children the influence of media on storytelling. First, read a storybook and then play a recording of the music. Ask questions about how the music introduces characters, builds excitement, and expresses Peter's feelings. How do children feel music added to the story?
CD: *Sergei Prokofiev: Peter and the Wolf* conducted by Leonard Bernstein and the New York Philharmonic Orchestra, CBS Records

MEETING INDIVIDUAL NEEDS FOR STUDENTS ACQUIRING ENGLISH

Children may be unfamiliar with stories like "Little Red Riding Hood." Choose that as the oral story you model telling the class. Once they are familiar with the story, you can ask them to retell the beginning, middle, or end. Then find some visuals for the story that you use to begin and end it.

Activity Master p. 103

Focus Skill: Oral Language Name _____

Little Red Riding Hood

Unit 6 Lesson 3: Telling a Story
Directions: Have children color the puppets, cut them out, glue them on sticks, and use them to tell the story of "Little Red Riding Hood."

Activity Master 103
Houghton Mifflin English Level K
Use with Teacher's Edition page 159

Poster Book p. 6B

Sample answer: A flower is too hot in the sun. The other

flower lassos the watering can and waters the droopy flower.

Unit 6 Lesson 4: Interpreting Pictures
Directions: Have children look at the pictures to understand the whole story and then the details. Then have them tell the story.
Houghton Mifflin English Level K
Use with Teacher's Edition page 160.   **6B**

 FOR STUDENTS ACQUIRING ENGLISH

Before looking at the pictures on Activity Master 104, discuss words that children can use to describe feelings, such as *sad, scared, happy*. Use facial expressions to help define these emotions. Then as children look at the pictures, ask choice questions, such as *Is the boy happy or sad?*

Activity Master 104

Focus Skill: Viewing   Name _____

Look for a Story   Sample answers:

Two trucks are left outside the sandbox.

The dump truck dumps sand.

The bulldozer makes a ramp.

The trucks go up the ramp to get back into the sandbox.

104 Unit 6 Lesson 4: Interpreting Pictures
Directions: Have children look at the pictures to understand the whole story and then the details. Then have children draw a picture of a possible solution.
Activity Master
Houghton Mifflin English Level K
Use with Teacher's Edition page 160.

---

④ Interpreting Pictures

Lesson Objective

Children will:
• obtain information from picture details

Materials

Jamaica Tag-Along, Poster Book p. 6B, dry erase marker, Activity Master 104, magazine or catalog pictures of groups of people in different settings and situations

---

Warm-Up

Display pages 10–11 from *Jamaica Tag-Along*. Tell children to look carefully at the picture. Have children point out details about the characters. (Example: Ossie tells Jamaica to go away, and Jamaica's feelings are hurt.)

Teach Poster Book p. 6B

• Display Poster Book page 6B. Tell children that if they look carefully, they can get information from pictures. Tell children to look first at the whole series of pictures and then at the details. Ask children to tell what happens in the story.

• To help children focus on important details in the pictures, ask questions beginning with *who, what, when, where, why*, or *how*. For this story, ask: *What characters do you see? Where are they? What problem do they have? How do they solve the problem?*

Try It Out Activity Master 104

Have children look at the pictures to understand the whole story. Then have them look for important details. Finally, have them draw a picture of a possible ending for the story.

Wrap-Up

Have volunteers share their drawings on Activity Master 104 with the class. Point out that when children write their own stories they may want to draw pictures to help them show details about the characters, the setting, and the problem.

 INFORMAL ASSESSMENT (*See* Activity Masters Plus p. 45)

 MEETING INDIVIDUAL NEEDS (*See* p. 170)

Grammar

⑤ Singular and Plural Nouns

Poster Book p. 6C

Lesson Objective

Children will:
• recognize regular singular and plural nouns

Materials

Jamaica Tag-Along, Poster Book p. 6C, dry erase marker, Activity Master 105

Warm-Up

Display pages 12–13 of *Jamaica Tag-Along*. Ask children to name the people, animals, places, and things they see. Have children tell whether the words name one or more than one.

Teach Poster Book p. 6C

• Display Poster Book page 6C. Have children name all the people, animals, places, and things they see in the picture. List each one they identify.

• Read the lists aloud. Remind children that these words are called naming words, or nouns, because they name people, animals, places, and things.

• Ask a volunteer to point to a picture of only one person, animal, place, or thing. (Sample answer: ranger) Then have a volunteer point to pictures of groups of more than one person, animal, place, or thing. (Sample answer: raccoons) Point out that many naming words for groups of more than one end with the letter *s*. Have volunteers point to the *s* at the end of each plural.

Try It Out Activity Master 105

Ask children to complete Activity Master 105. Have children listen carefully for the sound of *s* at the end of the words you say aloud. Then they should circle pictures of one or more than one. For each one, have children tell you how they decided which picture to circle. Say:

Row 1: *Circle the picture of the <u>tent</u>.*
Row 2: *Circle the picture of the <u>clowns</u>.*
Row 3: *Circle the picture of the <u>cars</u>.*
Row 4: *Circle the picture of the <u>dog</u>.*

Wrap-Up

Point out to children that they have circled pictures of one or more than one person, animal, place, or thing on Activity Master 105. Have children count to explain which pictures they chose. Tell children that they will use naming words for one and more than one when they write their stories.

 INFORMAL ASSESSMENT (*See* Activity Masters Plus p. 46)

 MEETING INDIVIDUAL NEEDS (*See* p. 170)

 FOR STUDENTS ACQUIRING ENGLISH

Teach plurals using hands-on activities. Give each child one or more blocks. Then hold up a block and say: *One block.* Hold up two blocks and say: *Two blocks,* exaggerating the *s*. Finally, ask each child how many blocks he or she has. Listen for correct pronunciation of the plural ending.

Poster Book p. 6D

Focus Skill: Grammar

Name the Actions

Sample
answers:

ride	run	sit
flip	play	watch

Unit 6 Lesson 6: Verbs
Directions: Have children name the actions in the picture as you list the action words on the lines below.

Houghton Mifflin English Level 6
Use with Teacher's Edition page 162. **6D**

 FOR STUDENTS ACQUIRING ENGLISH

During the picture walk for *Jamaica Tag-Along*, call on children to act out each verb. For example, when the children see Jamaica talking, point to a child talking. For the Wrap-Up, be sure the word cards have pictures of all the actions so children will be able to "read."

Activity Master 106

Focus Skill: Grammar   Name

Name the Actions

1. Children color picture.

2. Children color picture.

3. Children color picture.

4. Children color picture.

106 Unit 6 Lesson 6: Verbs
Directions: Have children color the pictures that show actions and name the actions.

Activity Master
Houghton Mifflin English Level K
Use with Teacher's Edition page 162.

Focus Skill   **Grammar**

⑥ Verbs

Lesson Objective

Children will:
• identify actions and name verbs

Materials

Jamaica Tag-Along, Poster Book p. 6D, dry erase marker, Activity Master 106

Warm-Up

Display pages 6–17 of *Jamaica Tag-Along*, having children identify a variety of actions as you ask what different characters are doing. Then have children use action words to name other things they might do at a playground.

Teach   Poster Book p. 6D

• Remind children they have already learned that words that name actions are called action words. Tell them that action words are also called verbs.

• Display Poster Book page 6D. Tell children that they are looking at a painting called *The Circus* by Georges Seurat. Have children share what they know about circuses.

• Then have children look closely at the picture. Ask: *What is the lady on the horse doing? What is the acrobat doing?* Write the base form of each verb on the poster.

• Read aloud the action words you listed on the Poster Book, tracking each word from left to right. Remind children that action words tell what people, animals, or things do.

Try It Out   Activity Master 106

Have children identify the pictures on Activity Master 106. Ask them to color only the pictures that show actions.

Wrap-Up

Ask children to share their answers on Activity Master 106. Have them name an action word for each picture they colored. (Sample answers: *ride, bounce, jump, build*) Make a picture-word card for each action word. Use these cards and other action words children name to begin an Action Word Wall. Tell children they can use these words when they write their stories.

 INFORMAL ASSESSMENT (*See* Activity Masters Plus p. 46)

 MEETING INDIVIDUAL NEEDS (*See* p. 171)

(7) Opposites

Lesson Objective

Children will:
• recognize opposites

Materials

Jamaica Tag-Along, Poster Book p. 6E, dry erase marker, Activity Master 107

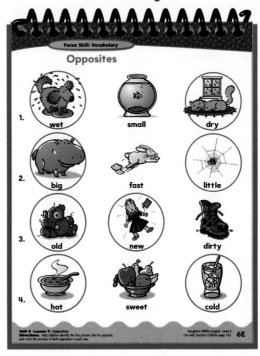

Poster Book p. 6E

Warm-Up

Display pages 18–19 of *Jamaica Tag-Along*. Remind children that Berto's mother told him, "Big kids don't like to be bothered by little kids." Point out that the word *little* means "not big," so *little* and *big* are opposites.

Teach Poster Book p. 6E

• Tell children that just as *big* and *little* are opposites, some other pairs of words are opposites.

• Remind children that on pages 16–17, Jamaica used wet sand to make a mound, while Berto sprinkled dry sand on the walls. Point out that *wet* and *dry* are opposites. Make the concept more concrete by showing children wet and dry paper towels. Make sure children understand that if the paper towel is wet, it is not dry, so the words *wet* and *dry* are opposites.

• Display Poster Book page 6E. Discuss the pictures in the first row with children. Use the labels to discuss the pictures. Ask: *Which word means "not wet"? Is it* small? (no) *Is it* dry? (yes) Explain that *wet* and *dry* are opposites. Repeat with the remaining rows of pictures and labels.

Try It Out Activity Master 107

Have children complete Activity Master 107. Help children identify the pictures for the words *big, long, fast,* and *high*. Then have children draw a picture that shows the opposite of each one. (Sample answers: <u>little</u> fly, <u>short</u> mouse, <u>slow</u> turtle, <u>low</u> ant)

Wrap-Up

Have children share their answers to Activity Master 107.

 INFORMAL ASSESSMENT (*See* Activity Masters Plus p. 47)

 MEETING INDIVIDUAL NEEDS (*See* p. 171)

 FOR STUDENTS ACQUIRING ENGLISH

Hands-on lessons to teach opposites are excellent for children acquiring English. Continue to use manipulatives throughout the exercises. When you ask children to illustrate opposites, provide examples that they can copy, such as *a hard block* and *a soft tissue*.

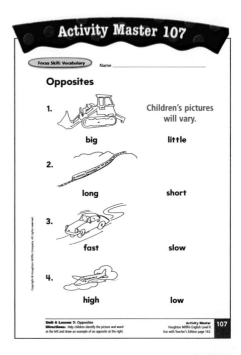

Poster Book p. 6F

Beginning

Middle

End

Sample answer: The painter uses the hose to wash off the dalmatian puppy.

Unit 6 Lesson 8: A Good Ending
Directions: Have children tell what is happening in the beginning and middle of the story. Then have children suggest an ending that will solve the character's problem.

Houghton Mifflin English Level K
Use with Teacher's Edition page 164. **6F**

 FOR STUDENTS ACQUIRING ENGLISH

Brainstorm vocabulary that children can use to discuss their endings. (My story ends with____.) For extra practice, use comic strips from newspapers. Cut out each scene from two comic strips, and have children order the scenes for good endings.

Activity Master 108

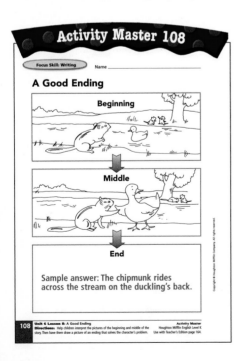

Focus Skill: Writing   Name ____

A Good Ending

Beginning

Middle

End

Sample answer: The chipmunk rides across the stream on the duckling's back.

108 Unit 6 Lesson 8: A Good Ending
Directions: Help children interpret the pictures of the beginning and middle of the story. Then have them draw a picture of an ending that solves the character's problem.

Activity Master
Houghton Mifflin English Level K
Use with Teacher's Edition page 164.

Focus Skill **Writing**

⑧ A Good Ending

Lesson Objective

Children will:

- contribute to a good story ending

Materials

Poster Book p. 6F, dry erase markers, Activity Master 108

Warm-Up

Recall with children the problem in *Jamaica Tag-Along*. (Sample answer: Jamaica wants to play with Ossie, but he does not want her to tag along.) Then ask children how the problem is solved. (Jamaica makes a new friend and does something special on her own.) Point out to children that Jamaica solves her problem at the end of the story.

Teach Poster Book p. 6F

- Remind children that a good story has characters who have an interesting problem to solve. Explain that a good story ending tells how the character solved the problem or how things worked out in a way that makes sense with the rest of the story.

- Display Poster Book page 6F. Point out that the pictures tell a story. Ask: *Who are the main characters? Where are they? What happens to them? How can the dalmatian solve his problem? How can the painter solve his problem?* Discuss children's suggestions for a possible solution, and agree on a story ending that shows how things worked out in a way that makes sense with the rest of the story. List key words, draw the ending, or ask volunteers to draw parts of the story ending.

Try It Out Activity Master 108

Ask children to look at the beginning and middle pictures on Activity Master 108. Ask: Who seems to have a problem? What is the chipmunk's problem? How could the chipmunk get across the stream? Remind children that the ending needs to make sense with the rest of the story. Children may suggest several reasonable endings. Then have them draw a good ending for the story.

Wrap-Up

Children can work with partners to share their story endings. They should discuss how their endings show the way the characters solved their problem. Tell children that when they write their own stories, they will write endings that show how their characters solve the problem.

 INFORMAL ASSESSMENT (*See* Activity Masters Plus p. 46)

 MEETING INDIVIDUAL NEEDS (*See* p. 171)

⑨ Story

Lesson Objectives

Children will:
- choose a topic and an audience for a story
- contribute to a story, using the steps of the writing process
- reflect on their writing experience

Materials

Poster Book p. 6G, Transparency 6–3 or chart paper, dry erase markers

Focus on Instruction

Explain to children that you are going to work together to write a story. Tell them that they are going to follow the steps that good writers use when writing something that others will read.

PREWRITING

Choose a Topic

- Help children decide what kind of story they will write and who will read or listen to it. Tell children that the story could be about something that could really happen or something make-believe. Ask them whom they will write the story for. Will it be their families? another class? friends?

- First, have children think of story characters that they would enjoy writing about. List the ideas on chart paper. Next, ask children to think about a problem each character might have. List it next to the character. Work together to generate three or four topic ideas. Then help children choose a topic. Ask: *Which topic do we have the most ideas about? Which one would we really enjoy writing about?*

Plan the Story Poster Book p. 6G

- Display Poster Book page 6G. Work together with children to list details for the story beginning, middle, and ending. Remind children to include where the story takes place and to name the main character and describe him/her/it. Prompt children to give some details by asking *who, what, why, when, where,* and *how* questions.

- Keep children focused on one main problem for the story, If they want to tell a lot of details unrelated to the story problem, explain that they don't need to tell everything—just the important details about how the characters solved the problem.

- Record children's ideas by writing key words or drawing simple pictures in appropriate places on the graphic organizers.

Topic Ideas

- a chipmunk has to find a birthday gift for a friend
- a dog forgets where he buried his favorite bone
- a child loses a library book
- a shy child has to perform in a class play
- a friendly giant gets lost in the forest
- a kangaroo becomes a basketball star

Poster Book p. 6G

Shared Writing: Prewriting
Planning Our Story
Title _Answers will vary._

Beginning

Middle

End

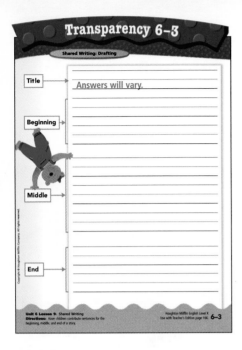

Transparency 6–3

Shared Writing: Drafting

Title — Answers will vary.

Beginning

Middle

End

Unit 6 **Lesson 9:** Shared Writing
Directions: Have children contribute sentences for the beginning, middle, and end of a story.

Houghton Mifflin English Level K
Use with Teacher's Edition page 166. **6–3**

NOTE As you draft, point out the correct use of capital letters and punctuation marks that children have learned. You may also wish to leave in several general verbs that children can replace with exact verbs when they revise the story.

DRAFTING   Transparency 6–3, Poster Book p. 6G

- Before drafting, review and discuss with children what makes a great story.

What Makes a Great Story?

- The story is about something make-believe.

- The story has a beginning, a middle, and an end.

- Details tell where the story takes place, who the characters are, and what problem they have.

- The story tells what happened in order.

- A good ending tells how the problem was solved or how things worked out.

- Now ask volunteers to contribute text ideas for each element of the draft, using the completed graphic organizer on Poster Book page 6G as a guide. Record children's suggestions on Transparency 6–3 or on chart paper. Help children generate the following:

  - an interesting **title** that will make people want to read the story

  - a **beginning** that introduces the **characters** and the **setting**

  - a **middle** that introduces a problem and describes how the characters deal with the problem

  - an **ending** that tells how the characters **solved the problem**

- Read the story together, and praise children for their contributions.

- Reread your draft together, asking children to evaluate their story by using the Questions for Revising. Make changes or additions children suggest to improve the story.

> **Questions for Revising**
>
> ✔ Does our story have a beginning, a middle, and an end?
>
> ✔ Did we tell what happens in order?
>
> ✔ Did we use details to tell who the characters are, where the story takes place, and what problem they have?
>
> ✔ Does our ending tell how the problem is solved or how things worked out?

- Remind children that exact action words will help their audience picture a character's actions. Together, find any general action words that can be replaced with more exact ones.

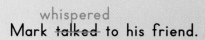

whispered

Mark ~~talked~~ to his friend.

PUBLISHING

Tell children you will make a clean final copy of the story for them. Have children illustrate their own copies. Help children plan how they will share their final copy of the story with their chosen audience.

 SCHOOL-HOME CONNECTION Suggest that children take their own copies home to use when they retell the story for family members.

REFLECTING

Praise children for planning and writing a story so thoughtfully. Discuss their writing experience with them. Ask:

- *What was easy about thinking of characters and their problems? What was hard?*

- *How did using the beginning, middle, and end chart help you write the story?*

- *What did you learn that will help you the next time you write a story?*

MEETING INDIVIDUAL NEEDS

FOR STUDENTS ACQUIRING ENGLISH
Make sure children can identify the beginning, middle, and end of a story. Review a story familiar to all by asking: *What happens at the beginning? What happens in the middle? What happens in the end?* Then ask children to identify what happens in the beginning, middle, and end of the story the group has written.

10 Story

Lesson Objectives	Materials
Children will: • tell, dictate, or write a story • listen and respond to the writing of peers	drawing paper, writing paper, Activity Master 109

Focus on Instruction

Tell children that now they will write their own stories. Explain that first they must decide what kind of stories they want to write and for whom they will write them. Here are some ideas you might use to help children plan, write, and share their work.

Planning Ideas

THINKING ABOUT TOPICS Help children list possible topics for stories by using their favorite stories as a springboard for ideas. What interesting characters, settings, and problems have they heard about? If individuals are having difficulty thinking of a topic, try reading one of the Writing Prompts on page 169. You might also read aloud some of the books in the Bibliography on page 154 to help spark a topic idea.

ORGANIZING IDEAS Before they begin writing, have children draw a picture of their character dealing with his or her problem. Then have children share their picture with a partner and tell how their character solves the problem.

Writing

Allow children to produce their stories in the format that is most appropriate to their own stage of development, as indicated in the chart below.

Writing Options		
Emergent Writers	**Early Beginning Writers**	**Late Beginning and Transitional Writers**
Have children draw pictures to represent the beginning, middle, and end of their stories. They can then add pretend or "scribble" writing and tell their stories to an adult, or they can dictate their stories to an adult to record.*	Children can draw pictures to represent the beginning, middle, and end of their stories. They can then label them with single words or phrases and tell their stories to an adult, or they can dictate their stories to an adult to record.*	Children can write their stories, using temporary spelling. They can add illustrations to support their text.
*Some children may feel their writing is not valid if an adult rewrites it.		

 INFORMAL ASSESSMENT (*See* Activity Masters Plus p. 46)

 FOR STUDENTS ACQUIRING ENGLISH

Remember that children acquiring English have different levels of proficiency. Children will be at emergent, beginning, and transitional levels for overall language acquisition. Children at all levels can be expected to draw pictures of their stories and label them with either real or scribble writing.

Writing Portfolio

If you are collecting samples of children's writing, decide if you want to save this piece.

Student Sample

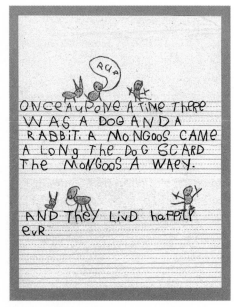

ONCE AUPONE A TIME THERE WAS A DOG AND A RABBIT. A MONGOOS CAME A LONG THE DOG SCARD THE MONGOOS A WAEY.

AND THEY LIVD HAPPLY EVR.

Late Beginning Writer

Ideas for Sharing

Have children share their completed stories with the whole class or with a classmate. They can share their work by "reading" it aloud or by using one of the suggestions below.

Write It Children can write the beginning, middle, and end of their stories on separate pieces of paper, add illustrations, and bind the pages to make a booklet.

Say It Have children make stick puppets with craft sticks and construction paper to represent characters in their stories. They can use these aids to enhance their oral storytelling.

Show It Have children draw illustrations for their stories in three panels, like a comic strip. They can use the comic strips as props while they tell the stories.

After each child shares his or her work, the listener or listeners should tell the author at least one thing they liked about the story. (Examples: I like the way you described your characters. Your character's problem was interesting. I really wanted to know how your character solved the problem.)

 INTERNET CONNECTION
See www.eduplace.com/rdg/hme/ for printable patterns for making shape paper booklets.

 FOR STUDENTS ACQUIRING ENGLISH
Remember that children acquiring English have different levels of proficiency. Children will be at emergent, beginning, and transitional levels for overall language acquisition. Children at all levels can be expected to draw pictures of their stories and label them with either real or scribble writing.

Writing Prompts

ART Activity Master 109

Color the pictures on Activity Master 109. Then use the pictures to dictate or write a story. Be sure to tell who the characters are, where the story takes place, what the problem is, and how the problem is solved.

SOCIAL STUDIES

Think about a worker in your neighborhood, such as a police officer, a firefighter, or a store owner. What is a problem the worker might have? What could be done to solve it? How could other people in the neighborhood help? Write a story about it. Be sure to begin by telling who your characters are and where the story takes place.

 INTERNET CONNECTION
See www.eduplace.com/rdg/hme/ for more writing ideas.

Meeting Individual Needs

Lesson 3 Focus Skill Oral Language: Telling a Story

RETEACHING Alternative Strategy
Tell a short, familiar story such as "The Three Little Pigs" twice. First tell the story in a monotone, disregarding all the storytelling tips. Then retell the story using good speaking skills, gestures, and facial expressions. Ask children to tell how you made the story more interesting the second time.

CHALLENGE
Have pairs take turns telling the same story. Children should make their versions special by adding details, sound effects, and hand gestures. They might even change the story events or the ending. Some children may wish to tell their stories for the rest of the class.

FOR STUDENTS ACQUIRING ENGLISH
Because children acquiring English may not be familiar with "typical" stories from the United States, try using a story that they enjoyed from a previous unit. Tell the story, stopping often to ask children to name the characters and recall what happens next.

Lesson 4 Focus Skill Viewing: Interpreting Pictures

RETEACHING Alternative Strategy
Show a picture book, and have children try to tell the story by looking at the pictures. Ask questions to draw children's attention to things in the pictures the children need to notice to understand the story, the characters, and the setting.

CHALLENGE
Provide children with series of pictures that tell stories, such as wordless books or cartoons. Have children ask themselves questions to interpret the pictures and then make up a retelling of the story. Pairs or small groups of children can tell their stories to each other.

FOR STUDENTS ACQUIRING ENGLISH
Because the first step in interpreting a picture is identification, help children do so. Use the magazine photos from the Challenge activity. Pass them to small groups of children and have them identify all the nouns and verbs they see. Then ask children to determine what's happening. Set up the pictures in simple sequences of three and guide children to retell a "story" by describing what's happening from picture to picture.

Lesson 5 Focus Skill Grammar: Singular and Plural Nouns

RETEACHING Alternative Strategy
Use math counters or small objects such as blocks, bears, cats, and dogs whose names form regular plurals by adding s. As you show one or more objects to children, have them name the objects using the singular or plural naming word. Write the singular word in one column and the plural word in a second column, pointing out the s ending on each plural.

CHALLENGE
Demonstrate this version of Concentration. Provide pairs of picture cards showing nouns that form regular plurals by adding s (ball/balls, cat/cats, doll/dolls). Have players mix up the cards and put them in a grid facedown. Then players take turns turning over two cards to find a matching pair. If the player can say the correct nouns, the player keeps the cards. The player with the most cards wins.

FOR STUDENTS ACQUIRING ENGLISH
Play a game of I Spy with the children, using either a book with busy illustrations or the classroom itself. Alternate spying singular and plural nouns. You begin by naming an object or objects, and the child who first finds what you named names the next noun. When plural nouns are named, stress the final s at the end of regular plurals and have children repeat after you.

Lesson 6 Focus Skill   Grammar: Verbs

RETEACHING ALTERNATIVE STRATEGY
Have children take turns pantomiming actions for others to guess. Record the action words that children name. Read the action words aloud. Remind children that the words tell about actions and are called action words, or verbs.

CHALLENGE
Help children create charts to fill in with action words they can act out. Use this sentence frame: *I can _____.* Have partners challenge each other to act out different actions, such as to hop, run, or sing. Then children can write or dictate action words, or verbs, to add to their charts. Have partners share their charts with the class, with one child acting out the verbs and the other reading the chart.

FOR STUDENTS ACQUIRING ENGLISH
Play a game of Charades. Form two teams. Have one player from each team come up to you. Whisper a verb to each player and have the child act it out for his or her team. The child who guesses correctly earns a point for his or her team and the opportunity to be the actor.

Lesson 7 Focus Skill   Vocabulary: Opposites

RETEACHING ALTERNATIVE STRATEGY
Demonstrate the opposites *on* and *off* by turning a light on and off. Say: *Now the light is on.* (Switch the light off.) *Now it is not on. It is _____.* (off) Repeat with other common pairs of opposites *right/left* (shown with hands), *in/out* and *go/come* (shown at classroom door), *fast/slow*, *cold/hot*, and *high/low*.

CHALLENGE
Have children work with partners to create opposite picture dictionaries. First, one partner names a word and the other dictates its opposite to make an opposites list. Then children illustrate as many opposites as they can. Help them label their drawings to create opposites picture dictionaries.

FOR STUDENTS ACQUIRING ENGLISH
Make sure that children understand that all the describing words used in the Reteaching activity are *opposites*. Present additional examples: *tall/short*, *clean/dirty*, *old/new* and demonstrate by using classroom objects as examples.

Lesson 8 Focus Skill   Writing: A Good Ending

RETEACHING ALTERNATIVE STRATEGY
Show pictures from a book, retelling a familiar story such as "The Gingerbread Man." Pause to show a picture in the middle of the story where people are chasing the Gingerbread Man. Ask: *Would this make a good ending? Does it show how the story turns out?* (no) Then show children the final picture of the fox gobbling up the Gingerbread Man. Ask: *Does this picture make a good ending?* (yes)*Why?*

CHALLENGE
Retell the beginning of a familiar story, such as "The Little Red Hen." Have children discuss the characters, the setting, and the problem. Then talk about the conventional ending of the story and how it solves the problem. Ask children to draw endings that show other ways to solve the problem.

FOR STUDENTS ACQUIRING ENGLISH
Cut out comic strips from newspapers. Separate the last scene from each one. Have the children form groups and give each one an unfinished comic scene. Then challenge the groups to figure out what is happening and to discuss and sketch two possible endings. Have a class sharing.

Unit 7
Instructions

In this unit, children are introduced to explanatory writing. They listen to a book about gardening and participate in the modeled writing of instructions that explain how to plant a garden. Then children work together with you to create a set of instructions, using the writing process. Unit skills develop language as well as relate to and support explanatory writing.

What You Will Find in This Unit . . .

Unit 7 Planning Guide
Instructions

	Poster Book	Transparency	Activity Masters Plus
DAILY COMMUNICATION LINKS **Daily Routines** *(176–177)* The oral language activities provide daily opportunities for children to develop the basic concepts and skills needed to compose instructions. • **Interactive Bulletin Board:** Calendar, Daily Message, Where Is the Bear? • **Daily Discussion Activity:** How to Make Butter *See also* Additional Resources *(253)* **Center Activities** *(178–179)* • Reading and Listening Center • Creative Arts Center • Block Center • Writing Center		7–1	
A Published Model ⏱ *1 day, 20 minutes* **Lesson 1** Listening to Instructions *(180–181)* *This Is Your Garden*			
Modeled Writing ⏱ *about 2–3 days, 20 minutes each day* **Lesson 2** Instructions *(182–184)*	7A	7–2	110
Focus Skills ⏱ *about 6 days, 20 minutes each day* **Lesson 3** Oral Language: Following and Giving Directions *(185)*	7B		111
Lesson 4 Viewing: Following Visual Instructions *(186)*	7C		112
Lesson 5 Grammar: Verbs *(187)*	7D		113
Lesson 6 Vocabulary: Exact Verbs *(188)*	7E		114
Lesson 7 Vocabulary: Positional Words: *on, in, under, behind, beside, over, in front of, between (189)*	7F		115
Lesson 8 Writing: Sequence *(190)*			116
Shared Writing ⏱ *about 2–3 days, 20 minutes each day* **Lesson 9** Instructions *(191–193)*	7G	7–3	
Independent Writing ⏱ *about 1–3 days, 20 minutes each day* **Lesson 10** Instructions *(194–195)* ✓ **Writing Prompts** *(195)*			117

 MEETING INDIVIDUAL NEEDS *(196–197)*

Activities for Special Needs/Inclusion, for Students Acquiring English, for Reteaching, and for Enrichment/Challenge

Meeting Individual Needs

▶ **FOR SPECIAL NEEDS/INCLUSION:** *Houghton Mifflin English* Audiotape ; *See also* Reteaching.

▶ **FOR STUDENTS ACQUIRING ENGLISH:**
- Notes and activities are included in this Teacher's Edition throughout the unit to help you adapt or use lessons with students acquiring English.
- Students can listen to the published model *This Is Your Garden* on audiotape.

▶ **RETEACHING**
- Activities for reteaching the focus skills are included on pages 196–197.

▶ **ENRICHMENT/CHALLENGE**
- Activities for challenge/enrichment that are correlated to focus skill lessons are included on pages 196–197.

All audiotape recordings are also available on CD.

Additional Resources

Audiotapes

 Technology Tools
CD-ROM: Curious George® Paint & Print Studio
Paint, Write & Play! (published by The Learning Company)
*Type to Learn Jr.™

*©Sunburst Technology Corporation, a Houghton Mifflin Company. All rights reserved.

INTERNET: http://www.eduplace.com/rdg/hme/
Visit Education Place for these additional support materials and activities:
- author biographies
- patterns for shape booklets
- writing prompts

 Informal Assessment
Activity Masters Plus, Assessment Checklists, pages 45–47

 Keeping a Journal
In kindergarten, journals can be blank notebooks or folders filled with paper. As children draw and write about school activities, important events, and special thoughts, they can watch their writing growth as the year progresses.

School-Home Connection
Suggestions for informing or involving family members in learning related to this unit are included in the Teacher's Edition throughout the unit.

Daily Routines

The oral language activities suggested here provide daily opportunities for children to develop basic concepts and skills they will need to compose instructions. Refer to the **Interactive Bulletin Board** and **Daily Discussion** ideas on pages 10–13 and 20–21 for help in establishing Daily Routines for your classroom.

Interactive Bulletin Board

The Calendar

Each day as you complete bulletin board routines, have different volunteers direct you by explaining what to do. Follow their instructions exactly, even if they are not accurate. Help children see that instructions must include all the steps in the proper order.

Daily Message

Push in your chair when you leave the table.

Daily Message

Children can help you compose a message that includes instructions each day.

Where Is the Bear?

Ask volunteers to find Claire Bear by following your instructions (*See* page 13).

Daily Discussion

Read aloud the instructions **How to Make Butter** below. Then discuss them with children, using the Think and Discuss questions. Do an activity like this daily, using different sets of instructions children may encounter in the classroom (*See also* Additional Resources page 253). You might, for example, present instructions that

- explain what to do during a fire drill,
- tell how to play a game, or
- explain how to operate a piece of equipment, such as a tape recorder.

Think and Discuss

- What do these instructions explain? Where might you find this kind of instructions?
- What do the instructions say to do?
- In what order are the steps? Are any steps missing?
- What words help make the order of the steps clear?
- Do you think these instructions are easy or hard to follow? Why?

ORDER WORDS As you read and discuss various instructions, have children identify order words such as *first*, *next*, *then*, *last*, and *finally*. Add these words to your word wall.

VERBS Keep a chart that categorizes common verbs used in different types of instructions. For example, workbook page instructions use verbs such as *write*, *draw*, and *cut*. Recipe instructions use verbs such as *mix*, *pour*, and *bake*. Allow volunteers to illustrate or pantomime the words on the chart.

Daily Discussion Activity

How to Make Butter

Making butter is easy and fun! All you need is whipping cream, salt, and a clean jar with a lid. First, leave the cream outside your refrigerator for two hours. Next, pour the cream into a jar, leaving space at the top. Then put on the lid and shake, shake, shake! You and your friends can take turns shaking the jar. Finally, when butter forms, pour off the extra cream and add a pinch of salt for taste. If you thought making butter was fun, just wait until you taste it on some bread or crackers!

Center Activities

Center Activities provide additional daily opportunities to develop and reinforce concepts and skills that support the composing of instructions.

Reading and Listening Center

PUBLISHED MODEL  Children can listen to the audiotape of *This Is Your Garden* as they follow along in the book. **Listening**

ORAL INSTRUCTIONS On a blank tape, pre-record drawing instructions for children to follow. For example, say: *First, draw a circle on your paper. Next, draw two little circles side by side in the top half of the big circle. Finally, draw a curved line under the two little circles. What have you drawn?* (a face) **Listening**

VISUAL INSTRUCTIONS Have children "read" copies of the illustrated instructions found in Additional Resources, page 253. **Viewing**

Block Center

EXPLAINING STEPS As children build constructions, have them explain what they are doing as they work. Challenge children to build a garden wall. Ask: *What do you do first, next, and last? What size block did you use first?* In addition, you can challenge one child to give another child instructions for building something, such as a high-rise apartment building or a circus ring. **Listening/Speaking**

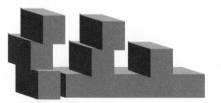

About the Author

Maggie Smith

Maggie Smith lives in a small apartment in New York City with her cat, Phoenix. The author makes pictures of flowers rather than weeding them! She has written and illustrated five other picture books.

Bibliography

You may wish to read aloud the following books that include well-written instructions.

- ***Planting a Rainbow***
  by Lois Ehlert
- ***It's Pumpkin Time***
  by Zoe Hall
- ***Growing Vegetable Soup***
  by Lois Ehlert
- ***One Bean***
  by Anne Rockwell

 FOR STUDENTS ACQUIRING ENGLISH

Before reading, hand each child or pair of children a picture-word card for a vocabulary word. Inform them that each time the item from their card is mentioned they should hold up the card for the class to see. Also as you read, pause often to ask questions: *What must you do first to start a garden? What comes next? What materials do you need for these steps?* (Answers will vary.)

A Published Model

1 Listening to Instructions

Lesson Objectives

Children will:
- listen to and discuss the characteristics of a published model of instructions
- listen for sequence
- understand the meaning of figurative language
- evaluate the relationship of visuals and text
- respond personally and critically to the selection

Materials

This Is Your Garden, tag board, crayons or markers

Reading the Model

The book *This Is Your Garden* includes explanatory text giving instructions for how to plant and tend a flower garden.

Building Background

Ask children to share what they know about gardens. Have they ever grown a garden? What tools do gardeners use? What do plants need to grow? Ask volunteers to name and describe different kinds of gardens. (Sample answers: flower garden, vegetable garden, herb garden, orchard)

Introducing Vocabulary

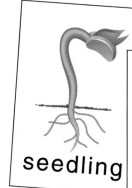

- Make a picture-word card for each key vocabulary word: *soil, seed, seedling, plant,* and *flower.* As you display each card, discuss what each word means.

- Describe how a seed becomes a flowering plant, using the picture-word card for each vocabulary word.

Predicting and Purpose Setting

PICTURE WALK Display *This Is Your Garden* and read the title aloud. Point out the author and illustrator's name. Take a picture walk through the selection, stopping at each page to allow children to tell what they see. Point out that the girl is holding seeds on page 5 and planting seeds on page 7. Then ask children to predict what they think the book will be about.

Tell children that good instructions are in an order that makes sense. Explain that as you read, children should listen carefully to find out how to grow a garden. Read *This Is Your Garden* aloud. Then ask: *How did your predictions about the book compare with what you heard?*

 This selection is also available on audiotape.

Listening As a Writer

Think About the Instructions

SEQUENCE Ask volunteers to retell in order the steps for growing a garden shared in the book. Discuss what would happen if a step were left out or if the steps were told in a different order. For example, what might happen if someone scattered the seeds first and then dug the bed? (The seeds would be moved around and not be in the right place.) Help children conclude that it is important that instructions include all the steps in the correct order.

ORDER WORDS Reread pages 6–9 of the selection, emphasizing the words *First, Then, Now,* and *Soon*. Discuss how these words help make the order of the steps and the passage of time clear.

First
Then
Now
Soon

Think About Writer's Craft

FIGURATIVE LANGUAGE Display and reread pages 6–7. The author describes making a "soft bed in the ground" and covering the seeds with "a blanket of earth." Discuss why the author compared the garden to a bed. Ask: *How is the bed for the seeds like your bed?* (The seeds lie in it.) *What kind of blanket should cover the seeds?* (dirt) *How is it like your blanket?* (It keeps the seeds warm.) *How is it different?* (Sample answer: The plants can grow through it.)

Think About the Pictures

Take another picture walk through the selection. Ask: *How do the pictures help make the instructions clearer?* (They show more details.)

NOTE If children are discussing and responding to *This Is Your Garden* on a day following your initial reading, reread the book.

Responding

- **Personal Response** Have children draw and then dictate or write about a garden they would like to plant. Encourage them to share their work with classmates.

- **Critical Thinking** Ask: *How did this story help you learn how to plant a garden?* (Sample answers: It told the steps in order.) *What else would you like to know about planting a garden?*

FOR STUDENTS ACQUIRING ENGLISH

Taking another picture walk through the book is an excellent way for the children who are acquiring English to review the steps. Pause at the description and illustration of each major step and ask the children to tell what is happening in the picture. For further practice, encourage small groups of volunteers to pantomime the step being described.

Modeled Writing

② Instructions

Lesson Objectives

Children will:

- recognize the purpose, use, and characteristics of instructions
- understand purpose and audience
- become familiar with the steps of the writing process
- help plan and draft a set of instructions

Materials

Poster Book p. 7A, Transparency 7–2 or chart paper, dry erase markers, Activity Master 110

Optional Materials

potting soil, planting container, hand trowel, seeds, watering can

Focus on Instruction

- Remind children that *This Is Your Garden* includes well-written instructions. Ask children what other instructions they have heard, such as instructions for what to do in a fire drill.

- Discuss reasons why people might write instructions. Help children understand that sometimes people write instructions for themselves so they can remember what to do at a later time, and sometimes people write instructions to help others learn how to do something.

MODELING PREWRITING

Choose a Topic

Tell children that you want to write some instructions and that you would like their help. Explain that first you need to decide what instructions you are going to write and for whom you are going to write them.

Think Aloud I have a young friend who loves flowers and wants to plant a garden. I would like to write instructions for how to grow a garden and send them to him.

Instructions

how to cook a . . .
how to build a . . .
how to fix a . . .
how to make a . . .
how to play . . .
how to use a . . .
what to do if . . .

Purpose
Audience

Plan the Instructions Poster Book p. 7A

- Tell children that before you begin to write, you need to make a plan.

Think Aloud Before I start writing my instructions, I want to think about what I want to say. I need to know what steps to tell about and in what order to tell them.

- Display Poster Book page 7A. Explain that the pictures show what to do to grow a garden. Have volunteers describe what is happening in each illustration. Ask children to help you number the pictures in order and then label them with the order words *First, Next, Then,* and *Last.* Be sure to use a dry erase marker.

MODELING DRAFTING Transparency 7–2, Poster Book p. 7A

To model drafting, use Transparency 7–2, or copy the frame from the transparency onto chart paper. As children dictate text, reinforce mechanics skills they have learned by pointing out specific capital letters and punctuation marks as you record them.

TITLE Explain that now you are ready to write your instructions. Display Transparency 7–2 and read the title aloud. Point out that the title tells what the instructions are about.

BEGINNING SENTENCE Tell children that good instructions need an interesting first sentence that tells the reader, or audience, the topic of the instructions. Read together the beginning sentence on the transparency.

Think Aloud This is a good beginning sentence because it tells what the instructions will be about and it makes me interested in reading more.

STEPS Have children help you draft the main text. Using the pictures and the order words on Poster Book page 7A as prompts, have volunteers suggest a sentence for each step of the instructions. Record their suggestions on the transparency. Remind children that you will need to write down all the steps in order.

ENDING SENTENCE Together, generate a good ending sentence. Record it on the transparency.

Think Aloud Now we need to think of a good ending sentence that shows I'm finished and that will make my friend want to follow the instructions.

FOR STUDENTS ACQUIRING ENGLISH

Use a brief think-aloud activity to model how to draft instructions for planting a garden. Say: *How would I begin?* Then write sentence stems featuring order words to structure the model: *First, _____. Next, _____. Then _____. Last, _____.*

How to Grow a Garden

How would you like to plant your own garden?

First, dig some holes in the ground.

Next, put the seeds in the holes.

Then cover the seeds with dirt.

Last, water the seeds.

Soon you will have a beautiful garden.

MODELING PUBLISHING

- Have children read the completed instructions chorally. Praise them for their help in writing the instructions.

- Explain that you plan to make a clean, neat copy of the instructions to send to your friend. Discuss different ways of sending the instructions, such as by regular mail or by e-mail.

 SCHOOL-HOME CONNECTION Activity Master 110

Have a classroom volunteer or assistant type the instructions. Children can illustrate and take home copies to share with family members. Have children complete Activity Master 110 and put the steps in order to show how to make a picture book.

MODELING REFLECTING

Help children think about their writing. Model the process of reflection.

Think Aloud I liked using the pictures in the Poster Book to help me plan my instructions. I learned how important it is to put all the steps in order.

Poster Book p. 7B

Focus Skill: Oral Language
Using Instructions

Unit 7 Lesson 3: Following and Giving Instructions
Directions: Have children follow several sets of three-step instructions you read from the Teacher's Edition. Then have them make up three-step instructions for other children to follow.

Houghton Mifflin English Level K
Use with Teacher's Edition page 185.   7B

Oral Language

③ Following and Giving Instructions

Lesson Objective
Children will:
• follow and give three-step oral instructions

Materials
Poster Book p. 7B, Activity Master 111, dry erase markers, crayons, drawing paper

Warm-Up

Tell children that people can give instructions by speaking as well as by writing. Ask children where they hear spoken instructions (at home, at school). Give volunteers simple two-step directions to get from one area of the classroom to another. For example, say: *From the classroom door, walk to the rug. Then turn left into the Reading Center.*

Teach Poster Book p. 7B

• Tell children it's important to listen carefully to spoken instructions. Say: *Listen for order words. Listen for words that tell you what to do, such as* Draw flowers. *Listen for details.*

• Display Poster Book page 7B, and ask children what they see. Tell them to listen carefully to the following instructions: *First, circle the boy. Next, draw a line from the boy to the flower garden. Then draw flowers in the garden.*

As you read the instructions again, have a volunteer use a dry erase marker to follow them. Together, check the result.

• Erase the drawings on the page, and give different instructions: *First, put an X on the bird. Next, draw a line from the bird to the vegetable garden. Then draw tomatoes in the garden.*

Erase the page again. Have volunteers make up their own three-step directions for others, using the words *first, next,* and *then.*

Try It Out Activity Master 111

Have children listen carefully as you read these directions aloud: *First, draw the missing flowers on the four stems. Next, draw the missing leaves. Then color the picture.* Read the directions aloud a second time.

Wrap-Up

Ask children to share their pictures. Discuss how important it is to give directions that are clear and to listen carefully when following spoken instructions.

INFORMAL ASSESSMENT (*See* Activity Masters Plus p. 45)

MEETING INDIVIDUAL NEEDS (*See* p. 196)

 FOR STUDENTS ACQUIRING ENGLISH

Understanding oral language instructions is a challenging part of learning a language. Use short, clear, and individual steps. (*Stand on the rug. Draw an X on the tree.*) Make sure each child has understood and completed a step before moving on. Try to repeat similar steps over and over.

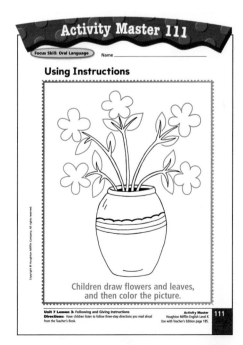

Activity Master 111
Focus Skill: Oral Language   Name
Using Instructions

Children draw flowers and leaves, and then color the picture.

Unit 7 Lesson 3: Following and Giving Instructions
Directions: Have children listen to follow three-step directions you read aloud from the Teacher's Book.

Activity Master   111
Houghton Mifflin English Level K
Use with Teacher's Edition page 185.

Poster Book p. 7C

Focus Skill: Viewing
Picture Instructions

Unit 7 **Lesson 4:** Following Visual Instructions
Directions: Have children discuss and follow simple picture instructions to complete a simple project.

Houghton Mifflin English Level K
Use with Teacher's Edition page 186. **7C**

 FOR STUDENTS ACQUIRING ENGLISH

Following visual instructions may be easier for children acquiring English because no vocabulary is involved and they can work at their own pace. If possible, make time for the plant pal activity. It will help reinforce the skills learned in the unit and show the usefulness and fun of following instructions.

Activity Master 112

Focus Skill: Viewing Name _____

Picture Instructions

1.
2.
3.
4.

Child pastes leaf rubbing here.

112 Unit 7 **Lesson 4:** Following Visual Instructions
Directions: Have children follow visual instructions to complete a simple project.

Activity Master
Houghton Mifflin English Level K
Use with Teacher's Edition page 186.

Focus Skill **Viewing**

④ Following Visual Instructions

Lesson Objective

Children will:
• use visual information to follow instructions

Materials

Poster Book p. 7C, Activity Master 112, a variety of leaves, thin paper, crayons, paste

Optional Materials

paper cup, markers, potting soil, water, grass seeds

Warm-Up

Display page 7 of *This Is Your Garden* and point to the girl in the picture. Have children look at the picture, and ask volunteers to pantomime what the girl is doing. Point out that pictures can show them what to do when they follow instructions.

Teach Poster Book p. 7C

• Display Poster Book page 7C. Help children recognize that the four pictures make up a set of instructions for a planting project. Read aloud the Viewing Tips on page 18 to guide children in careful viewing.

• Discuss the needed materials and the four steps in the project. Guide children to "read" the pictures and tell what they see in each step. Then ask volunteers to pantomime the steps in the correct order.

• If time permits, have children follow the directions to make their own plant pals.

Try It Out Activity Master 112

• Ask children to complete Activity Master 112. Distribute leaves, tracing paper, crayons, and paste. If leaves are not available, use pine needles, grasses, or other natural materials.

• Remind children to look at the pictures if they need help in remembering the order of the steps.

Wrap-Up

Ask children to share the leaf rubbings they made in completing Activity Master 112. Tell them that when they write their own instructions, they can add pictures that show the steps to follow.

 INFORMAL ASSESSMENT (*See* Activity Masters Plus p. 45)

 MEETING INDIVIDUAL NEEDS (*See* p. 196)

Focus Skill Grammar

⑤ Verbs

Lesson Objective

Children will:
- use picture clues to identify verbs

Materials

Poster Book p. 7D, dry erase marker, Activity Master 113

Warm-Up

Tell children that you are about to do something and you want them to say what you did. Then perform a simple action, such as jumping, standing, or walking. Have children name the action. Have volunteers perform actions, and instruct other children to name them.

Teach Poster Book p. 7D

- Explain that action words, or verbs, tell what people or things do.

- Show Poster Book page 7D. Have children talk about what action they see in the top row of pictures. Ask: *What does the girl do when she gets to the corner?* (stop) Say: *The girl stops at the corner.*

- Have children identify the action word in each of the next two rows and make up a sentence using the action word. Label the pictures with the correct words. (*look, walk*) Say: *The girl looks left and right. The girl walks across the street.*

Try It Out Activity Master 113

Ask children to complete Activity Master 113 by circling the picture in each row that shows an action.

Wrap-Up

Ask volunteers to name the actions pictured on Activity Master 113. Then have them make up sentences, using the action words to describe the pictures.

 INFORMAL ASSESSMENT (*See* Activity Masters Plus p. 46)

 MEETING INDIVIDUAL NEEDS (*See* p. 196)

Poster Book p. 7D

Focus Skill: Grammar

Name the Action Words

stop

look

walk

Unit 7 **Lesson 5:** Verbs
Directions: Have children help you identify the action in each picture, and write the action word on the line.

Houghton Mifflin English Level K
Use with Teacher's Edition page 187. **7D**

MEETING INDIVIDUAL NEEDS **FOR STUDENTS ACQUIRING ENGLISH**

Begin the Warm-Up by acting out all the verbs children may use in this lesson (*stop, look, walk…*). As you act out the verbs, name them several times. Then write them on the board, acting them out before and after writing. Finally, name a verb and have the class act it out.

Activity Master 113

Focus Skill: Grammar Name

Name the Action Words

1. throw
2. catch
3. run
4. jump

Unit 7 Lesson 5: Verbs
Directions: Have children look at each set of pictures and circle the one that shows an action.

Activity Master 113
Houghton Mifflin English Level K
Use with Teacher's Edition page 187.

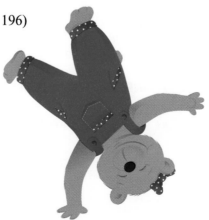

Poster Book p. 7E

Exact Action Words

Fix the fruit.

1. _____ Slice _____ the fruit.

Get the fruit into the blender.

2. _____ Scoop _____ the fruit into the blender.

Put the drink into a glass.

3. _____ Pour _____ the drink into a glass.

Unit 7 Lesson 6: Exact Verbs
Directions: Have children suggest an exact action word to describe the picture.
Write the word to complete the sentence.

Houghton Mifflin English, Level K
Use with Teacher's Edition page 188. **7E**

FOR STUDENTS ACQUIRING ENGLISH

Before beginning any of the activities, define or demonstrate the exact verbs to be used in this lesson. Children will understand *go*, but they may not understand *skip*, *tiptoe*, or *hop*. Act out each verb and then have children imitate you. Use the Poster Book illustrations to show the definitions of *slice*, *scoop*, and *pour*.

Activity Master 114

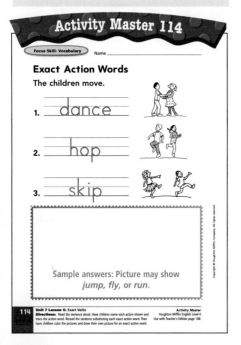

Focus Skill: Vocabulary   Name _____

Exact Action Words
The children move.

1. dance

2. hop

3. skip

Sample answers: Picture may show
jump, fly, or *run.*

114 **Unit 7 Lesson 6:** Exact Verbs
Directions: Read the sentence aloud. Have children name each action shown and trace the action word. Reread the sentence substituting each exact action word. Then have children color the pictures and draw their own picture for an exact action word.

Activity Master
Houghton Mifflin English Level K
Use with Teacher's Edition page 188.

Focus Skill Vocabulary

⑥ Exact Verbs

Lesson Objectives

Children will:
• generate exact verbs
• use exact verbs to give and follow instructions

Materials

Poster Book p. 7E, Activity Master 114, dry erase marker, art supplies (scissors, paste, paint, colored paper), 3 index cards per child

Warm-Up

Remind children that they have been learning about instructions. Give individuals the following instructions, telling them to listen carefully.

Go to the door.   *Skip to the door.*   *Tiptoe to the door.*

Point out that the words *skip* and *tiptoe* are more exact than the word *go*. They tell exactly, or more clearly, what action to do to go to the door.

Teach Poster Book p. 7E

• Tell children you will say instructions for making a fruit shake. Read aloud these instructions: <u>*Fix the fruit.*</u> <u>*Get the fruit into the blender.*</u> <u>*Put the drink into a glass.*</u> Have children discuss the pictures and suggest exact verbs, such as *slice* or *cut*, *scoop* or *spoon*, and *pour*, to replace *fix*, *get*, and *put*.

Try It Out Activity Master 114

• Help children complete Activity Master 114. First, read aloud the sentence at the top of the page: *The children move.*

• Next, ask children to look at each picture and name the exact action word. (*dance, hop, skip*) Repeat the sentence, substituting the exact action word for the general one. Have children trace the action words and color the pictures.

• Finally, have children draw a picture showing an action and dictate or write the exact action word to label the picture.

Wrap-Up

Have several volunteers share their pictures on the Activity Master. Tell children that using exact action words in instructions will help a person following them know what to do.

 INFORMAL ASSESSMENT (*See* Activity Masters Plus p. 47)

 MEETING INDIVIDUAL NEEDS (*See* p. 197)

Poster Book p. 7F

⑦ Positional Words

Lesson Objective

Children will:
• use positional words to describe location of objects and people

Materials

Poster Book p. 7F, dry erase marker, Activity Master 115, scissors, paste

Warm-Up

Display page 25 of *This Is Your Garden*. Ask children to point to the animal <u>on</u> the watering can. Ask where they would point if the animal were <u>in</u> the watering can. Have children tell how the words *on* and *in* made a difference in where they pointed.

Teach Poster Book p. 7F

• Explain that there are many other words besides *on* and *in* that tell where someone or something is.

• Display Poster Book page 7F. Have children name people, animals, and objects in the picture and identify their positions. Then have volunteers use the dry erase marker to follow these instructions. Say: 1. *Circle the animal <u>under</u> the picnic table.* 2. *Circle the person sitting <u>behind</u> a girl.* 3. *Circle the animal <u>in</u> a basket.* 4. *Circle the person kneeling <u>beside</u> a row of plants.* 5. *Circle the animal flying <u>over</u> the yard.*

• Continue by having children give additional instructions. Tell them to use the words *on, over*, *in front of,* and *between* in their instructions.

Try It Out Activity Master 115

Ask children to cut out the pictures at the bottom of Activity Master 115 and paste them in position by following these instructions as you read them. Say: 1. *Paste the bowl <u>on</u> the table.* 2. *Paste the butterfly <u>over</u> the flower.* 3. *Paste the boy <u>in front of</u> the children.* 4. *Paste the bush <u>between</u> the trees.*

Wrap-Up

Ask volunteers to share their work on Activity Master 115. As they include the words *on, over, in front of,* and *between,* have them describe the position of each picture. Tell children that using words that tell where someone or something is makes instructions easier to follow.

 INFORMAL ASSESSMENT (*See* Activity Masters Plus p. 47)

 MEETING INDIVIDUAL NEEDS (*See* p. 197)

 FOR STUDENTS ACQUIRING ENGLISH

Teach the positional words by having the children work with a chair. Then say *on* and sit on the chair, inviting all the children to do the same. Then say *in front of* and stand in front of the chair, asking all the children to join you. Repeat the activity until all the children understand the positional words.

Focus Skill Writing

⑧ Sequence

Lesson Objective	Materials
Children will:	Activity Master 116, crayons or markers
• use order words to sequence events	

Warm-Up

Discuss the order for a familiar daily activity, such as putting on socks and shoes. Ask a volunteer to describe the routine, using the order words *first, next,* and *last*. (Sample answer: First, I put on my socks. Next, I put on my shoes. Last, I tie my shoes.)

Repeat, having children describe other daily routines, such as fixing cereal or brushing teeth.

Teach

Explain that many everyday activities are done in a certain order, or sequence. Say: *When we talk about the order of doing things, we use words such as* first, next, *and* last. Ask: *What is the first thing you do to make toast for breakfast? What is next? What do you do last?*

Ask a volunteer to follow these instructions: *First, put on your coat. Next, put books away in the Reading Center. Last, line up to go outside.*

Ask children what is wrong with these instructions. (The steps are out of order.) Point out that if the steps are done out of order, they don't make sense.

Try It Out Activity Master 116

Ask children to complete Activity Master 116 by numbering each set of pictures 1, 2, and 3.

Wrap-Up

Ask volunteers to share the pictures they drew on Activity Master 116. Have them use sentences beginning with *First, Next,* and *Last* to describe the three pictures in each group.

INFORMAL ASSESSMENT (*See* Activity Masters Plus p. 46)

MEETING INDIVIDUAL NEEDS (*See* p. 197)

FOR STUDENTS ACQUIRING ENGLISH

To help the children with the vocabulary needed to describe activities like putting on shoes and brushing teeth, act out both activities and name your actions. Say: *First, I take my socks from their drawer. Next, I put them on. Last, I put on my shoes.* If necessary, write on the board important words like *take, unroll,* and *put on.* Children can refer to them as they act out the activities.

Shared Writing

⑨ Instructions

Lesson Objectives

Children will:

- choose a topic and audience for instructions
- contribute to a set of instructions, using the steps of the writing process
- reflect on their writing experience

Materials

Poster Book p. 7G, Transparency 7–3 or chart paper, dry erase markers

Focus on Instruction

Tell children that you are going to work together to write instructions. Remind them that good writers usually follow certain steps when they write something that others will read. Explain that you are going to follow these same steps.

PREWRITING

Choose a Topic

- Help children think about the kind of instructions they want to write.

Think Aloud First, we need to decide what to write about. What could we tell someone else how to do or make? Whom do we want to read our instructions? Will they be for another class, for a friend, or for our parents?

- Brainstorm topic ideas. Record children's suggestions on chart paper. Then discuss each topic idea. Ask: *What are the steps? Can we explain the steps clearly?*

- Together, decide on a topic and an audience.

Plan the Instructions Poster Book p. 7G

- Display Poster Book page 7G. Write the topic for the instructions at the top of the graphic organizer and read it aloud.

- Have volunteers name the materials needed to complete the instructions. Record them in the Materials space, using pictures and/or key words.

- Help children recall the steps for the instructions by having a volunteer pantomime or demonstrate the steps in order.

- Draw simple pictures, or write key words, in the four frames on the poster to represent the steps. Have children help you number the frames in order and then label them with the order words *First, Next, Then,* and *Last.*

Topic Ideas

how to make a taco

how to ride a bike

how to wash a car or a lunchroom table

how to line up for recess

how to make a picture book

how to use the water fountain

how to play a computer game

Poster Book p. 7G

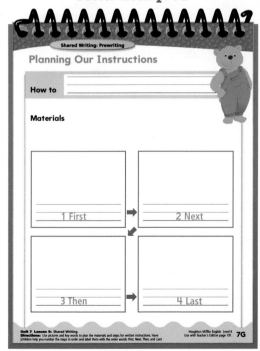

FOR STUDENTS ACQUIRING ENGLISH

Children acquiring English can be helpful during many parts of the Shared Writing lesson. Have them fill in the charts during the drafting session. Then ask them to pantomime the instructions to check for missing steps during the revision session.

DRAFTING   Transparency 7–3, Poster Book p. 7G

- Before drafting, review with children what makes great instructions, using the elements listed below.

What Makes Great Instructions?

- A good beginning sentence tells the topic.
- The steps tell the reader what to do.
- The steps are in order and have order words.
- A good ending sentence shows you are done.

- Then ask volunteers to contribute text ideas for each element of the draft, using the graphic organizer on Poster Book page 7G as a guide. Record children's suggestions on Transparency 7–3 or on chart paper. Help children generate the following:

  - a **title** that tells what the instructions will be about

  - an interesting **beginning sentence** that tells the topic of the instructions

  - sentences that tell the **steps in order** and that use **order words**

  - a good **ending sentence** that finishes the instructions and that will make the reader interested in following them

- Read the instructions together and praise children for their contributions.

REVISING

- Reread your draft together, asking children to review the instructions by using the Questions for Revising.

Questions for Revising
✔ Do the steps tell the reader what to do?
✔ Are the steps in order?
✔ Did we use order words?
✔ Do we have good beginning and ending sentences?

- Together, see if any vague action words should be replaced with more exact action words.

glue
Next, ~~put~~ the yarn on the paper plate.

Make a clean final copy of the instructions on chart paper. Ask volunteers to add illustrations. Post the finished product or add it to a class Big Book of shared writing. Encourage children to share the instructions with the intended audience.

 SCHOOL-HOME CONNECTION You may want to have a classroom volunteer or assistant type the instructions and reproduce them for children to illustrate and take home to share with family members.

REFLECTING

Praise children for the instructions they wrote. Ask:

- *What was easy to do? What was hard?*
- *What did you like about writing the instructions?*
- *What did you learn that will help you the next time you write instructions?*

Independent Writing

⑩ Instructions

Lesson Objectives

Children will:
• tell, dictate, or write instructions
• listen and respond to the writing of peers

Materials

drawing paper, writing paper, Activity Master 117

Focus on Instruction

Tell children that now they will write their own instructions. Explain that first they must decide what instructions they want to write and for whom they will write them. Here are some ideas you might use to help children plan, write, and share their work.

Planning Ideas

THINKING ABOUT TOPICS Some children may benefit from brainstorming topic ideas with a partner. If individuals are having difficulty thinking of a topic, try reading one of the Writing Prompts on page 195. You might also read aloud some of the books in the bibliography on page 180 to help spark a topic idea.

ORGANIZING IDEAS Before children begin writing, have them "rehearse" by telling and/or demonstrating their instructions for a partner.

Writing

Allow children to produce their instructions in the format that is most appropriate to their own stage of development, as indicated in the chart below.

Writing Options		
Emergent Writers	**Early Beginning Writers**	**Late Beginning and Transitional Writers**
Have children draw pictures to represent the steps for their instructions. They can then add pretend or "scribble" writing to describe them and tell the steps to an adult, or they can dictate their instructions to an adult to record.*	Children can draw pictures to represent the steps for the instructions. They can label them with single words or phrases and tell the steps to an adult, or they can dictate their instructions to an adult to record.*	Children can write their instructions using temporary spelling. They can add illustrations to support their text.

*Some children may feel their writing is not valid if an adult rewrites it.

 INFORMAL ASSESSMENT (*See* Activity Masters Plus p. 46)

 FOR STUDENTS ACQUIRING ENGLISH

Remember to consider the children acquiring English according to their reading and writing abilities in any language, English or another. If they can write in another language, challenge them to do so in English. If not, do not expect them to write in English yet. Encourage the children to work in pairs, pantomiming the steps as they draw to make sure they include all the necessary tasks.

Writing Portfolio

If you are collecting samples of children's writing, decide if you want to save this piece.

Ideas for Sharing

 INTERNET CONNECTION See www.eduplace.com/rdg/hme/ for printable patterns for making shape-paper booklets.

Have children share their instructions with the class or with a classmate by "reading" them aloud or by using one of the suggestions below.

Write It Write each step of the instructions on a separate sheet of paper, add illustrations, and bind the pages to make an instruction booklet.

Say It Do a demonstration, giving the instructions orally.

Show It Make the instructions into an illustrated poster.

After each child shares, the listener or listeners should tell the writer at least one thing they liked about the instructions. (Examples: Your instructions are clear. You told all the steps in order.)

Writing Prompts

MATH

Do you like to make things with clay? Make clay beads for counting. Roll bits of clay into 10 balls. Thread a blunt needle with yarn and poke through all the beads. Then dictate or write instructions telling someone else how to make a clay bead necklace.

ART Activity Master 117

Color the pictures on Activity Master 117. Then tell or dictate the labels for order words *First*, *Next*, *Then*, and *Last*. Use the pictures to give instructions that tell how to make a puppet. You might want to try using the instructions to make some puppets of your own.

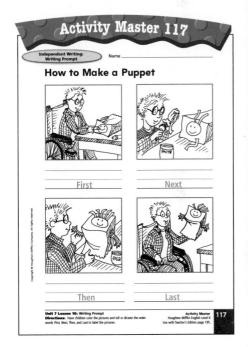

 INTERNET CONNECTION See www.eduplace.com/rdg/hme/ for more writing ideas.

Meeting Individual Needs

Lesson 3 Focus Skill   Oral Language: Following and Giving Instructions

RETEACHING ALTERNATIVE STRATEGY

Tell children to listen carefully to order words as you sing "Hokey Pokey." Explain that good instructions use order words such as *first, next, then*, and *last*. Ask children to describe their movements in singing "Hokey Pokey." (Example: First, we put our right hand in. Next, we took our right hand out. Then we put our right hand in. Last, we shook it all about.)

CHALLENGE

Have partners take turns giving and following oral three-step directions. (Example: Draw a dog. Next, give it a red collar. Then color the dog brown.) Then have partners check each other's pictures.

FOR STUDENTS ACQUIRING ENGLISH

Teach the children a version of Simon Says in which Simon says everything. In other words, the children follow each instruction you give and are only dropped from the game when they don't follow your instructions. By naming the body parts and repeating words like *put, in, out*, and *shake*, you can prepare children to participate in the singing of "Hokey Pokey."

Lesson 4 Focus Skill   Viewing: Following Visual Instructions

RETEACHING ALTERNATIVE STRATEGY

Display one card and have children look at each figure, noting the details of hands, feet, or head positions. Have them mimic the figure on the card. Then show two cards, having children mimic what they see on the two cards. Explain that when they follow picture instructions, they should look at picture details to help them understand what they see.

CHALLENGE

Additional Resources page 253 provides four-step instructions for making a paper doll. Duplicate the instructions and distribute them as a handout or place them in the Art Center for children to follow.

FOR STUDENTS ACQUIRING ENGLISH

Play a version of Red Light, Green Light. Make three circles colored red, yellow, and green with the words *Stop! Slow!* and *Go!* printed on them respectively. Line up the children at one side of the room and stand at the other holding up circles alternately. Children should follow the instructions until one reaches you. Then that child becomes the stoplight.

Lesson 5 Focus Skill   Grammar: Verbs

RETEACHING ALTERNATIVE STRATEGY

Say three action words such as *jump, stretch, walk*. Tell children these words describe actions. The words are called action words, or verbs. Play Simon Says using directions that use only verbs. (Examples: Simon says, hop. Simon says, kick.) Then play Simon Says. Explain that everyone has to follow Simon's instructions by listening for the action word and then doing the action.

CHALLENGE

Have children work in pairs. One child draws a picture of an action; the partner writes or dictates the verb. Then partners switch roles.

FOR STUDENTS ACQUIRING ENGLISH

Play Charades. Write or draw simple action words on cards (*jump, look, walk, run, skip, hop, tiptoe*). Without showing the card, act out one of the action words for the class to guess. The child who guesses correctly comes up to take a card and act out an action word. Play continues until all words are acted out or all the children are familiar with them.

Lesson 6 Focus Skill   Vocabulary: Exact Verbs

RETEACHING ALTERNATIVE STRATEGY

Tell children to touch their faces. Then use exact verbs for different ways to touch their faces, such as *tickle, rub,* and *tap.* Tell children these words are more exact than *touch.* Tell children to listen as you say this sentence: *The horse moved down the road.* Ask them to change the action word *move* to one that is more exact. (Sample answers: *ran, walked, trotted*)

CHALLENGE

Draw three sketches on the board that show the steps for making a peanut butter cracker sandwich. Then give oral instructions, using general verbs. Ask children to substitute exact verbs. (Sample answer: *Put the peanut butter on one cracker. Spread*)

FOR STUDENTS ACQUIRING ENGLISH

Review the exact verbs from the exercises by playing a game called Silly Walk. Have all the children walk in a circle. You shout "Tiptoe!" and they must all begin to tiptoe in a circle. Then you shout "Skip!" and they must all begin to do so. Play continues until all the verbs have been reviewed. Be sure to change the direction of movement so the children don't get dizzy.

Lesson 7 Focus Skill   Vocabulary: Positional Words

RETEACHING ALTERNATIVE STRATEGY

Tell children that some words tell <u>where</u> people or things are. As you use a small block and a box to demonstrate the meaning of *in, on, over, under, behind, in front of, beside,* and *between,* have children describe where the block is. (Sample answer: The block is <u>beside</u> the box.)

CHALLENGE

Have children dictate or write short instructions that tell where to find things in the classroom. Remind them to use the words *in, on, over, under, behind, in front of, beside,* and *between.* Then they can draw pictures to make these instructions into a classroom visitor's guide.

FOR STUDENTS ACQUIRING ENGLISH

Use classroom objects to demonstrate the use of positional words. Say with emphasis: *The book is <u>in</u> the bookcase. The pencil is <u>on</u> the desk. The jacket is <u>over</u> the chair,* etc. Then ask for three volunteers to demonstrate other positional words by having them stand *behind, in front of, beside,* and *between* each other. Finally, ask two of the volunteers to join both hands and raise them while the third volunteer goes *under* the arch that is formed. Repeat the actions and have children call out the appropriate positional word for each action.

Lesson 8 Focus Skill   Writing: Sequence

RETEACHING ALTERNATIVE STRATEGY

As a child acts out simple instructions, such as putting on his or her coat for recess, describe them orally, using order words. (Example: <u>First</u>, take your coat off the closet hook. <u>Next</u>, put it on. <u>Last</u>, zip it up.) Ask: *What would happen if you did the steps out of order?*

CHALLENGE

Activity Master 118 provides a six-frame sequence of pictures for making stick puppets. Duplicate the page, cut the frames apart, mix them up, and have children put them in order. Provide materials, and have children follow the instructions.

FOR STUDENTS ACQUIRING ENGLISH

Write a simple rhyme such as "Jack and Jill" on chart paper and guide children to chant it. Explain that "broke his crown" means "hurt his head" and that "tumbling" means that Jill fell down after Jack. Then ask children to help you write order words next to each line, for example: *First*: Jack and Jill went up the hill/to fetch a pail of water. *Next*: Jack fell down and broke his crown. *Last*: Jill came tumbling after. Then chant the rhyme as volunteers act out the lines in sequence. Model "broke his crown" by rubbing your head and "tumbling" by appearing to fall down quickly on a chair.

Unit 8
Report

In this unit, children learn about informative writing. They listen to a nonfiction book about fish and participate in the modeled writing of a report about sea horses. Then children work together with you to create a class report, using the writing process. Unit skills develop language as well as relate to and support informative writing.

What You Will Find in This Unit . . .

Unit 8 Planning Guide
Report

	Poster Book	Transparency	Activity Masters Plus
DAILY COMMUNICATION LINKS **Daily Routines** *(202–203)* The oral language activities provide daily opportunities for children to develop the basic concepts and skills needed to compose reports. • **Interactive Bulletin Board:** Weather Chart; Color, Number, Size Wheels; Daily Message • **Daily Discussion Activity:** All About Spiders *See also* Additional Resources *(254–255)*			
Center Activities *(204–205)* • Reading and Listening Center • Math Center • Writing Center • Creative Arts Center		8–1	
A Published Model ⏱ *1 day, 20 minutes* **Lesson 1** Listening to Informative Writing *(206–207)* *What's It Like to Be a Fish?*			
Modeled Writing ⏱ *about 2-3 days, 20 minutes each day* **Lesson 2** Report *(208–210)*	8A	8–2, 8–3	
Focus Skills ⏱ *about 2–3 days, 20 minutes each day* **Lesson 3** Oral Language: Sharing Information *(211)*	8B		
Lesson 4 Listening and Viewing: Information and Media *(212)*	8C		
Lesson 5 Grammar/Usage: Subject-Verb Agreement *(213)*	8D		120
Lesson 6 Grammar/Usage: Comparing with Adjectives *(214)*	8E		
Lesson 7 Writing: Fact and Opinion *(215)*			
Lesson 8 Study Skills: ABC Order *(216)*			121
Lesson 9 Study Skills: Finding Information *(217)*	8F		
Lesson 10 Study Skills: Using Charts and Graphs *(218)*	8G		122–123
Shared Writing ⏱ *about 2–3 days, 20 minutes each day* **Lesson 11** Report *(219–221)*	8H	8–4	
Independent Writing ⏱ *about 1–3 days, 20 minutes each day* **Lesson 12** Report *(222–223)* ✓ **Writing Prompts** *(223)*			

MEETING INDIVIDUAL NEEDS *(224–227)*

Activities for Special Needs/Inclusion, for Students Acquiring English, for Reteaching, and for Enrichment/Challenge

Meeting Individual Needs

▶ **FOR SPECIAL NEEDS/INCLUSION:** *Houghton Mifflin English* Audiotape ; *See also* Reteaching.

▶ **FOR STUDENTS ACQUIRING ENGLISH:**
- Notes and activities are included in this Teacher's Edition throughout the unit to help you adapt or use lessons with students acquiring English.
- Students can listen to the published model *What's It Like to Be a Fish?* on audiotape.

▶ **RETEACHING**
- Activities for reteaching the focus skills are included on pages 224–227.

▶ **ENRICHMENT/CHALLENGE**
- Activities for challenge/enrichment that are correlated to focus skill lessons are included on pages 224–227.

 All audiotape recordings are also available on CD.

Additional Resources

Audiotapes

 Technology Tools
CD-ROM: Curious George® Paint & Print Studio
Paint, Write & Play! (published by The Learning Company)
*Type to Learn Jr.™

*©Sunburst Technology Corporation, a Houghton Mifflin Company. All rights reserved.

INTERNET: http://www.eduplace.com/rdg/hme/
Visit Education Place for these additional support materials and activities:
- author biographies
- patterns for shape booklets
- writing prompts

 Informal Assessment
Activity Masters Plus, Assessment Checklists, pages 45–47

 ### Keeping a Journal
In kindergarten, journals can be blank notebooks or folders filled with paper. As children draw and write about school activities, important events, and special thoughts, they can watch their writing growth as the year progresses.

 School-Home Connection
Suggestions for informing or involving family members in learning related to this unit are included in the Teacher's Edition throughout the unit.

Daily Routines

The oral language activities suggested here provide daily opportunities for children to develop basic concepts and skills they will need to compose reports. Refer to the **Interactive Bulletin Board** and **Daily Discussion** ideas on pages 10–13 and 20–21 for help in establishing Daily Routines for your classroom.

Interactive Bulletin Board

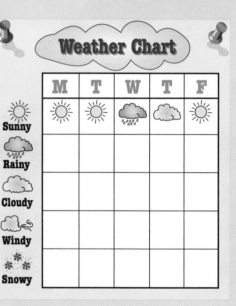

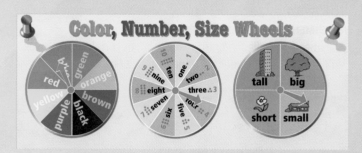

Color, Number, Size Wheels

Have volunteers spin one of the spinners and use the word that it lands on in a sentence that tells something true about an object in the classroom. (Example: The ball is <u>blue</u>.) Point out that because the sentence is true, it tells a fact about the object.

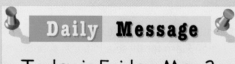

Today is Friday, May 3.

Daily Message

After updating the Calendar or Weather Chart, write a fact on the board that gives information about the date or the weather. Read the sentence aloud. Explain that it is true, so it is a fact. As you write, point out the use of capital letters at the beginning of sentences and at the beginning of names of days and months.

Weather Chart

Each day as you work with the Weather Chart have different volunteers state true information about the weather. (Examples: It is <u>rainy</u>. It is <u>windy</u>. It is a <u>cloudy</u> day.) Explain to children that these are facts. If time allows, ask volunteers to gather additional facts about the day's weather, using thermometers, rain gauges, windsocks, or other devices, and to report their findings to the class.

Daily Discussion

Explain that some writing tells about real things and real happenings. These real things are called facts. Have children listen as you read aloud the text **All About Spiders** below. Then discuss the information, using the Think and Discuss questions. Do this daily. Have children listen to factual information about a different topic each day and then discuss the facts. You can use a variety of different sources for the information. You might

- call on volunteers to talk about a hobby or a place they have visited,
- play an informative video or audio recording,
- invite speakers to talk to the class about their jobs or hobbies, or
- read nonfiction picture books or articles. (*See also* Additional Resources, pages 254–255)

Think and Discuss

- What was the writing about?
- What facts did you learn? Which facts were the most interesting?
- What else would you like to know about this topic?

ASKING QUESTIONS Help children ask *Who, What, Where, When, Why,* and *How* questions to find out more about the topic or to clarify their understandings. Record and post any questions that cannot be answered from the information available. Challenge one or two volunteers to find the answers to these questions during school time or outside of school and then report their findings.

FINDING INFORMATION After children listen to factual information about a topic, ask where they would find out more about it. Record their responses in a running list that you can post. Have volunteers draw or cut out pictures to show each resource named. Display these pictures on the classroom list.

 INFORMAL ASSESSMENT (*See* Activity Masters Plus pp. 45, 47)

Daily Discussion Activity

All About Spiders

What is a spider? A spider is a kind of arachnid. It has eight legs.

There are many kinds of spiders, and they live everywhere. They live in cold places, hot places, dark places, rainy places, and dry places. One kind of spider even lives underwater.

All spiders can make silk from their bodies. Their bodies have two sections, a head and an abdomen. The silk comes from the abdomen. Spiders use this silk to spin webs, to build nests, or to move away from danger.

Spiders come in different colors, shapes, and sizes. For example, some cellar spiders have small bodies with long skinny legs. There are the tarantula spiders that are the largest of all spiders.

Most spiders are not poisonous to people and are truly interesting creatures to watch and learn more about.

Center Activities

Center Activities provide additional daily opportunities for children to develop and reinforce concepts and skills that support the composing of reports.

Reading and Listening Center

PUBLISHED MODEL Children can listen to *What's It Like to Be a Fish?* on audiotape as they follow along in the book. **Listening**

FACT CLUES Provide partners with pictures of familiar animals and plants. One partner uses information from the picture to tell facts about the animal or plant without identifying it. The other child uses the factual clues to guess the animal or plant in the picture. **Viewing/Listening/Speaking**

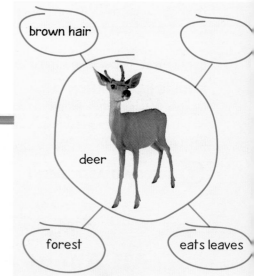

Writing Center

FACT WEBS Provide children with pictures of animals in their natural habitats. Have each child select an animal and then create a fact web. Help children write the name of the animal in the center of the web. Then have children use viewing skills they learned on page 18 as they look at the picture and tell facts about the animal. Children can draw pictures and dictate or write labels to complete their fact webs. **Viewing**

QUESTIONS Help children think of a topic about which they would like to learn more. You may provide them with pictures of places, animals, things, or activities they could research. Have children select a topic, and then help them list questions about it. Children can then use classroom resources or the library to begin to answer their questions.

JOURNAL Children can use their journals to draw or list topics they would like to know more about. Also encourage them to write or dictate specific questions they have about the topics. Tell children they can refer to these lists and questions when they pick a topic for writing their reports.

1234 Math Center

TALLY CHARTS AND GRAPHS Explain to children that people often organize factual information that involves numbers in tally charts and graphs to make the information easier to understand. Display pages 4 and 5 of *What's It Like to Be a Fish?* at the center. Have children make a tally chart or graph to show how many of each fish are pictured. **Viewing**

How Many Fish?

	Tally	Total Number
Lake Whitefish	II	2
Common Shiners	₩₩ III	8
Smallmouth Buffalo	IIII	4
Coho Salmon	I	I
Grass Pickerel	I	I

Creative Arts Center

STORY RETELLING Use Transparency 8–1 to project underwater background scenery against a white surface. Ask volunteers to act out different fish behaviors they learned from *What's It Like to Be a Fish?*, such as how fish breathe and how fish swim. Viewers should look for fish behaviors they recall from the book and explain what they saw after the presentation. **Viewing/Speaking**

1 Listening to Informative Writing

About the Author

Wendy Pfeffer

Besides writing books for children, Wendy Pfeffer also gives writing workshops to children and adults. She lives in New Jersey.

INTERNET CONNECTION
See www.eduplace.com/kids/ for information about Wendy Pfeffer.

Bibliography

You may also wish to read aloud the following nonfiction books.

- *From Tadpole to Frog*
  by Wendy Pfeffer
- *Snow Is Falling*
  Franklyn M. Branley
- *Wonderful Worms*
  by Linda Glaser
- *Life in a Pond*
  by Allan Fowler

 FOR STUDENTS ACQUIRING ENGLISH

During the picture walk, help children focus on key details by such questions as *Where are the fish on this page? What are they doing? What would you like to know more about?* Record their responses to the third question in the W column of the K-W-L Chart. Finally, pause at pages 4, 5, 11, 13, and 18. Have the children name the parts of the fish's body. Help them with words such as *fins, scales,* and *gills.*

Lesson Objectives

Children will:
- listen to a published model and discuss characteristics of informative writing
- listen for sentence fluency
- understand the use of sensory adjectives
- evaluate the relationship of visuals and text
- respond personally and critically to the selection

Materials

What's It Like to Be a Fish?, chart paper, drawing paper

Reading the Model

What's It Like to Be a Fish? is an informational text that explains how fish eat, breathe, swim, and rest in water.

Building Background

Ask volunteers to act like fish. Point out the fish movements demonstrated. Begin a K-W-L chart with children. Have them share what they know about fish and what they want to find out. Discuss how living underwater differs from living on land.

What We Know	What We Want to Know	What We Learned
• Fish live in water.	• How do fish breathe?	

Introducing Vocabulary

- Discuss these key vocabulary words: *aquarium, fin, scales, slime, gills, lungs,* and *oxygen.* Draw on the board a simple fish inside an aquarium. Point out and label these key vocabulary words: *aquarium, fin, scales, slime,* and *gills.* Then ask children to put their hands on their chests as they take a deep breath. Explain that when they breathe they take *oxygen* from the air into their *lungs.* Ask: *What happens to your chest when you breathe?* (It moves.)

Predicting and Purpose Setting

PICTURE WALK Display *What's It Like to Be a Fish?* and read aloud the title and author, Wendy Pfeffer. Take a picture walk through the selection, pausing so that children can tell what they think the book will be about. On page 11, point out the diagram.

Explain that this is an informational book that gives true information, or facts, about one big idea or topic. As you read the book, children should listen carefully for facts about fish.

 This selection is also available on audiotape.

Listening As a Writer

Think About Informative Writing

TOPIC Have children identify the one big idea, or topic, of the selection. (fish)

FACTS Ask volunteers to recall facts they learned about fish from the selection. Add to the K-W-L chart.

What We Know	What We Want to Know	What We Learned
• Fish live in water.	• How do fish breathe?	• Fish breathe with their gills.

GOOD ENDING Reread page 29. Ask children why they think this is a good ending for the book. (Sample answer: It sums up the important facts about fish.)

Think About Writer's Craft

SENTENCE FLUENCY Display and reread page 20. Then read it again and change the sentence structure so that each sentence begins with *Fish*. (Example: <u>Fish</u> need food. <u>Fish</u> flip their tails at feeding time. <u>Fish</u> race to the top of the bowl. <u>Fish</u> need only a tiny pinch. . . .) Help children understand that it is more interesting to begin sentences in different ways.

WORD CHOICE: ADJECTIVES Read aloud phrases from *What's It Like to Be a Fish?* pages 10–12 that describe how a fish looks or feels. (Examples: *sleek body*; *smooth, slick scales*; *delicate skin*) Help children recognize the adjectives by asking questions, such as the following: *How does a fish's body look?* (sleek) *How do a fish's scales feel?* (smooth, slick)

Think About the Pictures

Allow children to look at pages 4, 5, and 11. Track the labels and captions. Discuss how this information helps the reader understand what different kinds of fish look like, what a fish's body parts are called, and where the body parts are.

Responding

- **Personal Response** Children can draw and dictate or write about one thing they learned about fish. They can share their responses at group time.

- **Critical Thinking** Ask children how writing an informative book about fish is different from writing a make-believe story about fish. (Sample answer: An informative book has true facts about fish. In a make-believe story you can write things about a fish that aren't true.)

NOTE If children are responding to the prompts below on a day following your initial reading of *What's It Like to Be a Fish?*, reread the book.

FOR STUDENTS ACQUIRING ENGLISH

The Word Choice: Adjectives exercise is a good chance to focus on the words that the children may not know. On the board, write *smooth*, *slick*, *delicate*, and *slime*. Then run your hand across a child's desk. Say: <u>*Smooth*</u>. *The desk is* <u>*smooth*</u>. Encourage children to repeat the action and word. Repeat this with other words: <u>*slick*</u> (soapy fingers), <u>*delicate*</u> (paper), <u>*slime*</u> (oil).

Fish don't sleep. They rest with their eyes open.

Modeled Writing

② Report

Lesson Objectives

Children will:

• recognize the purpose, use, and characteristics of a report
• understand purpose and audience
• become familiar with the steps of the writing process
• help plan and draft a report
• use a diagram

Materials

Poster Book p. 8A, Transparencies 8–2 and 8–3 or chart paper, dry erase markers, Activity Master 119

Optional Materials

Nonfiction books or nature magazines that include information on sea horses, children's encyclopedia, sea horse model

Kinds of Reports

about an animal

about the weather

about a news event

about a place

about a famous person

Focus on Instruction

• Remind children that *What's It Like to Be a Fish?* tells true information, or facts, about one topic, fish. Explain that a report also tells facts about one topic.

• Then discuss reasons why people write reports. Help children understand that sometimes people write reports because they are interested in finding out more about something and they want to write down the information to share what they have learned with others.

MODELING PREWRITING

Choose a Topic

• Tell children that you would like their help to write a report. Explain that first you have to decide what you are going to write a report about. You also have to decide who your audience will be.

Topic Ideas

sharks

whales

seals

jellyfish

sea horses

Think Aloud Reading the book *What's It Like to Be a Fish?* has made me interested in the other animals that live in the sea. One sea animal that is really interesting is the sea horse. My brother saw a sea horse at a saltwater aquarium. I know that he would like to read more about them. I think I'll write my report for my brother.

• You may prefer to write about another topic that you know more thoroughly.

Before showing Transparency 8–2, share nonfiction books or encyclopedias with pictures of sea horses, or display a plastic model. Ask children to generate *What, Where, Why, and How* questions about the sea horse.

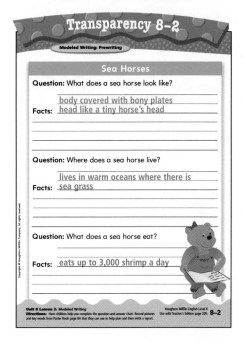

Plan the Report Transparency 8–2, Poster Book p. 8A

- Tell children that before you begin to write a report, you need to plan it.

Think Aloud Before I start writing, I want to think about the questions that I want to answer. What does a sea horse look like? Where does it live? What does it eat?

- Display Transparency 8–2 or copy the questions on chart paper. After you read the questions, explain that you now have to find the answers. Display Poster Book page 8A. Ask: *What animal do you see?* Have a volunteer point to the labels on the poster. Tell children that these words provide facts about sea horses. Read aloud each label, tracking the words as you read. Ask children to listen carefully as you read the additional facts below aloud.

> Sea horses live in warm oceans where there is sea grass. Sea grass is a home for the tiny shrimp that sea horses eat.
>
> **head**—A sea horse's head looks like a tiny horse's head. That is how the sea horse got its name.
> **snout**—Its long snout may suck up nearly 3,000 tiny shrimp in one day.
> **tail**—The sea horse uses its tail to hang onto sea grass and other plants.
> **plates**—Spiny, bony plates cover the sea horse's body. These plates protect it.
> **body color**—The sea horse can change the color of its body to match the rocks or sea grass around it.

- Remind children to look at the poster as they help you answer the questions on Transparency 8–2. Write in key vocabulary words and/or draw pictures for the facts.

Poster Book p. 8A

FOR STUDENTS ACQUIRING ENGLISH

Display Poster Book page 8A. Say: *Here are facts on sea horses. I need to read them and write down the facts in my own words. This is called taking notes.* Then model taking notes on the board. Read a few lines and jot down the facts. Then encourage the children to "take notes" by listening to what you read and saying what they remember.

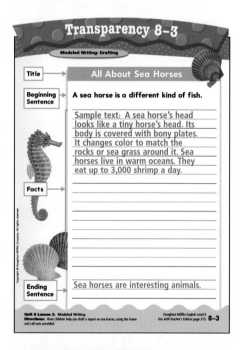

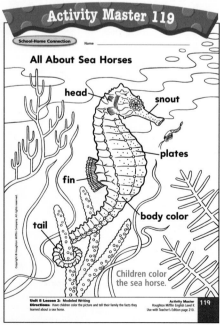

MODELING DRAFTING   Transparency 8–3

To model drafting, use Transparency 8–3, or copy the frame from the transparency onto chart paper. As children dictate text, reinforce mechanics skills that they have learned by pointing out specific capital letters and punctuation marks as you write.

TITLE Explain that now you are ready to write your report. Display Transparency 8–3 and read the title aloud. Point out that the title tells what the report is about.

BEGINNING SENTENCE Tell children that a good report needs a beginning sentence that will make the reader want to read the report. Read together the beginning sentence on the transparency.

Think Aloud The beginning sentence tells my topic and says something interesting about it.

FACTS Have children help you draft the main text. Tell them you will use what you recorded on the question-answer chart on Transparency 8–3 to give facts that answer the question. Record their suggestions on the transparency. Remind children that you will follow the order of the questions on Transparency 8–3 to write these facts.

ENDING SENTENCE Together, generate and record a good ending sentence.

Think Aloud I need to write an ending sentence that shows that I'm finished and says one big idea about my topic.

MODELING PUBLISHING

Read the report chorally with children. Then thank them for their help in writing it. Praise their good work. Explain that you plan to make a neat, clean copy to send to your brother.

SCHOOL-HOME CONNECTION You may want to have a classroom volunteer or assistant type the report. Children can draw a cover and take home the report to share with family members. Children can also complete Activity Master 119 to share with their families.

MODELING REFLECTING

To help children think more about the writing experience, model the process of reflection.

Think Aloud I liked learning about the sea horse. I had to think about how to tell those facts in a way that would be easy for my brother to understand without a picture to look at.

Focus Skill Oral Language

③ Sharing Information

Lesson Objectives

Children will:
- share factual information orally, using appropriate language, volume, and rate
- use gestures and facial expressions effectively when speaking

Materials

Poster Book p. 8B

Warm-Up

Whisper: *Sharks have several rows of teeth*. Ask children what you said. When children say that they couldn't hear, repeat the fact but mumble. Ask what you should do so that they can hear. (speak loudly, clearly)

Teach Poster Book p. 8B

- Review the Speaking Tips on page 16. Explain that it sometimes helps their audience understand information more clearly if children use their hands to help explain facts. Have them show how they could use their hands to show how a fish swims.

- Display Poster Book page 8B. Repeat the fact that sharks have several rows of teeth, and point to the shark's teeth on Poster Book page 8B. Ask how your pointing to the picture helps you share the fact more clearly. (You are pointing out the part of the picture that matches the fact.) Ask how they could use their hands and face to show how the shark's teeth look if they didn't have a picture. Then read aloud the following text.

> Sharks live in oceans all over the world. Most sharks like to stay in warmer waters. Most sharks have several rows of teeth. Gills help sharks breathe. Most sharks have gray skin, but they can also be blue or black. Fins help a shark keep its balance while swimming. A shark's tail helps it swim very quickly.

- Ask volunteers to share facts about sharks and to point to the Poster Book page or use their hands in another way. Remind them of the Speaking Tips.

Try It Out

Have children take turns sharing facts they know about other topics. Class members should praise the speakers when they follow the speaking tips or use their faces and hands effectively.

Wrap-Up

Have children review what they learned about sharing information orally.

 INFORMAL ASSESSMENT OPPORTUNITY (*See* Activity Masters Plus p. 45)

 MEETING INDIVIDUAL NEEDS (*See* p. 224)

Topic Ideas
- our classroom pet
- baseball
- dinosaurs
- our school
- soccer

Poster Book p. 8B

Focus Skill: Oral Language
All About Sharks

skin
tail
fins
fin
gills
teeth

Unit 8 Lesson 3: Sharing Information
Directions: Have children look at the Poster Book as you read the informational text in the Teacher's Edition. Then have children take turns sharing this information orally.

Houghton Mifflin English Level K
Use with Teacher's Edition page 211. **8B**

FOR STUDENTS ACQUIRING ENGLISH

Before asking the children to give an oral report, have them read aloud together all of Poster Book page 8B. Then model giving a report yourself, showing children which parts of the poster you will use yourself. Finally, have the children present a report in small groups or pairs so they feel comfortable speaking to the class. Give them time to practice.

Poster Book p. 8C

Focus Skill: Viewing

Comparing What We See

Unit 8 Lesson 4: Information and Media
Directions: Have children discuss and compare information they get from the photo to information they get from a book illustration and text.

Houghton Mifflin English Level K
Use with Teacher's Edition page 212. **8C**

  FOR STUDENTS ACQUIRING ENGLISH

Children acquiring English may know the name of an animal but may not possess the vocabulary needed to describe the animal. Referring to photos or drawings, brainstorm words children can use to describe animals such as a fish or a bear. Assist with vocabulary for body parts such as *paws, claws, fins,* and *scales* as needed. You may want to make stick-on labels for the various body parts as well.

 Focus Skill **Listening and Viewing**

④ Information and Media

Lesson Objectives

Children will:
• gain information by looking at pictures and photographs
• describe how the information in photographs can differ from that of book illustrations or videos

Materials

What's It Like to Be a Fish?, Poster Book p. 8C

Optional Materials

Videotape such as National Geographic, *Jewels of the Carribbean Sea, 1994*

Warm-Up

Display page 6 of *What's It Like to Be a Fish?*. Discuss what children think it would be like to live underwater. Ask volunteers to describe what they see. Ask: *How could you find out more about the fish you see pictured?* (Sample answers: Read the words. Look at other books. Look at photographs of fish.)

Teach Poster Book p. 8C

• Tell children that they can find out facts about fish or other subjects by using the information they see in book illustrations or by looking at photographs. Explain that each source will show different facts or show the same facts in a different way that helps them understand more about the subject.

• Display Poster Book page 8C. Explain that the page shows a photograph of real fish. Ask: *What can you learn about fish by looking at the photograph?* (Sample answers: Fish are different colors. Fish have scales.)

• Have children compare the information they learned by looking at the photograph with the information in the illustration on page 6 of *What's It Like to Be a Fish?*. (Sample answers: The book illustration has word labels that tell the names of the fish. The fish photo shows more details, such as scales and gills.)

• If possible, show a video about tropical fish. Ask: *How is the information in the video different from the book illustration and the photograph?* (Sample answer: The video shows how fish move. You hear a voice or music.)

Try It Out

Show pictures in nonfiction books. Ask children what facts they learn from them. Then show a photograph of the same subject as the nonfiction books. Ask children to compare the information that each source gives.

Wrap-Up

Help children summarize that they can learn facts by looking at illustrations, by reading books, and by looking carefully at photographs and informational videos.

 INFORMAL ASSESSMENT (*See* Activity Masters Plus p. 45)

 MEETING INDIVIDUAL NEEDS (*See* p. 224)

⑤ Subject-Verb Agreement

Lesson Objectives

Children will:

- listen for different forms of verbs in the present tense
- use the correct form of present tense verbs

Materials

What's It Like to Be a Fish?, Poster Book p. 8D, Activity Master 120

Warm-Up

Display page 15 from *What's It Like to Be a Fish?*. Direct children to listen for the action word, or verb, in the following sentences: *The girls look. The boy looks.* Emphasize each verb. Ask children how it is different in the second sentence. (ends in *s*) Explain that they will learn when an action verb ends in *s*.

Teach Poster Book p. 8D

- Display Poster Book page 8D. Ask children what the boys in the pictures in row one are doing. (swimming) Have a volunteer tell how many people are in each picture of row one. Then read aloud the sentences, using *swims* and *swim*. Read the sentences again, asking children to tell with which picture you used *swims* and how many people are shown in that picture. (one) Help children summarize that the action word *swim* ends with *s* when it tells about one person or animal.

- Have children use the pictures to identify the action words for the sentences in the other rows. (bark, hop, eat) Have children tell you which present tense form of the action word to use in each sentence.

Try It Out Activity Master 120

Distribute Activity Master 120. Have children look at the two pictures in row one. Tell them that you will say two sentences for each picture. Read aloud the pairs of sentences below for row one. Have children tell you which sentences are correct and say the correct sentences chorally. Repeat with the other pictures and sentences. 1. *The girl digs. The girl dig.* / *The girls dig. The girls digs.* 2. *The bird fly. The bird flies.* / *The birds fly. The birds flies.* 3. *The dolphin jumps. The dolphin jump.* / *The dolphins jump. The dolphins jumps.* 4. *The boy play. The boy plays.* / *The boys plays. The boys play.* Have children color the pictures.

Wrap-Up

Have children repeat the correct sentence for every picture on the Activity Master.

 INFORMAL ASSESSMENT (*See* Activity Masters Plus p. 46)

 MEETING INDIVIDUAL NEEDS (*See* p. 225)

Poster Book p. 8D

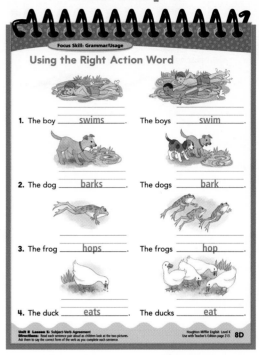

 FOR STUDENTS ACQUIRING ENGLISH

Subject-verb agreement for third person singular and plural is especially problematic for children acquiring English because of the contrasting functions of the -*s* ending. Call attention to the -*s* endings, and make sure children are aware that they mean two different things. Provide additional examples relating to classroom objects and people.

Poster Book p. 8E

Compare and Describe

Focus Skill: Grammar and Usage

1.	long	longer	longest
2.	small	smaller	smallest
3.	young	younger	youngest
4.	big	bigger	biggest

Unit 8 Lesson 6: Comparing with Adjectives
Directions: Have children help you to label the pictures in each row using the comparative and superlative forms of the adjective.

Houghton Mifflin English Level K
Use with Teacher's Edition page 214. **8E**

FOR STUDENTS ACQUIRING ENGLISH

Use sets of three classroom objects for additional comparing with adjectives. For example, hold up a heavy book. Use actions to demonstrate that it is heavy. Say: *This book is heavy.* Continue with a heavier book. Say: *This book is heavier than that book.* Finally with the heaviest of the three say: *This book is the heaviest of the three books.* Have children repeat the phrases with you. Continue with other objects.

Focus Skill Grammar and Usage

6 Comparing with Adjectives

Lesson Objective

Children will:

• recognize and use comparative and superlative forms of adjectives

Materials

What's It Like to Be a Fish?, Poster Book p. 8E; sets of three classroom objects, such as blocks, books, pencils

Warm-Up

Display page 22 of *What's It Like to Be a Fish?*. Point to and identify the striped anchovy as a <u>big</u> fish. Ask a volunteer to point to a <u>bigger</u> fish. Ask another to point to the <u>biggest</u> fish in the picture. Ask children which words let them know which fish you wanted them to point to. *(big, bigger, biggest)*

Teach Poster Book p. 8E

• Display Poster Book page 8E. Point to the first whale and identify it as <u>long</u>. Ask a volunteer to point to a <u>longer</u> whale and the <u>longest</u> whale. Explain that when we compare animals, objects, or people to one another we use special describing words. Ask children to describe the whales in order of length as you write the labels *long, longer,* and *longest*. Then together read the labels as you point to the pictures in order.

• Repeat the procedure with the remaining items: salmon: *small, smaller, smallest*; children: *young, younger, youngest*; beach balls: *big, bigger, biggest*.

Try It Out

Have small groups put three classroom objects in order by height, length, or size and describe them, using comparative adjectives. (Example: *I put these books in order by size. The book on the top is <u>big</u>. The book in the middle is <u>bigger</u>. The book on the bottom is the <u>biggest</u> book.*)

Wrap-Up

Invite each group to describe one arrangement of items. Remind children that they can use these special describing words, or adjectives, in their reports when they compare more than one thing.

 INFORMAL ASSESSMENT (*See* Activity Masters Plus p. 46)

 MEETING INDIVIDUAL NEEDS (*See* p. 225)

Focus Skill Writing

⑦ Fact and Opinion

Lesson Objectives

Children will:
- distinguish between fact and opinion
- state facts and opinions about classroom objects

Materials

What's It Like to Be a Fish?

Warm-Up

Review the book *What's It Like to Be a Fish?*. Have children recall facts that they learned. Then ask them what they thought about the book.

Teach

- Tell children that a fact is true information. An opinion is what we think or feel about something. An opinion uses words such as *I think* or *I like*.

- Read aloud the following sentences, and have children decide which one tells a fact and which one gives an opinion.

  This is a dolphin. (fact) *I love to watch dolphins swim.* (opinion)

- Continue with the following sentences.

  1. *The turtle is big and green.* (fact)

     Turtles are the most interesting animals. (opinion)

  2. *I like to build sandcastles.* (opinion)

     The children are building two sandcastles. (fact)

  3. *I would not like an octopus for a pet.* (opinion)

     An octopus has eight legs. (fact)

Try It Out

Have pairs of children take turns giving facts and opinions about classroom objects. (Examples: *The blue chair has four legs.* (fact) *I think the blue chair is soft.* (opinion))

Wrap-Up

Review with children the difference between fact and opinion. Then have pairs share some of the facts and opinions they generated together.

 INFORMAL ASSESSMENT (*See* Activity Masters Plus p. 46)

 MEETING INDIVIDUAL NEEDS (*See* p. 226)

 FOR STUDENTS ACQUIRING ENGLISH

With children, brainstorm a list of words that are used to express feelings. Begin with strong words in context sentences. Say: *I love chocolate. I hate peas.* Use facial expressions to show the strong feelings. Be sure to include common adjectives such as *good, great, beautiful, terrible, awful, ugly.* Emphasize that all of these words are clues to feelings or opinions. Then contrast feelings and opinions with facts.

Focus Skill **Study Skills**

⑧ ABC Order

Lesson Objectives	**Materials**
Children will:	*What's It Like to Be a Fish?*, Activity Master 121, letter cards, index cards, drawing paper, scissors, paste
• arrange letters in alphabetical order	
• alphabetize words using the first letter	

Warm-Up

Ask children to identify the alphabet on your classroom border. Then say the alphabet with children as you point to each letter on the classroom alphabet banner or display.

Teach

- Remind children that the order in which letters appear in the alphabet is called ABC order. Point to the first names of the author and illustrator of *What's It Like to Be a Fish?*, and have children identify the first letters in their names. Ask: *Which letter comes first,* W *or* H*? (H)* Then have children look at the first letters of the last names. Ask: *Which letter comes first,* P *or* K*? (K)*

- Have children write their first names on index cards, circling the first letter. Then call four children to the front of the room, and help them use the classroom alphabet banner to put themselves in ABC order. Repeat until all children have had a chance to participate.

Try It Out Activity Master 121

Have children complete Activity Master 121 by naming the words on the picture-word cards, circling the first letter in each word, cutting out the cards, and gluing them in ABC order on a separate sheet of paper.

Wrap-Up

Ask children to share their work by "reading" and pointing to the words in order. Remind them that the order in which the pictures and words appear on their page is called ABC order.

 INFORMAL ASSESSMENT (*See* Activity Masters Plus p. 46)

 MEETING INDIVIDUAL NEEDS (*See* p. 226)

FOR STUDENTS ACQUIRING ENGLISH

Say each of the letters of the alphabet clearly and distinctly so that children acquiring English can better distinguish the sounds. Have children say the letters with you. You may also want to teach or review the alphabet song. Make sure children understand that ABC order relates to the first letter of a word. Use phrases such as A *is for apple* to reinforce this concept.

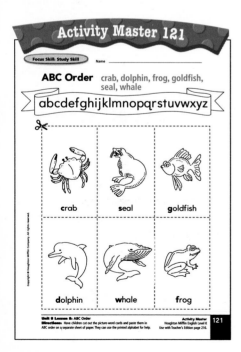

Activity Master 121

Focus Skill: Study Skill Name _____

ABC Order crab, dolphin, frog, goldfish, seal, whale

abcdefghijklmnopqrstuvwxyz

crab | seal | goldfish

dolphin | whale | frog

Unit 8 Lesson 8: ABC Order
Directions: Have children cut out the picture-word cards and paste them in ABC order on a separate sheet of paper. They can use the printed alphabet for help.

Activity Master
Houghton Mifflin English Level K
Use with Teacher's Edition page 216.
121

Focus Skill | Study Skills

⑨ Finding Information

Lesson Objectives

Children will:

- identify which resources they can use to find information
- ask and answer relevant questions and make contributions in group discussion

Materials

What's It Like to Be a Fish?, Poster Book p. 8F, encyclopedia, children's picture dictionary, newspaper

Optional Materials

nonfiction books, videos

Warm-Up

Display *What's It Like to Be a Fish?*, an encyclopedia, and a children's picture dictionary for children to examine. Then show or tell children where each resource can be found in the school library.

Teach   Poster Book p. 8F

- Explain to children that when they have a question they can find answers in different places, such as encyclopedias and dictionaries. Display Poster Book page 8F. Name the resources and, if possible, provide samples of them.

- Ask children to listen as you describe what kind of information can be found in each resource.

  A **dictionary** gives the meanings of words. The words are arranged in ABC order. An **encyclopedia** gives information about many different topics. The topics are arranged in ABC order. A **nonfiction book** gives information on a topic. A **newspaper** tells about what is happening. **Videos** show and tell facts about many topics. **The Internet** has dictionaries, encyclopedias, newspapers, magazines, and many sites about special topics.

- Mention that people and television can also be sources of information.

Try It Out

Ask children what resources they could use to find the answers to these questions: *What is a lobster?* (encyclopedia, video, Internet, book, person) *What does the word* sprint *mean?* (dictionary) *What will the weather in your town be like today?* (newspaper, Internet, television) Use resources to find the answers together. Then have children ask questions about facts they want to know and discuss where they could find the answers. If possible, use available resources to find some or all of the answers.

Wrap-Up

Ask volunteers to review the resources they learned about.

 INFORMAL ASSESSMENT (*See* Activity Masters Plus p. 46)

 MEETING INDIVIDUAL NEEDS (*See* p. 227)

 FOR STUDENTS ACQUIRING ENGLISH

As you present each type of resource, say the name and have children repeat after you. Allow the children ample time to examine each type and then afterward ask yes-no, choice, and information questions about the resources. Ask: *Is this a dictionary or an encyclopedia? What's this? Is an encyclopedia in ABC order?*

Poster Book p. 8F

Poster Book p. 8G

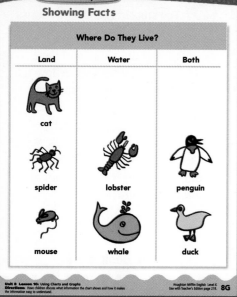

Focus Skill: Study Skill
Showing Facts

Where Do They Live?

Land	Water	Both
cat		
spider	lobster	penguin
mouse	whale	duck

Unit 8 Lesson 10: Using Charts and Graphs
Directions: Have children discuss what information the chart shows and how it makes the information easy to understand.
Houghton Mifflin English Level K
Use with Teacher's Edition page 218. **8G**

Activity Masters 122–123

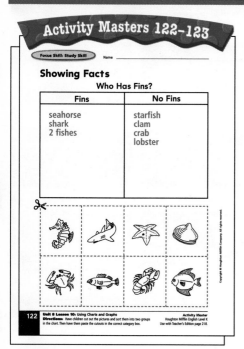

Focus Skill: Study Skill   Name _____

Showing Facts
Who Has Fins?

Fins	No Fins
seahorse	starfish
shark	clam
2 fishes	crab
	lobster

122 Unit 8 Lesson 10: Using Charts and Graphs
Directions: Have children cut out the pictures and sort them into two groups in the chart. Then have them paste the cutouts in the correct category box.
Activity Master
Houghton Mifflin English Level K
Use with Teacher's Edition page 218.

FOR STUDENTS ACQUIRING ENGLISH

Children will be able to sort the sea creatures but will need vocabulary support. As you present words such as *chart*, *graph*, and *creature*, have children repeat after you. Reinforce vocabulary by encouraging the children to use the words and by asking questions. Ask: *Is this a chart or a graph?*

⑩ Using Charts and Graphs

Lesson Objective

Children will:
• use charts and graphs to get information

Materials

What's It Like to Be a Fish?, Poster Book p. 8G, Activity Masters 122–123, masking tape, drawing paper, scissors, paste

Warm-Up

Display page 11 of *What's It Like to Be a Fish?* and tell children that this is a diagram. Ask: *What information does it show?* (Sample answer: It shows the names of the different parts of a fish.)

Teach   Poster Book p. 8G

• Explain that a diagram is just one way to show information so that it is easy to understand. Display Poster Book page 8G and tell children that this is a chart. Read the title and chart headings. Ask: *What does the chart show? How does it make the information easier to understand?* (Sample answers: It tells the different places animals live. Sorting the pictures by place makes it easy to see where each animal lives.)

• Let each child draw a picture of his or her favorite animal. Create a graph grid (3 x 6 squares) on the floor with masking tape. Number the left side with number cards 1–6, and label the other with the category words *Land*, *Water*, and *Both*. Help children sort their animal pictures by where they live, placing their pictures on the graph grid in one of the labeled categories.

• Then point to the graph and explain that this is called a graph. Ask: *What does our graph show?* (Sample answer: It shows how many of our favorite animals live on land, water, or both.) *Where do most of our favorite animals live? How many live in water? How does the graph help answer these questions?* (Sample answer: You can compare the numbers without counting.)

Try It Out   Activity Masters 122–123

Have children complete Activity Master 122 by cutting out the sea creatures and pasting them on the sorting chart. Then have children cut out the sea creatures on Activity Master 123 and sort and paste them on the graph.

Wrap-Up

Remind children that charts and graphs order facts in a way that can be seen. Explain that people often use charts and graphs when they write reports.

✓ **INFORMAL ASSESSMENT** (*See* Activity Masters Plus p. 46)

 MEETING INDIVIDUAL NEEDS (*See* p. 227)

11 Report

Lesson Objectives

Children will:
- choose a topic and audience for a report
- contribute to a report, using the steps of the writing process
- reflect on their writing experience

Materials

Poster Book p. 8H, Transparency 8–4 or chart paper, dry erase markers, nonfiction resource material for a chosen animal or Additional Resources, pp. 254–255

Focus on Instruction

Tell children that you are going to work together to write a report about an animal. Explain that good writers usually follow certain steps when they write something that others will read. Tell them that you will follow these same steps.

PREWRITING

Choose a Topic

- Help children think about their audience as they brainstorm topic ideas. (Examples: Is another class learning about a certain animal that we think is interesting? Do some of our family members really like certain animals?)
- Record children's topic suggestions on the board or on chart paper. Together, decide on an animal and an audience for the report.

Plan the Report   Poster Book p. 8H

- Display Poster Book page 8H. Have children suggest a title for the report that includes the name of the animal. Write it at the top of the page, using a dry erase marker.
- Write the name of the animal in each blank. Read the questions aloud. Then have children suggest resources in which they can find the answers. Provide the appropriate resources, and find the answers as a class. Alternately, assign questions to groups of children and help them to find the answers.
- Draw simple pictures or write key words on Poster Book page 8H to record children's answers.

INTERNET CONNECTION
Go to www.eduplace.com/kids/hme/ for Internet links to sites with information for research topics.

NOTE If you are unable to find information on a particular animal, there is information on manatees, horses, alligators, and tigers in Additional Resources, pages 254–255. Read aloud or tape record the material, and let children use this information to write a report.

Topic Ideas
- tigers
- elephants
- dolphins
- cats
- manatees
- alligators

Poster Book p. 8H

Shared Writing: Prewriting
Planning Our Report

Title _____

Question: What does a _____ look like?

Facts: _____

Question: Where does a _____ live?

Facts: _____

Question: What does a _____ eat?

Facts: _____

NOTE As you draft, point out the correct use of capital letters and end marks that children have learned. You may also wish to use the animal name at the beginning of most sentences so children can replace it to improve sentence fluency during the revising stage.

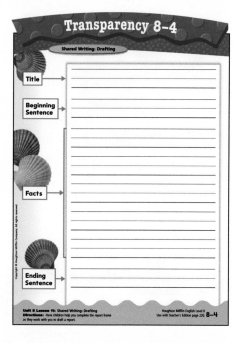

Transparency 8–4

Shared Writing: Drafting

Title
Beginning Sentence
Facts
Ending Sentence

Unit 8 Lesson 11: Shared Writing: Drafting
Directions: Have children help you complete the report frame as they work with you to draft a report.

Houghton Mifflin English Level K
Use with Teacher's Edition page 220. 8–4

Questions for Revising

✔ Does our beginning ask a question about the topic?

✔ Did we give facts about our topic?

✔ Does our ending tell one big idea about the topic to finish the report?

DRAFTING   Transparency 8–4, Poster Book p. 8H

• Before drafting, review what makes good written reports.

What Makes a Great Report?

- A good beginning tells something interesting about the topic.

- Facts give true information about the topic.

- A good ending tells the important facts or makes a final comment about the topic.

• Have volunteers contribute ideas for the draft, using Poster Book page 8H as a guide. Record children's suggestions on Transparency 8–4 or on chart paper. Help children orally compose text by asking the following questions:

- What can we write for a **title** that tells what our report is about?

- What **beginning sentence** can we write that will say something interesting about the topic?

- Which **facts** answer questions about this animal?

- What **ending sentence** can we write to say one big idea about the topic and to show that the report is finished?

• Then read your draft together.

REVISING

• Tell children that they need to think about whether their report will be clear and interesting to their audience. Read aloud the Questions for Revising. Reread the report chorally with the class, answering one question at a time.

• Ask children if any facts or details could be added to make the report clearer or more interesting for the audience. Make any agreed upon revisions.

• Then remind children what they have learned about sentence fluency. Together, see if any of the words at the beginning of sentences should be replaced to make the report flow more smoothly or sound better.

They
Cats are small animals. ~~Cats~~ are smaller than most dogs.

PUBLISHING

Make a clean final copy of the report.

● Ask volunteers to add illustrations or diagrams of the animal with captions on chart paper, or have the class make the report into a booklet.

● Help children plan a way to share the report with their intended audience. Afterward, the report can be put in the class Reading and Listening Center.

SCHOOL-HOME CONNECTION You may want to have a classroom volunteer or assistant reproduce the report. Have children illustrate the pages and take the report home to share with family members.

REFLECTING

Praise children for planning and writing a report. Discuss their writing experience. Ask:

● *What books and materials did we use to answer questions about our topic?*

● *What was easy to do? What was difficult?*

● *What things might we do differently the next time we have to write a report?*

Good Report

⑫ Report

Lesson Objectives

Children will:
• tell, dictate, or write a report
• listen and respond to the writing of peers

Materials

drawing paper, writing paper

Focus on Instruction

Tell children that they are going to write their own report about a topic that interests them. They should think about who will read their report. Here are some ideas you might use to help children plan, write, and share their reports.

Planning Ideas

THINKING ABOUT TOPICS Help children list possible topics for reports. Suggest that they brainstorm topics in areas that interest them, such as places they have been, animals, or famous people. Children can also use their journals as a source for topic ideas. Children who are having trouble thinking of their own topics can use one of the Writing Prompts on page 223. They may also find topics by reading one of the books in the Bibliography on page 206.

ORGANIZING IDEAS Have children develop their topics by asking and answering questions with a partner. One child names the topic, and the other child asks questions about it to help extract information.

Writing

Allow children to produce their reports in the format that is most appropriate to their own stage of writing development as indicated in the chart below.

Writing Options		
Emergent Writers	**Early Beginning Writers**	**Late Beginning and Transitional Writers**
Children can draw pictures to represent the facts for their topics. They can add pretend or "scribble" writing to describe them, and then dictate their text for an adult to record.*	Children can draw pictures to show the facts about their topic. They can label them with single words or phrases and tell the facts to an adult, or they can dictate their report to an adult to record.*	Children can write the topic of their report and one or two facts about that topic using temporary spelling. Have children illustrate their sentence or sentences.

*Some children may feel their writing is not valid if an adult rewrites it.

 INFORMAL ASSESSMENT (*See* Activity Masters Plus p. 46)

 FOR STUDENTS ACQUIRING ENGLISH

Be sure that children acquiring English understand that they are going to write their own reports about any topic they want. To help them choose a topic, ask, *What is your favorite animal? What is your favorite sport? Is there a game or a type of food from your or your parents' country of origin that you would like to share with the class?* Help them dictate or write a list.

 Writing Portfolio

If you are collecting samples of children's writing, decide if you want to save this piece.

Student Sample

Early Beginning Writer

Ideas for Sharing

Have children share their completed reports by "reading" them aloud or by using one of the suggestions below.

Write It Children can make their reports into booklets. Have children write report titles and their names on the cover. Place their reports in the Reading and Listening Center.

Say It Have children present their reports as if they were television broadcasters.

Show It Ask children to draw diagrams about their topic. Have children use the diagrams to explain their topic.

After each child shares his or her work, the listeners should tell at least one thing they liked about the report. (Examples: Your topic was interesting. The question in the beginning made me want to know more about the topic.)

 FOR STUDENTS ACQUIRING ENGLISH

Have children read the first draft aloud in chorus. Then ask a few volunteers to read it. Reviewing the draft in this way may help children find parts of the report that need revision and it will provide good oral reading practice. Assign children acquiring English the role of illustrators for the final report.

 INTERNET CONNECTION

See www.eduplace.com/rdg/hme/ for printable patterns for making shape paper booklets.

Writing Prompts

FINE ART Poster Book p. 2D

Display Poster Book page 2D. Ask volunteers to identify the different animals on the poster. Then have children choose one of them. Ask: *What do you know about this animal from looking at this painting? What does the animal look like? Is there anything you want to learn about this animal? Find out more about it.*

SOCIAL STUDIES

Ask children where they would like to go on a trip. Would they like to visit the mountains or the desert? a river or an ocean? Tell them to think of a place that they would like to visit and find out more about it. Tell them to write about what they learn, and to draw pictures of what the place looks like.

 INTERNET CONNECTION

See www.eduplace.com/rdg/hme/ for more writing ideas.

Meeting Individual Needs

Lesson 3 Focus Skill   Oral Language: Sharing Information

RETEACHING ALTERNATIVE STRATEGY

Display pages 18–19 in *What's It Like to Be a Fish?*. Tell children that when they tell facts about a topic, they need to speak clearly and loudly enough for others to hear. Model good speaking by using your hands to point to the gills on the diagram as you tell one fact about gills. Speak clearly and distinctly. Then have children draw detailed pictures of the classroom or one of the centers. Each child can use the picture as a prop to share facts about the kindergarten classroom to a small group.

CHALLENGE

Have small groups form teams to report the kindergarten news, sports, and weather, just as they have seen on television news programs. Have them share the information in the form of a newscast. Remind them to follow the Speaking Tips on page 16.

FOR STUDENTS ACQUIRING ENGLISH

Allow children to watch several presentations before they present to the group. Ask children to pay special attention to speaking loudly and clearly, using gestures and facial expressions.

Lesson 4 Focus Skill   Listening and Viewing: Information and Media

RETEACHING ALTERNATIVE STRATEGY

Display a magazine photograph of a cat and a picture book illustration of a cat. Explain that both give the viewer information. Ask how information or facts from the photo differ from the information in the drawing of the cat. (Sample answers: The photo shows light in the cat's eyes, the true color of fur, the details of claws or whiskers. The illustration may give a sense of movement or show expression on the cat's face.)

CHALLENGE

Provide pairs of children magazines and picture books that show the same things, such as household items (brooms, chairs), wild animals, or forms of transportation. Ask children to dictate or write the facts that each image provides. Then have volunteers explain how the information differs.

FOR STUDENTS ACQUIRING ENGLISH

Show photos of fish in different settings, and brainstorm words about their surroundings (for example, *among seaweed; in dark waters; near the shore*).

Lesson 5 Focus Skill Grammar: Subject-Verb Agreement

RETEACHING ALTERNATIVE STRATEGY

Hold up a picture of at least two people performing an action. Give an oral sentence that tells what the people in the picture are doing. (Use a verb that has a singular form that ends in *s*.) Then cover up all but one person in the picture and say a second sentence that tells what that person is doing. Explain how you changed the action word by adding *s*. Then show another picture of people in action. Ask volunteers to say sentences describing the actions, using both singular and plural subjects.

CHALLENGE

Ask children to draw pictures of three classmates doing different playground activities. Then have them dictate or write captions that tell about what one and more than one classmate is doing. Ask them to explain how the action word changes when it tells about one.

FOR STUDENTS ACQUIRING ENGLISH

Contrast *run/runs*, *hide/hides*, and *sit/sits* using sample sentences that show proper agreement.

Lesson 6 Focus Skill Grammar: Comparing with Adjectives

RETEACHING ALTERNATIVE STRATEGY

Show three strips of paper of varying lengths. Put them in order from shortest to longest. Help children describe the arrangement, using comparative language. (Example: This one is long. This one is longer. This one is the longest.) Then pass out a set of three strips to pairs of children. Have them arrange the strips and explain the arrangement, using the words *short/shorter/shortest* and *long/longer/longest*.

CHALLENGE

Have pairs of children measure classroom objects by cutting lengths of yarn to match. Have them label each length of yarn and then put the pieces in order by length. Ask children to describe the measurements using the words *long*, *longer*, and *longest*.

FOR STUDENTS ACQUIRING ENGLISH

Choose a page in *What's It Like to Be a Fish?* and have children compare the sizes of fish using comparative and superlative forms.

Meeting Individual Needs

Lesson 7 Focus Skill   Writing: Fact and Opinion

RETEACHING ALTERNATIVE STRATEGY
Play a piece of music that children know. Ask them to tell a fact, or one true thing, about the song. (Possible answers: title, who or what it is about, whether it is a fast or a slow song) Then have children move to the music. Ask them to give opinions, explaining that opinions tell how someone feels. Help children use phrases such as *I think* or *I feel* when they give opinions.

CHALLENGE
Have children select a picture from a nonfiction book that shows something they know about, such as a pet or a food. Ask them to tell one fact and one opinion about the picture to a partner. Have partners trade pictures, giving a different fact and opinion about the subject of each other's pictures.

FOR STUDENTS ACQUIRING ENGLISH

Use facial expressions to compare statements beginning with *I think* or *I feel* against statements beginning with *I love* or *I hate*. Explain that all these statements express opinion, and center attention to the word *I* that is common to all.

Lesson 8 Focus Skill   Study Skills: ABC Order

RETEACHING ALTERNATIVE STRATEGY
Display chart paper with the alphabet listed in 2–3 rows with space below each letter. Hand out groups of four picture-word cards in ABC order. Start by asking the person who has the *A* card to tape it to the chart under *A*. Then ask what letter comes next. Tape *B* on the chart. Continue for *C* and *D*. Then hand out the next four letter cards, and ask children to place the cards in ABC order. Explain that the words are in ABC order because they follow the alphabet.

CHALLENGE
Have children work in small groups to find examples of words in ABC order in classroom books and references, such as dictionaries, encyclopedias, and indexes in texts and nonfiction books. Ask the groups to share their findings with the class.

FOR STUDENTS ACQUIRING ENGLISH

Use the materials described in the Reteaching note to reinforce letter sequence. Guide children in singing "The Alphabet Song" again, grouping the picture-word cards according to the letter sequence in the song. Remain silent while they sing out the appropriate letter at each pause, using the letters on the chart as necessary.

Lesson 9 Focus Skill   Study Skills: Finding Information

RETEACHING ALTERNATIVE STRATEGY

Tell children you have seen robins eat worms, but you wonder if robins eat other kinds of food. Display a nonfiction book about birds, the *R* volume of an encyclopedia, a children's picture dictionary, and a CD-ROM encyclopedia. Explain what each resource offers to help you answer this question. Then hold up a daily newspaper and discuss why you would probably not find an answer to your question in this resource. (Most articles in newspapers are about things that happen each day.)

CHALLENGE

Help children set up a resource center in your classroom to get ready for writing an animal report. Arrange for them to work with the school librarian to gather a variety of resources. Then they can organize the resources by making signs and labels for each type of resource.

FOR STUDENTS ACQUIRING ENGLISH

Use a picture dictionary to help children suggest the names of animals that live in water, for example, *goldfish, crab, frog,* and *dolphin.* Ask children where they might find more information on each animal (an encyclopedia), and have them arrange the items alphabetically before looking them up.

Lesson 10 Focus Skill   Study Skills: Using Charts and Graphs

RETEACHING ALTERNATIVE STRATEGY

Randomly pin up six animal pictures, two animals without tails and four with tails. Write *Tails* and *No Tails* labels on chart paper. Ask children to sort the pictures into the two groups. Tell them this is a sorting chart. Then place the two category titles to the left of a 2 x 6 block grid and add numerals from 1 to 6 under the grid to make a graph. Have children tell you how many blocks to color to graph the information shown in the chart.

CHALLENGE

Have the children work together to record information from six classmates who tell the kind of pet they own or would like to own. Then have children use the information to make a graph that shows this information. Suggest they create a graph, using the graph on Activity Master 123 as a model. Ask children to share their completed graph with the class.

FOR STUDENTS ACQUIRING ENGLISH

Review vocabulary such as *chart, graph, more,* and *fewer* using the chart described in the Reteaching activity: *There are _____ animals with tails than animals without tails.*

Additional Resources

The following materials support activities in the Houghton Mifflin English kindergarten program. You may use the chants, finger plays, poems, songs, stories, and other materials during Daily Discussion or as part of your read-aloud time. Some of the resources will be referenced in the Teacher Edition. The unit, lesson, and Teacher Edition page references are provided on those selections that are connected to particular units.

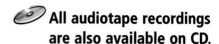 **All audiotape recordings are also available on CD.**

Counting Rhymes, Chants, Songs, Finger Plays, and Poems

The Alphabet Song

Unit 1, Building Background, p. 30.

One, Two, Buckle My Shoe

Mother Goose

Unit 2, Daily Discussion, p. 51

One, two,
Buckle my shoe;
Three, four,
Knock at the door,
Five, six,
Pick up sticks;
Seven, eight,
Lay them straight;
Nine, ten,
A good fat hen;
Eleven, twelve,
Dig and delve;
Thirteen, fourteen,
Maids a-courting;
Fifteen, sixteen,
Maids in the kitchen;
Seventeen, eighteen,
Maids a-waiting;
Nineteen, twenty,
My plate's empty.

Engine, Engine
Jump Rope Chant
Unit 2, Daily Discussion, p. 51

Engine, engine, number Nine,
Going down the Chicago line.
See it sparkle, see it shine,
Engine, engine, number Nine!

Five Little Pumpkins
A Counting Song
Unit 2, Daily Discussion, p. 51

Five lit-tle pump-kins sit-ting on a gate.   First one said, "Oh my, it's get-ting late."

Sec-ond one said, "There's a frost in the air." The third one said, "But we don't care." The

fourth one said, "Let's run and run and run." The fifth one said, "I'm rea-dy for some fun." "Oo-

oo," went the wind and out went the light, And the five lit-tle pump-kins rolled out of sight.

Two Blackbirds Sitting on a Hill

A Finger Play

Unit 2, Daily Discussion, p. 51

There were two blackbirds (*Put hands in fists in front of chest.*)
Sitting on a hill,
The one named Jack, (*Open right hand.*)
And the other named Jill. (*Open left hand.*)
Fly away, Jack! (*Move right hand in fluttering motion behind back.*)
Fly away, Jill! (*Move left hand in fluttering motion behind back.*)
Come again, Jack! (*Bring right hand back in front of chest.*)
Come again, Jill! (*Bring left hand back in front of chest.*)

Five Little Chickadees

Unit 2, Daily Discussion, p. 51

Verse — Lightly

G   C
Five lit-tle chick-a-dees peep-ing at the door,

D7   G
One flew a-way and then there were four;

Chorus   G   D7
Chick-a-dee, chick-a-dee, hap-py and gay,

                                 G
Chick-a-dee, chick-a-dee, fly a-way.

Five Little Ducks

Unit 2, Daily Discussion, p. 51

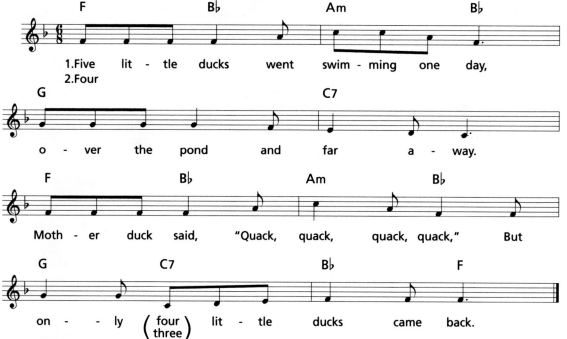

F   B♭   Am   B♭

1.Five lit - tle ducks went swim - ming one day,
2.Four

G   C7

o - ver the pond and far a - way.

F   B♭   Am   B♭

Moth - er duck said, "Quack, quack, quack, quack," But

G   C7   B♭   F

on - - ly (four / three) lit - tle ducks came back.

3. Three little ducks went swimming one day,
    Over the pond and far away.
    Mother duck said, "Quack, quack, quack, quack,"
    But only two little ducks came back.

4. Two little ducks went swimming one day,
    Over the pond and far away.
    Mother duck said, "Quack, quack, quack, quack,"
    But only one little duck came back.

5. One little duck went swimming one day,
    Over the pond and far away.
    Mother duck said, "Quack, quack, quack, quack,"
    But that day no little ducks came back.

6. Five little ducks came back one day,
    Over the pond and far away.
    Mother duck said, "Quack, quack, quack, quack,"
    And the five little ducks came back.

Hippety Hop

A Nursery Rhyme

Unit 2, Daily Discussion, p. 51

Hippety hop to the barber shop,
To get a stick of candy,
One for you and one for me,
And one for Sister Mandy.

Baa, Baa, Black Sheep

A Nursery Rhyme

Unit 2, Daily Discussion, p. 51

Baa, baa, black sheep, have you any wool?
"Yes, Sir, yes, Sir, three bags full;
One for my master, one for my dame,
And one for the little boy that lives in the lane."

This Old Man

An English Folk Song

Unit 2, Daily Discussion, p. 51

This old man, he played ONE,
He played nick-nack on my drum.

CHORUS
With a nick-nack, paddy whack,
give a dog a bone,
This old man came rolling home.

This old man, he played TWO,
He played nick-nack on my shoe.

CHORUS

This old man, he played THREE,
He played nick-nack on my tree.

CHORUS

This old man, he played FOUR,
He played nick-nack on my door.

CHORUS

This old man, he played FIVE,
He played nick-nack on my hive.

CHORUS

This old man, he played SIX,
He played nick-nack on my sticks.

CHORUS

This old man, he played SEVEN,
He played nick-nack on my oven.

CHORUS

This old man, he played EIGHT,
He played nick-nack on my gate.

CHORUS

This old man, he played NINE,
He played nick-nack on my line.

CHORUS

This old man, he played TEN,
He played nick-nack on my hen.

CHORUS

Animals

A Movement Rhyme

Unit 3, Daily Discussion, p. 75

Can you hop like a rabbit?
I can hop like a rabbit.
Can you jump like a frog?
I can jump like a frog.
Can you walk like a duck?
I can walk like a duck.
Can you run like a dog?
I can run like a dog.
Can you swim like a fish?
I can swim like a fish.
And still be like a quiet child, as still as this.
I can still be a quiet child, as still as this.

Here Are My Ears

A Finger Play

Unit 3, Daily Discussion, p. 75

Here are my ears.
Here is my nose.
Here are my fingers.
Here are my toes.
Here are my eyes,
Both open wide.
Here is my mouth
With white teeth inside.
Here is my tongue
That helps me speak.
Here is my chin,
And here are my cheeks.
Here are my hands
That help me play.
Here are my feet
For walking today.

The Friendly Cow

by Robert Louis Stevenson

Unit 5, Daily Discussion, p. 125

The friendly cow all red and white
I love with all my heart:
She gives me cream with all her might,
To eat with apple-tart.

The Star

by Jane Taylor

Unit 5, Daily Discussion, p. 125

Twinkle, twinkle, little star,
How I wonder what you are!
Up above the world so high,
Like a diamond in the sky.

Butterflies, Butterflies

Native American Pueblo Song

Unit 5, Daily Discussion, p. 125

Butterflies, butterflies,
Fly away to the flowers,
Fly, blue wing,
Fly, yellow wing,
Fly away to the flowers!

The Swing

by Robert Louis Stevenson

Unit 5, Daily Discussion, p. 125

How do you like to go up in a swing,
Up in the air so blue?
Oh, I do think it the pleasantest thing
Ever a child can do!

Up in the air and over the wall,
Till I can see so wide,
Rivers and trees and cattle and all
Over the countryside—

Till I look down on the garden green,
Down on the roof so brown—
Up in the air I go flying again,
Up in the air and down!

Who Has Seen the Wind?

by Christina Rossetti

Unit 5, Daily Discussion, p. 125

Who has seen the wind?
Neither I nor you:
But when the leaves hang trembling,
The wind is passing thro'.

Who has seen the wind?
Neither you nor I:
But when the trees bow down their heads,
The wind is passing by.

There Was an Old Man with a Beard

by Edward Lear

Unit 5, Daily Discussion, p. 125

There was an Old Man with a beard,
Who said, "It is just as I feared!—
Two Owls and a Hen, four Larks and a Wren,
Have all built their nests in my beard!"

I've Got a Dog

Anonymous

Unit 5, Daily Discussion, p. 125

I've got a dog as thin as a rail,
He's got fleas all over his tail;
Every time his tail goes flop,
The fleas on the bottom all hop to the top.

Stories and Folktales

Unit 6, Daily Discussion, p. 151

The Little Red Hen and the Wheat

A Traditional Tale

Once there was a little red hen, and she found a grain of wheat in the barnyard and said, "Who will plant this wheat?"

"Not I," said the dog.

"Not I," said the cat.

"Not I," said the goose.

"Not I," said the turkey.

"I will, then," said the little red hen, and so she did.

She planted the grain of wheat. Pretty soon the wheat began to grow up out of the ground. The sun shone and the rain fell and the wheat kept growing until it was a tall, strong stalk and had a big head of ripe grain at the top.

"Who will harvest or cut this wheat?" said the little red hen.

"Not I," said the dog.

"Not I," said the cat.

"Not I," said the goose.

"Not I," said the turkey.

"I will, then," said the little red hen, and so she did. She harvested the wheat.

"Who will prepare this wheat?" said the little red hen.

"Not I," said the dog.

"Not I," said the cat.

"Not I," said the goose.

"Not I," said the turkey.

"I will, then," said the little red hen, and so she did. She prepared the wheat.

"Who will take this bundle of wheat to the mill to have it ground into flour?" said the little red hen.

"Not I," said the dog.

"Not I," said the cat.

"Not I," said the goose.

"Not I," said the turkey.

"I will, then," said the little red hen, and so she did. She took the wheat to mill, and by and by she came back with the flour.

"Who will make this flour into bread?" said the little red hen.

"Not I," said the dog.

"Not I," said the cat.

"Not I," said the goose.

"Not I," said the turkey.

"I will, then," said the little red hen, and so she did. She baked the dough and made a loaf of bread.

"Who will eat this bread?" said the little red hen.

"I will," said the dog.

"I will," said the cat.

"I will," said the goose.

"I will," said the turkey.

"Only I will," said the little red hen, and she ate the loaf of bread all up by herself.

The Elves and the Shoemaker

**A Fairy Tale by Wilhelm Grimm,
translated by Edgar Taylor**

Unit 6, Daily Discussion, p. 151

There was once a shoemaker who, though he worked very hard and was very honest, yet could not earn enough to live on. At last all his money was gone, and he had the leather for only one more pair of shoes. That evening he cut the leather to have it ready to make into shoes the next day. "Alas," said he, "things are in a bad way; but I've done the best I could, and now I may as well go to bed."

So he went to bed and fell asleep. Early in the morning, he sat down to do his work. To his great astonishment, there stood the shoes all made on the table. The good man knew not what to say or think of this strange event. He looked at the workmanship. "Not a false stitch in the whole job. It is better work than I can do myself."

Presently a customer came in, and the shoemaker showed him the new pair of shoes. The customer examined them and was so much pleased that he willingly paid a higher price for the shoes than usual. With this money the shoemaker bought leather enough to make two pairs more. In the evening he cut out the work and went to bed early, in order that he might be up and start making the shoes at daybreak. But when he rose with the first light in the morning, there on the table were the two pairs of shoes all finished. Buyers came in who paid him handsomely for their shoes, and he had the money to buy the leather for four pairs more. He cut out the work again in the evening and found it finished the next morning. Thus matters went on, and the shoemaker became wealthy.

One evening as the shoemaker and his wife were sitting by the fire chatting together, he said, "I would like to stay up and watch tonight and see who it is that comes and does my work for me."

"I think that is a very good plan," said his wife, "and I will stay up with you."

So they left the light burning and hid themselves in a corner of the room behind a curtain and watched what would happen. They saw nothing unusual until the clock struck twelve. Then little elves slipped in at the door and went to work at the shoemaker's bench. They took up the work that was cut out, and how their fingers flew! They rapped and tapped and stitched away at such a rate that the shoemaker was all amazement. Not once did they stop until the job was finished and the shoes stood ready for use on the table. Then the elves looked at their work and bustled off.

The next day the wife said to the shoemaker, "Those little men made us rich and we ought to be thankful to them. I will make them each a coat and you can make each of them a little pair of shoes."

"Yes," said the shoemaker, "a great idea."

So the shoemaker made the little shoes, and his wife made the coats and that night they laid out these things on the table, instead of the leather that was usually there. Then they hid behind the curtain to watch what the little elves would do. The clock struck twelve, and in they came, about to do their work. Then they saw the coats and the shoes. They picked them up and laughed and danced and were greatly delighted. All night they jumped about as merry as could be.

Then with the morning sun, the little elves danced out of the door and never came to the shoemaker's house again. But everything went well with the shoemaker and his wife from that time as long as they both lived, and they lived a long, long time.

The Rabbit and the Hungry Coyote

A Folktale from Mexico

Unit 6, Daily Discussion, p. 151

In the foothills of Mexico there once lived a young rabbit. In the daytime the rabbit munched on clover or chased his brothers and sisters through the tall grass. In the evening, the little rabbit would rest on a bridge that overlooked a pond. He never went into the water, for rabbits don't like to swim. But sometimes he would hop onto the bridge and look at his reflection in the glassy surface of the pond.

One evening when Rabbit was resting near the bridge, a coyote came along. Now Rabbit was smart enough to be afraid, because a coyote is very much like a wolf. And this coyote looked hungry. But Rabbit knew that if he ran, the coyote would surely chase him. So Rabbit stamped his feet to send a warning to his brothers and sisters. *Thump-thump!* And then he stood absolutely still.

"Good evening, Señor!" said Rabbit in a friendly voice.

The coyote was a little surprised at the rabbit's boldness—he was used to little rabbits running away from him. He took another look, just to make sure Rabbit really was a rabbit.

"Good evening," said Coyote.

"What brings you to our little pond?" said Rabbit.

"Well, I'm very hungry. I've been up and down this mountain all day, and I've seen nothing but snakes and beetles and spiders, and that isn't much of a meal." Just then Coyote gave Rabbit a long, hungry look. Rabbit knew just what that look meant! Quickly, he tried to get Coyote interested in something else.

"What luck!" said Rabbit. "Do you see what is in the middle of the pond?"

Through the darkness, Coyote saw something round and yellow glowing in the water.

"You won't be hungry much longer," said Rabbit. "It's cheese! A big, round, delicious wheel of cheese. It must have fallen off a wagon as someone was passing over the bridge."

"Is that really cheese?" said Coyote, taking a closer look. "I've often wondered what that was. I've seen one before in another pond, but it was only half a cheese. My, that does look delicious." Coyote was beginning to drool a little from hunger.

"It's a pity I'm not much of a swimmer," said Rabbit sadly, "and I suppose you aren't either. Someone else will soon be enjoying that big wheel of cheese."

When he heard this, Coyote stood up and hurried over to the pond. *Splash!* Coyote jumped right into the cold water and swam toward the golden circle of cheese, his jaws wide open. Coyote snapped away hungrily, but each time he swam closer to the middle, the cheese seemed to wobble and break into pieces.

The coyote swam in circles, snapping away in vain. Exhausted, he swam back to the side of the pond, where Rabbit was watching.

"It's no use!" cried Coyote. "The cheese has broken into little pieces, and I can't catch them."

"Are you sure?" the clever Rabbit said, looking out at the dark water, which was just becoming smooth and calm again. Looking up, Coyote could hardly believe his eyes. The cheese, whole and round, was back in the middle of the pond.

Continued on page 244

"But I'm sure it was broken into pieces!" exclaimed the confused Coyote.

"It's just as whole as ever. But here is the problem," said Rabbit. "The cheese is at the bottom of the pond. You'll have to dive for it."

"Very well," said Coyote, who by now was so hungry that he would have dived to the bottom of the ocean if he had to. Back into the pond he went. After each dive, Coyote would come up for breath, but he never caught the cheese. At last he gave up and swam ashore.

"I couldn't find it!" Coyote gasped. "I saw nothing but weeds and rocks at the bottom. The fish must have taken all the cheese."

Rabbit said nothing but only stared at the pond. As the surface grew more and more still, the animals noticed something taking shape in the middle of the pond. Sure enough, the cheese was back, and this time it looked bigger, rounder, and more delicious than ever!

"There is one more thing you could try," said Rabbit thoughtfully. "It may take some time, though."

"What? What?" said Coyote, so hungry he could hardly bear to look at the cheese.

"Well, if you drink all the water in the pond, it will be easy to find the cheese."

"That's true," said Coyote. "I'm very thirsty from all that exercise, and my belly is completely empty. I'm sure I could drink up the pond in no time!"

With that, the hungry coyote ran to the edge of the pond and began to drink greedily. *Lap, lap, lap, lap, lap!*

"Good, good!" said Rabbit, encouraging him. "See now—the cheese is looking bigger by the minute! The water must be getting lower. The cheese will soon be all yours, Coyote!"

Rabbit settled back to watch as Coyote continued to drink. But after a while, Coyote began to slow down. His belly was feeling very heavy and uncomfortable. At that moment Rabbit's brother came looking for him.

"Here you are, Brother!" he exclaimed. "Did you see the full moon? It makes a beautiful reflection, doesn't it?" And he pointed right to the middle of the pond.

Rabbit began to laugh. When Coyote heard why they were laughing, he became very angry.

"You tricked me!" he said. "Just for that, I'll gobble you up!" Coyote swam to shore, but he was too full of water to take a single step. The rabbits scampered off, still laughing. When they returned later, the moon was still shining brightly in the pond. But Coyote was never seen again.

The Two Silly Kittens

A Folktale from Japan

Unit 6, Daily Discussion, p. 151

A long time ago in Japan, there were two kittens who were brothers. Meiku (meh ee koo) was the big kitten and Timuchi (tee moo chee) was the little one. They got along very well most of the time, until one day when they found two pancakes cooling on a windowsill.

"Yum!" said Meiku. "My favorite—cherry pancakes! Look how round and brown mine is!" and he took the pancake lying on top.

Timuchi took the other pancake. "Yes—and mine is still warm! How wonderful it smells!"

The two kittens looked over their shoulders to make sure no one else was around. They were very hungry and in no mood to share. Then they held up their pancakes to compare them.

"Wait!" cried Meiku. "Your pancake is bigger, and I am the bigger kitten. So I should have yours. Let's trade."

Little Timuchi held on tightly to his pancake. "Mine might be a little bigger," he said, "but since I am the smaller kitten, I need more food so that I can grow up to be a big, strong cat. Besides, your pancake has more cherries."

"Yes," returned Meiku. "But yours is warmer because it was sitting under the other one."

"It isn't warm any longer," growled Timuchi. "It has grown completely cold since you started arguing with me!"

"I didn't start it. You did!" said Meiku.

"Oh?" retorted Timuchi. "You are the one who started off saying that mine was bigger and you wanted to trade."

"And why won't you trade?" demanded Meiku. "You greedy, selfish kitten!"

"You silly, stubborn kitten!" answered Timuchi.

Meiku pounced on Timuchi and began to chase him. Round and round they went, hissing and swatting at each other. After a long time, the kittens grew too tired to run any more, but they had not given up their argument.

"Well then," said Meiku, "Since you can't be reasoned with, perhaps we can ask our sister Keiku (keh ee koo) to help settle this argument."

Timuchi agreed, because he was getting very hungry, and he wanted to eat his pancake. So the two kittens scampered off to find their older sister.

"Keiku!" they cried. "Can you help us decide which of us should get to eat the bigger pancake?"

"It's good you came to see me," said Keiku, "for I have a lot of experience in

Continued on page 247

these matters. Give me the pancakes so that I can decide which one is bigger."

Keiku examined the pancakes, one in each paw, turning them over carefully. "I can see why you were arguing," she said. "One of the pancakes is a little bigger, though the other one has more cherries. A difficult choice. Hmm."

Then, much to the kittens' dismay, Keiku took a bite out of the bigger pancake. She held up the pancakes again, to see which one was bigger. "Oh dear, I must have taken too large a bite! Now the other one is bigger," she said with a sigh, and she took a bite out of the other pancake.

As Keiku held out the pancakes again for inspection, the kittens could see that she had taken far too much.

"Well, I must take another bite!" she said cheerfully.

"Don't you think they must be equal by now?" asked Meiku nervously.

Instead of answering, Keiku just kept on taking bites, one pancake at a time, and the poor little kittens kept turning their hungry faces from the bigger pancake to the smaller one, crying "Now mine is smaller!" "Now MINE is smaller!" until there were no pancakes left to divide. Keiku had eaten every last crumb, every last cherry!

"There!" said Keiku, licking her paws. "Both pancakes are gone now. I've settled your argument, because you have nothing left to fight over."

The two kittens looked very disappointed. They slouched away, tails drooping. All that arguing had done no good, and the two kittens felt very silly indeed!

Then the kittens noticed a deliciously familiar smell wafting from their mother's kitchen. Could they be imagining it? It smelled like . . . pancakes!

"Meiku! Timuchi!" called Mother Cat out the window. "Time to eat!"

The kittens raced inside.

"Mine looks a little bigger," said Timuchi when he saw his pancake. "But I'll trade if you want to."

"No, thank you," said Meiku. "Mine will do just fine."

They quickly gobbled up their pancakes. And the two silly kittens never argued over food again.

The Yam That Talked

A West African Folktale

Unit 6, Daily Discussion, p. 151

One sunny day in Africa, a boy was digging in his family's garden. He saw a yam peeking out of the dirt. Now a yam is something like a sweet potato, and this boy liked yams.

"This yam looks good and ripe," said the boy. "I'll take it home and my mother can cook it for dinner."

Then the boy heard a small voice coming from the dirt.

"Whoa!" said the yam. "How would you like it if someone pulled you up and dropped you into a pot of boiling water? Leave me alone!"

"I didn't know that yams could talk," said the boy.

"Yams talk all the time. You just haven't been listening," said the yam.

The boy couldn't believe his ears. A yam that talked? He couldn't wait to spread the news. The boy dropped the yam and ran off to tell his sister.

"What's the matter?" asked his sister. She was playing with her doll.

"I was digging in the garden, and a yam said, 'Whoa!'" the boy told her.

"That's the craziest thing I ever heard," said the sister. "Yams can't talk."

Then the girl heard a small voice coming from her lap.

"Ouch! You're pulling my curls!" said the doll.

"I didn't know that dolls could talk," said the girl.

"Dolls talk all the time. You just haven't been listening," said the doll.

The girl couldn't believe her ears. A doll that talked? She couldn't wait to spread the news. The girl dropped her doll and ran off with the boy to tell their mother.

"What's the matter?" asked their mother. She was stirring a pot of stew.

"His yam said, 'Whoa,' and my doll said, 'Ouch,'" the girl told her.

"That's the craziest thing I ever heard," said the mother. "Yams and dolls can't talk."

Then the mother heard a small voice coming from the stew pot.

"Hurray for the yam! I'd like to meet him," said the stew.

"I didn't know that a stew could talk," said the mother.

"Stews talk all the time. You just haven't been listening," said the stew. The mother couldn't believe her ears. A stew that talked? She couldn't wait to spread the news. The mother dropped her spoon and ran off with the girl and the boy to tell their father.

"What's the matter?" asked the father.

He was carving some wood with a carving knife.

"His yam said, 'Whoa,' her doll said 'Ouch,' and my stew said, 'Hurray,'" the mother told him.

"That's the craziest thing I ever heard," said the father. "Yams and dolls and stews can't talk."

Then the father heard a small voice coming from below.

"Look out! You nearly cut yourself," said the carving knife.

"I didn't know that a knife could talk," said the father.

"Knives talk all the time. You just haven't been listening," said the knife.

Continued on page 250

The father couldn't believe his ears. A carving knife that talked? He couldn't wait to spread the news. The father dropped the carving knife and ran off with the mother and the girl and the boy to tell the grandfather.

"What's the matter?" asked the grandfather.

He was scratching his dog's ears.

"His yam said, 'Whoa,' her doll said, 'Ouch,' her stew said, 'Hurray,' and my knife said, 'Look out,'" the father told him.

"That's the craziest thing I ever heard," said the grandfather. "Yams and dolls and stews and carving knives can't talk."

Then the grandfather heard a voice coming from under his hand.

"Excuse me! Could you scratch my other ear, please?" the dog said.

"I didn't know that dogs could talk," said the grandfather.

"Dogs talk all the time. You just haven't been listening," said the dog.

The grandfather couldn't believe his ears. A dog that talked? He couldn't wait to spread the news. The grandfather left the dog and ran off with the father, the mother, the girl, and the boy to tell the grandmother.

"What's the matter?" asked the grandmother. She was sitting in her favorite chair.

"His yam said, 'Whoa,' her doll said, 'Ouch,' her stew said, 'Hurray,' his carving knife said, 'Look out,' and my dog said, 'Excuse me,'" the grandfather told her.

"That's the craziest thing I ever heard," said the grandmother. "Yams and dolls and stews and carving knives and dogs can't talk. Now go back home, all of you."

So they went back home. The grandmother sat down in her chair and had a good laugh.

Then the grandmother heard a voice coming from right underneath her.

"If you think that's crazy, you should hear what the footstool has to say!" said the chair.

The Legend of Johnny Appleseed

Unit 6, Daily Discussion, p. 151

Have you ever heard of a man called Johnny Appleseed? He was born more than two hundred years ago, and his real name was John Chapman. Johnny loved nature, and he always looked for adventure. He decided to explore the American Northwest, a part of our country where only Native Americans had lived. Some people called that land the "frontier." There are many stories about Johnny's adventures. These stories, handed down from one family to another over many years, make up the legend of Johnny Appleseed.

When he was twenty-three, Johnny left his home in Massachusetts and began walking west. People say he carried a sack of cornmeal, a stew pot, and a few tools for cutting wood and making fires. Sometimes he wore the stew pot on his head so that he wouldn't have to carry it. Johnny's feet were bare, and after he had walked at least 100 miles, it started to snow. He tore some scraps off his coat and wrapped them around his feet to keep them warm. When the snow got too deep, Johnny made snowshoes out of bark and branches. Sometimes he traveled by canoe, following the rivers west.

By springtime, Johnny had traveled all the way to Pennsylvania. Back then, only a few white people lived in the Pennsylvania countryside. There were no towns, no stores, no schools. Johnny noticed that there were no apple trees, either. It was beautiful country, and he was sure that some day, people would want to live there. As soon as the snow melted, Johnny planted his first apple seed, and as he continued walking along the river valleys, he planted more apple seeds.

People were grateful for the trees that grew from Johnny's seeds. They gave him a new name—Johnny Appleseed.

Johnny Appleseed cared for animals who were sick or hurt. Once he came upon some horses who had been abandoned in the woods. Johnny found homes for them so the horses wouldn't starve. Another time he discovered a wolf in a trap, and after setting the wolf free, he took care of its wounds.

Johnny kept on walking until he reached Ohio, where he lived for the next twenty years. He earned enough money from his apple business to buy land and build his own home, but Johnny preferred to live simply, sleeping outdoors and growing his own food. He spent some of his money on books, which he liked to loan to the people he met on his travels.

On Johnny's last trip, he walked all the way to Indiana. Knowing that the settlers would soon follow, he cleared land and planted apple trees along the way. Many nights he slept under the stars, and other times he made friends with people and stayed with them. Johnny Appleseed was staying in Indiana at the house of a friend when he died. He was buried in Ohio. On his gravestone are the words, "He lived for others."

Johnny Appleseed has never been forgotten. The children who heard his stories grew up and passed the stories on to their children and grandchildren. And if you ever travel to Pennsylvania, Ohio, or Indiana in the springtime, you can see clouds of pink and white apple blossoms all along the river valleys, where Johnny Appleseed planted the first apple trees.

Instructions

How to Make a Board Game

Unit 7, Daily Discussion, p. 177

   Board games are fun and easy to make from a file folder. First, open the folder and place it so the longest side faces you. Next, draw a square on the left side of the folder and another square on the far right side. Next, starting at the left square, draw a path of squares winding around the folder until they stop at the square on the right. Then draw a scene around the path. You could make it a garden, a forest, a town, or city. Finally, cut two different colored papers into squares for game pieces. Roll a number cube to see how many squares to move the game pieces. Invite a friend to play your board game with you.

How to Make a Paper Doll

Unit 7, Daily Discussion, p. 177

Informational Writing

Manatees

Unit 8, Daily Discussion, p. 203

Manatees are large, peaceful water animals. Manatees are found along the coasts and inlets of Florida. They live in warm shallow water where there are plenty of water plants to eat. A manatee's mouth has a special shape that helps it eat a lot of plants. That is why manatees are sometimes called sea cows. They are big heavy animals who graze a lot like cows do. Manatees usually weigh about 1,500 pounds. But instead of hoofs, manatees have very short front legs that look like paddles and round flat tails. Manatees spend all of their lives in the water.

Horses

Unit 8, Daily Discussion, p. 203

Horses have been helping people for hundreds of years. Before the days of cars and trains, people used to ride horses to go from place to place. People still ride horses now but mostly for fun, exercise, or as a sport. Horses are useful to people because they are strong and fast. They can run fast to help people round up cattle. People can also teach horses to pull carts or do tricks. Horses work with and entertain people all over the world.

Tigers

Unit 8, Daily Discussion, p. 203

Tigers are big, powerful cats. They have orange fur with black stripes. These stripes make them hard to see when they are hunting in the forests and grasslands where they live. Many people are afraid of tigers because they have long teeth and sharp claws, but tigers are shy and try to stay away from people. They like to spend most of their time hiding in the shade. When they get hungry, they use their teeth and claws to catch other animals for food. Their speed and strength make them good hunters.

Alligators

Unit 8, Daily Discussion, p. 203

Alligators are big lizards that spend their time on land and in the water. They live in or near rivers, lakes, and swamps. They have thick bodies and tails that help them run and swim very quickly. Their tough, scaly skin protects them in the water. They have strong muscles and powerful jaws with many sharp teeth that make them excellent hunters. Alligators can move very quickly into the water when they are looking for food. They usually eat smaller animals.

Index

Scope and Sequence of Skills for Level K

LISTENING

Following directions
All lessons; Unit 1 34, 42; Unit 7 176, 178, 185, 196

To fiction
Unit 2 52, 54; Unit 4 100, 102; Unit 5 126, 128;
Unit 6 151, 152, 154, 159

To nonfiction
Unit 1 28, 30; Unit 3 76, 78; Unit 7 177, 178, 180;
Unit 8 203, 204, 206

To poetry
Unit 2 51; Unit 3 84, 85; Unit 5 125

For rhyme
Unit 2 51, 55, 56, 58, 66

For different types of sentences
Unit 3 78, 79, 80, 82, 90; Unit 4 110, 119

To compare media
Unit 6 159; Unit 8 212

SPEAKING

Having a conversation or discussion
Getting Started 17, 21; All lessons

Making introductions
Unit 1 34, 42

Using the telephone
Unit 2 54, 58, 66

Telling/Retelling a story
Unit 2 54; Unit 6 152, 153, 159, 169, 170;
Unit 7 179; Unit 8 205

Choral speaking
Unit 2 65; Unit 3 89; Unit 5 140; Unit 7 184;
Unit 8 210, 213, 220

Using telling sentences
Unit 3 75, 76, 77, 78, 84, 88, 89, 90, 91;
Unit 4 98, 101, 112, 119; Unit 5 124, 136, 137, 145;
Unit 6 150; Unit 7 187; Unit 8 225

Asking questions
Unit 3 74, 75, 76, 77, 78, 82, 84; Unit 4 101;
Unit 8 203, 222

Dramatizing
Unit 3 84; Unit 4 100; Unit 5 127; Unit 6 153, 159;
Unit 7 179

SPEAKING (continued)

Using polite language/Formal and informal language
Unit 4 100, 107, 118

Giving an opinion
Unit 6 151; Unit 8 215, 226

Giving instructions
Unit 7 176, 178, 179, 185, 195, 196

Sharing information
Unit 8 211, 224

VIEWING

Nonverbal cues
Unit 1 35, 42; Unit 6 155, 159, 170

Comparing and contrasting
Unit 1 35, 43; Unit 2 59, 67; Unit 3 83, 90; Unit 5 134

Identifying signs
Unit 1 59, 66

Using pictures for meaning/information
Unit 2 55; Unit 3 79; Unit 4 103; Unit 5 129;
Unit 6 155, 160, 170; Unit 8 207, 212

Identifying cause and effect
Unit 3 83, 91

Identifying main idea/details
Unit 4 108, 118

Observing
Unit 5 127, 134, 144

Following visual directions
Unit 7 178, 186, 196

Comparing media
Unit 8 212, 224

GRAMMAR/USAGE

NOUNS

People and places
Unit 1 27, 31, 33, 36, 43; Unit 2 64; Unit 3 91;
Unit 4 99, 100, 101, 109, 111, 118, 119; Unit 6 161,
170

Animals and things
Unit 2 51, 55, 56, 60, 64, 67; Unit 3 91;
Unit 4 99, 100, 109, 111, 118, 119; Unit 6 161, 170

Plural nouns
Unit 1 26, 27, 29, 31, 33, 36, 38, 40, 43, 45;
Unit 4 99

GRAMMAR/USAGE (continued)

NOUNS (continued)

Proper nouns
Unit 3 89; Unit 6 150, 151, 161, 170; Unit 8 213, 225

PRONOUNS

I, me, we
Unit 1 36, 43; Unit 4 99, 103, 114

ADJECTIVES

Describing words
(See also other entries in ADJECTIVES below)
Unit 1 31, 32, 33

Color words
(See also ADJECTIVES: Sensory words; VOCABULARY: Color words)
Unit 2 60, 61, 64, 67, 68; Unit 3 74, 80, 83;
Unit 4 100, 112, 119; Unit 5 124, 135; Unit 6 150;
Unit 8 202

Number words
(See also ADJECTIVES: Sensory words;
VOCABULARY: Number words)
Unit 2 60, 64, 67; Unit 4 112, 119; Unit 5 124, 135;
Unit 6 150; Unit 8 202

Words for sizes and shapes
(See also ADJECTIVES: Sensory words)
Unit 2 61, 68; Unit 3 74, 83; Unit 4 100, 112, 119;
Unit 5 124, 135; Unit 6 150; Unit 8 202

Sensory words
(See also ADJECTIVES: Color words, Number words,
Words for sizes and shapes)
Unit 4 99, 100; Unit 5 124, 125, 126, 127, 128, 129,
130, 131, 132, 135, 136, 138, 139, 143, 144, 145;
Unit 8 207

Comparative and superlative forms
Unit 8 214, 225

VERBS

Action words
Unit 3 84, 91; Unit 6 155, 162, 167, 171;
Unit 7 177, 187, 188, 192, 196, 197

Present tense
Unit 8 213, 225

Subject-verb agreement
Unit 8 213, 225

GRAMMAR/USAGE (continued)

SENTENCES

Telling sentences
(See also LISTENING: Using telling sentences)
Unit 3 74, 75, 76, 77, 79, 80, 81, 82, 84, 86, 88, 89, 90,
91, 93; Unit 4 98, 110, 119

Questions
(See also LISTENING: Asking questions)
Unit 3 74, 75, 76, 77, 78, 79, 80, 81, 82, 84, 86, 88, 89,
90, 91, 93; Unit 4 110, 119;
Unit 8 203, 204, 209, 210, 222

Exclamations
Unit 3 79, 81; Unit 4 110, 119

MECHANICS

CAPITALIZATION

Pronoun I
Unit 1 36; Unit 4 103, 105; Unit 5 131; Unit 6 157;
Unit 7 183, 192; Unit 8 210

Proper nouns
Unit 1 26, 28, 29, 33, 36, 38, 40, 43, 45; Unit 4 99, 105;
Unit 5 131; Unit 6 157; Unit 7 183, 192; Unit 8 210

Beginning of a sentence
Unit 2 50; Unit 3 74, 81, 84, 89, 91;
Unit 4 98, 105, 110; Unit 5 124, 131; Unit 6 157;
Unit 7 183, 192; Unit 8 210

PUNCTUATION

Period (to end a sentence)
Unit 2 50; Unit 3 74, 79, 81, 82, 84, 86, 89, 91, 93;
Unit 4 98, 105, 110, 119; Unit 5 124, 131; Unit 6 157;
Unit 7 183, 192; Unit 8 210

Question mark
Unit 3 74, 78, 79, 81, 82, 84, 86, 89, 91, 93;
Unit 4 105; Unit 5 105, 110, 119, 131; Unit 6 157;
Unit 7 183, 192; Unit 8 210

Exclamation point
Unit 3 79, 81; Unit 4 105, 110, 119; Unit 5 131;
Unit 6 157; Unit 7 183, 192; Unit 8 210

VOCABULARY

Positional words
Unit 1 (*top, middle bottom*) 37, 44;
Unit 2 (*left, right*) 57; Unit 3 (*left, right*) 85, 92;
Unit 5 (*top, middle, bottom, left, right*) 125;
Unit 7 (prepositions) 189, 197

Same and _different_
Unit 1 35, 43; Unit 2 59, 67

Words that name feelings
Unit 1 37, 44; Unit 4 100

Rhyming words
Unit 2 51, 52, 55, 56, 58, 61, 62, 64, 66, 68

Color words
(*See also* GRAMMAR/USAGE/*ADJECTIVES*: Color words)
Unit 2 50, 51, 52, 53, 55, 56, 57, 59, 61, 64, 68;
Unit 3 74, 80, 83; Unit 5 135, 145; Unit 6 150;
Unit 8 202

Number words
(*See also* GRAMMAR/USAGE/*ADJECTIVES* Number words)
Unit 2 50, 51, 52, 53, 54, 55, 56, 57, 64, 68

Words that name size and shapes
Unit 2 61, 68; Unit 3 83; Unit 4 100, 112;
Unit 5 135, 145; Unit 6 150; Unit 8 202

Words that name body parts
Unit 3 85, 92

Time words
Unit 3 74; Unit 4 98, 99; Unit 5 128

Exact nouns
Unit 4 111, 119

Weather words
Unit 5 124; Unit 8 202

Onomatopoeia
Unit 5 133, 144

Synonyms
Unit 5 137, 145

Exact verbs
Unit 6 155, 167; Unit 7 188, 192, 197

Opposites
Unit 6 163, 171

WRITING

WRITING SKILLS

Alliteration
Unit 1 31

Handwriting
Unit 1 29, 37, 38, 44, 45

Good titles
Unit 1 33, 41; Unit 2 57, 65; Unit 3 89; Unit 4 114;
Unit 5 131, 140; Unit 6 157, 166; Unit 7 185, 192;
Unit 8 210, 219, 220

Beginning, middle, ending
Unit 4 99, 101, 102, 103, 105, 106, 113, 114;
Unit 5 132, 140, 141; Unit 6 150, 151, 155, 156, 157,
158, 164, 165, 166, 167, 168, 171; Unit 7 183, 184, 192;
Unit 8 207, 210, 220

Using details
Unit 4 106, 112, 114, 115, 119;
Unit 5 132, 138, 139, 140, 141, 145; Unit 6 155, 166

Dialogue
Unit 4 100, 103, 115

Simile/Figurative language
Unit 5 127, 129, 138, 141, 145; Unit 7 181

Mood
Unit 5 129

Story elements (plot, setting, character)
Unit 6 150, 152, 155, 156, 157, 158, 164, 165, 166, 167,
168, 169

Sequence
Unit 7 176, 181, 183, 184, 190, 191, 192, 197;
Unit 8 220

Order words
Unit 7 177, 181, 183, 190, 191, 192, 195, 196, 197

TYPES OF WRITING

Message
Unit 1 26; Unit 2 50; Unit 3 74, 86; Unit 4 98;
Unit 5 124; Unit 6 150; Unit 7 176; Unit 8 202

Lists
Unit 1 29; Unit 2 52, 62, 67, 69; Unit 7 179;
Unit 8 204

Journal
Unit 1 29; Unit 2 52; Unit 3 76; Unit 4 101;
Unit 5 126; Unit 6 152; Unit 7 179; Unit 8 204

Name book
Unit 1 32–33, 40–41

WRITING (continued)

TYPES OF WRITING (continued)

Captions/Labels/Signs
Unit 2 52; Unit 3 85, 86, 92; Unit 5 125, 126; Unit 8 204

Counting book
Unit 2 56–57, 64–65

Poems
Unit 2 62, 68

Question/Answer book
Unit 3 80–81, 88–89

Thank-you note
Unit 3 86, 93

Personal narrative
Unit 4 104–106, 113–115, 116

Description
Unit 5 126, 130–132, 138, 139–141, 142

Story
Unit 6 153, 156–58, 165–167, 168

Instructions
Unit 7 182–184, 191–193, 194

Report
Unit 8 208–210, 219–221, 222

WRITING PROCESS

Prewriting, Drafting, Revising, Publishing
Unit 1 32–33, 40–41; Unit 2 56–57, 64–65;
Unit 3 80–81, 88–89; Unit 4 104–106, 113–115;
Unit 5 130–132, 139–141; Unit 6 156–158, 165–167;
Unit 7 182–184, 191–193; Unit 8 208–210, 219–221

WRITING TRAITS

Ideas
Unit 1 32, 40; Unit 2 56, 64; Unit 3 80, 88;
Unit 4 104, 113, 116, 117; Unit 5 130, 139, 142, 143;
Unit 6 156, 165, 168, 169; Unit 7 182, 191, 194, 195;
Unit 8 208, 219, 222, 223

Organization
(See WRITING/WRITING SKILLS: Beginning, Middle, Ending; Sequence)

Word choice
(See VOCABULARY: Exact Nouns; Exact Verbs;
GRAMMAR/USAGE/ADJECTIVES)

Sentence fluency
Unit 8 207, 220

Conventions
(See GRAMMAR/USAGE/NOUNS: Plural nouns; VERBS: Subject-
verb agreement; ADJECTIVES: Comparative and superlative
forms; MECHANICS)

WRITING (continued)

WRITING TRAITS (continued)

Presentation
Unit 1 33, 41; Unit 2 57, 65; Unit 3 89;
Unit 4 106, 115, 117; Unit 5 132, 141, 143;
Unit 6 158, 167, 169; Unit 7 184, 193, 195;
Unit 8 210, 221, 223

THINKING AND STUDY SKILLS

Making letter/sound associations
Unit 1 31; Unit 2 57

Letter recognition/ABC order
Unit 1 26, 28, 29, 30, 32, 35, 40, 43, 44;
Unit 7 179; Unit 8 216, 226

Understanding concepts of print
Unit 1 33; Unit 2 57; Unit 3 81

Predicting
Unit 1 30; Unit 2 54; Unit 3 78, 80; Unit 4 102;
Unit 5 128; Unit 6 152, 154; Unit 7 180

Comparing and contrasting
(See VIEWING: Comparing and contrasting, Comparing media;
LISTENING: Comparing media)

Recognizing parts of a book
Unit 1 39, 45

Using a keyboard
Unit 1 39, 45 Unit 2 63, 69

Categorizing/classifying
Unit 2 51, 63, 64, 69; Unit 3 87, 93; Unit 5 125, 144

Recognizing cause and effect
(See also VIEWING: Identifying cause and effect)
Unit 3 75

Using charts and graphs
Unit 3 87, 93; Unit 8 205, 206, 218, 219, 223, 227

Solving problems
Unit 6 155

Distinguishing between real and make-believe
Unit 6 156, 166 Unit 8 207

Differentiating between fact and opinion
Unit 8 202, 203, 204, 207, 209, 210, 211, 215, 220, 226

Finding information
Unit 8 203, 204, 217, 227